The Family and the Bible

To my sisters in Christ
at Carmel —
who have loved the
Word of God —
and wed Him —

Mary Reed Newland

THE
FAMILY
AND
THE BIBLE

Mary Reed Newland

RANDOM HOUSE · NEW YORK

FIRST PRINTING

© *Copyright, 1963, by Mary Reed Newland*

All rights reserved under International and Pan-American Copyright
Conventions. Published in New York by Random House, Inc., and
simultaneously in Toronto, Canada, by Random House of Canada, Limited.

Library of Congress Catalog Card Number: 63-11624

MANUFACTURED IN THE UNITED STATES OF AMERICA BY
The Colonial Press Inc., Clinton, Massachusetts

For all the families everywhere
who have wanted help
reading the Bible

Acknowledgments

I wish to thank all the scholars whose works have helped our family to find its way at last through the story of salvation in the Bible. Without them we could not have done it; but to name each one and his works would be impossible. Particularly, I do want to thank Father Barnabus Ahern, C.P., for his encouragement, enthusiasm and criticism, and Father Carroll Stuhlmueller, C.P., for painstakingly reading the manuscript page by page and making corrections and criticism which have been invaluable, in spite of his own heavy schedule of classes, lectures, retreats and writing. My gratitude goes also to my pastor, Father Richard Hoey of St. Patrick's parish, Monson, Massachusetts, and his assistant, Father Edward Kennedy, who in friendship and help have been unendingly patient; to Miss Sylvia de Santis, friend and librarian at the library we love—the Monson Free Library—for searching out material; and to all the other friends who listened and offered advice. I am grateful to Father Francis N. Wendell, O.P., editor of the *Torch*, where a number of these chapters were first published as articles; to the Confraternity of Christian Doctrine, Washington, D. C., for permission to quote from its translations of both the Old and New Testaments; and to Sheed & Ward, New York, for the Scripture quotations which are taken from the Old Testament in the translation of Monsignor Ronald Knox (Copyright 1948 and 1950) with the kind permission of the Archbishop of Westminster. Last, I want especially to thank Paul Lapolla and his assistant, Mrs. Jean Stewart, of Random House, not only for all the help they have given me but for being incredibly understanding and patient about the manuscript.

Foreword

A family Bible enhances the living room of many a home and genuinely Christian families want to read their Bible intelligently and religiously. Some start on the project; a few heroic ones do so repeatedly. Most families, however, finally give it up, and in time the Bible becomes another antique—revered, but not particularly useful.

Glowing tributes to the Word of God exist, but the average Christian, unfamiliar with the Bible, is obliged to accept them on faith. He may have heard, for instance, St. Paul's encomium: "All Scripture is inspired by God and useful for teaching, for reproving, for correcting, for instructing in justice, that the man of God may be perfect, equipped for every good work." Scripture, therefore, does more than enrich a person for a cultured life. It equips him to be "perfect in every good work," and this is an ideal that appeals to every father and mother. They want to provide their children with a personal regard for God which infuses enthusiasm and gratitude into every moment of life.

But parents ask themselves, almost desperately at times, how their family Bible can ever be the source of these things and be what Jesus said it is: "spirit and life." How can it become a "lamp shining in the dark place" of the needs and wants of their family? St. Jerome has said: "To be ignorant of Scripture is to be ignorant of Christ." His words only echo Christ's: "Is not this why you err, because you know neither the Scripture nor the power of God?"

Many fathers and mothers will honestly protest: "We want to read the Bible and we have tried to, but it never works. Much of what we read we don't understand. Some parts of it seem almost scandalous, while other parts seem unrealistic. Often it's impossible to detect any kind of sequence, the children begin to fidget, we become irritated, and in the end the whole thing is a failure."

Bible reading, we must admit, is not easy. Jesus himself had to explain "the law of Moses and the Prophets and the Psalms" to three Jewish men who were walking from Jerusalem to Emmaus on the morning of the first Easter, arguing among themselves. On another occasion an Ethiopian statesman was asked by the deacon Philip if he understood what he was reading from the book of Isaia. The Ethiopian turned and replied, almost with consternation: "How can I, unless someone shows me?" He then asked Philip to get into the chariot in which he was riding and sit with him. As they travelled slowly along the road, Philip began to preach Jesus to him from the Scriptures.

"But isn't it enough," someone will surely ask, "simply to listen to the Sunday sermon in order to know the Bible?"

To answer very bluntly, "No." Many families have been going to church regularly for years and can even claim an excellent training in religion, and yet flounder in the reading of the Bible. I do not hesitate to say that Mrs. Newland's way of opening up the Scriptures is charged with conviction and shows an insight seldom if ever found in even the best sermons and catechism classes. The Church never takes the place of the home, and Sunday sermons never substitute for family study and reading.

Mary Reed Newland answers the desperate cry of many families today: "How can we ever understand the Bible unless someone helps us?" The fire of Christ burns within her words, illuminating, warming, enticing. Whenever she speaks or writes, a swell of enthusiasm moves through the audience as though they were saying, almost as the three men on the way to Emmaus did: "Was not our heart burning within us, while she was explaining to us the Scriptures?" This enthusiasm accounts for her busy schedule of lecturing and her heavy backlog of requests for articles and books. Scholars find her words balanced with solid, scientific research, and everyone is enlightened by the simple but vigorous clarity of her writing.

Mrs. Newland stresses—in fact, she insists—what a priest could not even suggest. "It can be done. Our family reads the Bible, and loves it." An old Latin proverb is once more proven true: *Ab esse ad posse.* Translated freely in our present context, it means: What one family has done, your family can do.

Mrs. Newland provides successful recipes and practical suggestions for serving the food of God's word. Effort, preparation and timing are still necessary to put these recipes and suggestions to good use. But when God's word is known and understood within the family, a new bond of family loyalty, a new depth and a new vigor of family life in Christ are possible. Parents thus bestow on their children not only a physical life but also a spiritual life by which their bodies will one day rise from the grave of death to live eternally with God in heaven.

This heavenly life begins on earth. "Now this is everlasting life," St. John wrote, "that they may know thee, the only true God, and whom thou has sent, Jesus Christ."

Louisville, Kentucky
May 1963

Carroll Stuhlmueller, C. P.
Passionist Fathers Seminary

Contents

The Family and the Bible

·I·

ABOUT READING
THE BIBLE

"We've tried to read the Bible aloud in our family, many times, but sooner or later we run into things we don't understand and can't explain and we always give it up. It's just too difficult."

How many times one hears this said (how many times did we say it ourselves?) by families who desire to know and love God more fully and suspect that a knowledge of the Bible is part of this knowing and loving. After all, it is God's book, one ought not ignore it, but—"It's so difficult."

Yes—and no. The Bible, especially the Old Testament, can be very difficult if we do not know what it is. It can seem to be a relic of the past, dead and behind us with the arrival of Christ, unnecessary now that we have the Gospels, and struggling to read it we may groan like the woman who said, "We're dragging ourselves through the days of the kings. Now really, what have they got to do with anything—and there's not a name among them that we can pronounce!"

Or we may think of it as a collection of Bible stories with familiar heroes and exploits which, to be honest, become somewhat commonplace with too frequent telling. After a while David endlessly killing Goliath is no more entertaining than Jack endlessly hacking down the giant on the beanstalk. If the Old Testament is simply a collection of hero tales without any significant connection or procession, it is no wonder people outgrow them and they fall into disuse.

Perhaps we have thought the real value of the Old Testament

lies in its inspirational content. Here is a huge volume of texts which one can open by design or at random and find rich passages in beautiful language which often seem to be providentially selected especially to suit us (although to be sure there are long sections which seem to have no message for us at all). Maybe it should be read principally for its ancient wisdom and noble thoughts.

Then again, we have always envied a little those people who can quote the Old Testament—but even that is almost a thing of the past. Few people quote scripture these days, still fewer are impressed by hearing it quoted; and even as we think wishfully of being able to cite chapter and verse right out of our head, we suspect that in itself is not why we should read the Old Testament.

More often than not, the closest we come to the reason for reading this book is a vague scruple that hints that what we are has much to do with what happened in the Old Testament, and therefore we should find out what *is* there, a scruple that starts to attention when an Old Testament text appears in the prayers of the liturgy, or we see Old Testament figures on the windows and walls of churches, or some reference to the prophets and the patriarchs reaches out to us from the pages of the Gospels. "We really should read it," we say, "because . . ." And there we are again, still unable to put a finger on exactly the right reason, the most important reason. Much of our failure in the past has been because we did not know what to look for or what we might expect to find.

Why Read the Old Testament?

The Old Testament contains God's word, it is alive with His presence, and this is something we cannot afford to miss. It is God's story, telling of His love for man, man's betrayal of this love, and God's determination to win man back. It is our story also, the story of our creation and fall and of our salvation. It is a mirror to be held in front of us so we may study the way of men with God and God with men, and see ourselves in it, and learn from it. But best of all, the Old Testament is our means of coming to focus at last on the meaning of the greatest of the mysteries—that we are the people of God who belong to Him and share His life and now bear part of the responsibility for His work, the continuing redemption of mankind.

We must read the Old Testament, not alone because of its hallowed antiquity, its beautiful prose and poetry, its inspiring stories, its spiritual nourishment, its classic images; but because we cannot see ourselves clearly as members of the divine community until we trace our way back to the beginnings of this community. We must see Israel being made into such a people, becoming inspirited with God, being prepared so God might be brought forth out of their humanity to enter men at last, as He planned in the beginning, and make them like Himself. This is the destiny of man, that he become like God and share in God's joy forever. This is the meaning of salvation: that we are saved after being lost to Him. This is the meaning of the Christian vocation: that we are the new people of God, the new generation who live His life and like the men of old are the chosen instruments He uses to extend His life to the men who still do not possess it.

Only when we scan the vista from Genesis to now can we appreciate what it means to exist in this final stage of the working out of God's promise, made long ages ago to a mankind God loved and wanted in spite of its disobedience. The Old Testament is an adventure with God, the real life story, as the children say, of how God entered human history to make men His dearly beloved sons again. There are plot, clues, heroes, and villains, and through it the Lord moves unremittingly down the centuries like a hunter in search of His prize. We are His prize.

How Much of the Old Testament for Family Reading?

A family settling down to read the Old Testament will want to read principally the historical books—Genesis, Exodus, part of Leviticus, Numbers, part of Deuteronomy, Josue, Judges, I and II Samuel, III and IV Kings, I and II Ezra, and I and II Machabees. These books tell the history of Israel, which is the history of our salvation, and it is impossible to make the most of the Bible, either the Old or the New Testament, if we do not have this background. Christ was the fulfillment of what was promised to men throughout the years spanned by these books.

We will not read the prophets in their entirety, but when we reach their period in the history of Israel, we will select passages from their books which help describe each prophet and his relation to the situation in Israel at his time. Thus we will make the prophets' acquaintance within the context of salvation history.

We will read the "story books"—Ruth, Tobias, Esther, Judith, Daniel and Jona—separately, for they are like modifiers of the main subject, and as we become ever better acquainted with the history of God's people, the Psalms will almost demand a part in family prayer. We will dip into the Wisdom books momentarily to see what they are like, but since they are not suitable for family reading, we will save them for a time when each of us wants to explore these wise sayings at leisure.

When? Who? How?

Each family in its own circumstances can best determine how to go about their Bible reading: who will read, how often and at what hours. We have done most of our reading in the evenings, sitting before the fireplace in the living room, although during summer vacations we read many times in the afternoon outdoors under a favorite tree. It is the mother who usually reads aloud in our family because of the evening working hours which keep the children's father from joining us. But he long ago established his reputation as a reader, and the evenings when he is able to be home are especially delightful. We follow such reading with night prayers, using Psalms which echo the spirit of the scripture passage we have read. Then, of course, there are evenings when it is impossible, for various reasons, to read at all.

To whom do we read? About three and a half years before the writing of this book, when we began to read the historical books in order (we had read parts of the Old Testament for years, passages related to the liturgical seasons), our audience included all seven of the children. In time, one child left for college, three entered high school, homework assignments became heavier all around and the quite normal distractions of adolescent life began to claim the attention of a good half of our audience. On the one hand, this is disappointing to parents, and on the other it is to be expected. We had started late with family Bible reading, so we were not too surprised that the older children did not cling to it with the same eagerness as the younger. This is the way children are. Some children of high school age might be very eager to listen to scripture read aloud, and if so—grand; but as our eldest said when we discussed this one time. "You know, there comes a time when you just don't want to be read to." And we had to agree.

From time to time each one of us has endured the exquisite irritation of being read to—and has always sworn silently never to afflict this on anyone else. The ideal time for beginning to hear scripture read aloud is very young—perhaps six or seven.

So, rather than regret that the audience for family Bible reading may dwindle in time, let us rest content that at least the uncoerced are not going to set up a resistance to the Word of God. The one thing worse than having children absent themselves from family scripture reading is the sullen presence of children who are there against their will. They have the whole of their lives ahead of them and there will be time to read it themselves, and if the family learns to know and love the scriptures, its lessons will seep into thinking and speech and will subtly affect each member. It is surprising the amount of listening the homework-bound members will do from the dining room while the rest of the family is reading in the living room. We have found bits and pieces of scripture popping up in all sorts of ways. Not long ago one lad, referring to a friend who was in a spiritual dilemma, said, "Don't worry. Some afternoon we'll take a walk in the woods and we'll wrestle—like Jacob and the angel—and we won't stop until God gets His way." He was hardly aware that he had summed up his friend's crisis perfectly in that great struggle between Jacob and the Lord on the night of Jacob's conversion.

Are the conditions for family Bible reading always perfect in our house? No, frequently they are far from perfect. Take the time that Christopher came to listen to a new chapter of Kings wearing a football helmet. To be honest, Stephen was wrapping and unwrapping his legs, like an eggbeater, around a baseball bat; and Philip was rotating a wheel from a model car between his teeth with the help of his tongue, but these seemed hardly likely to interfere with *hearing*. The football helmet? We were not sure. We suggested he take it off.

"But I can hear, honest I can, I can hear."

We hesitated—and we submitted. Reading had been under way for some minutes when Christopher began to fidget. He removed the helmet, examined its inside, put it back on. There were frowns and noises of disapproval. Minutes passed, the story unfolded, and Christopher removed his helmet again. He explored its interior once more; he put it back on his head. Another few minutes, and in the middle of reading he removed it again. Enough! We closed the book and said, somewhat sternly, "Christopher, take off that football helmet. It's distracting everyone."

But Christopher, having taken it off, pounced on something he at that moment discovered inside it and returned it to his head with an air of great success.

"There! I knew there was something in it. A cricket—but I got him. Now I can hear good. Go ahead and read some more."

Who knows what delight may be associated with the books of Kings all his life for the joy of having heard them read while wearing a football helmet?

Difficulties with Language

Wouldn't it be better to read Bible stories written in children's language than struggle through the many big words they might not understand? No, it would not. This is the Word of God and its impact on us is unique; there is no substitute for it. Bible stories are very good, it is true, but they are not the same as holy scripture. However, there *are* many passages with words beyond the understanding of small children, and in such cases we can substitute easier words. This is quite permissible. For this reason, it is important that the reader at least scan the text—or better yet, read it carefully—and prepare for the difficulties before the reading begins. One develops a great facility for this in no time. For example, Genesis 42:6 says: "Joseph's brothers also came and prostrated themselves before him." We might read, "Joseph's brothers also came and they bowed down low (or fell on their faces) before him."

What about the many delicate situations for which the Old Testament is so famous—the multiple wives, the fornications, adulteries, and all the rest? (Would it were as famous for its mighty lessons.) These pose less trouble than one would think. Throughout this book we have tried to give explanations and even words that might be used to clarify these things. Indeed, such passages give us an opportunity to teach lessons about chastity, marriage, morality, which all children must learn.

Differences in Names

Why is it that the names in the Old Testament appear with so many different spellings? We find Noe instead of Noah, Josue instead of Joshua, and so on. The differences between the spellings of the names in Catholic translations and those in the Jewish and Protestant translations go all the way back to the translation of the Bible into Latin, at which time basically the names from the ancient Greek translation which were used by the New Testament (Greek) writers were more or less taken over into the Latin Bible. Jewish and Protestant translations use the Hebrew names. A simple rule for the family is to use whichever names are most familiar. (Throughout this book we have used the names as they appear in the Catholic Confraternity of Christian Doctrine translation and, where no CCD translation is available, the Knox translation; but when reading we use the more familiar Hebrew names. For example, we are used to saying *Joshua* so we continue to say it.)

As for pronouncing the names, we have appended a pronunciation guide at the back of the book for help with this.

The Use of Maps, Charts, Texts

In our enthusiasm at the start of our reading, we provided ourselves with several excellent maps in addition to those found in the back of the texts we were using for reference. One particularly handsome relief map of Palestine promised wonderful adventures in the third dimension and we marveled at the distances Our Lord and Our Lady traveled on their journeys, at the low level of the Dead Sea, at the rocky heights of Juda—called "the hill country" in the Gospel of the Visitation. But strangely, trying to trace out the localities of the Old Testament did not seem to help us at all. It constantly broke the smooth flow of our reading and, as we were not yet sufficiently acquainted with the story, its places were only strange names without familiar associations. We did not even enjoy finding them on the map. Perhaps not all families go about things the way this one does (hind end to, some say), but it was necessary for us to know the patriarchs and their high places, to know Josue and his battles, the kings and their struggles, the Machabees and their heroism before we cared to find their sites on the map. To try to learn the names of towns, districts, rivers, lakes before we have a story to weave with them is too much like a geography lesson, and family Bible reading is not meant to be a chore. It is meant to be an adventure.

There are many books published currently which are of enormous help to families and, needless to say, we pored over them continually. Some are more suitable for first time readers of scripture than others, but in all of them the scholars have generously poured out their treasures to help light our way through these sacred pages. Certainly one does not have to read all these books in order to know the Bible, but as time goes on one may want to read them, just to learn more and more. A list of books for family reading also appears at the end of this book.

The Scriptures and the Liturgy

One of the most glorious of all the rewards for reading the Old Testament is the light it spreads over the texts of the liturgy, the great blessings and ceremonies with which we have been familiar from our youth but about which we have often understood very little. The Mass is made almost entirely of texts from the scriptures, and figures from its pages appear everywhere, full of meaning if one knows their stories, meaningless if one does not. Teaching children about the Mass will be completely transformed against this background of the story of man the creature, and his relation to God the creator. Sacrifices, blessings, the Law, the covenant, signs, symbols, types—all these provide us with lessons on every aspect of the Mass and make it much easier to show them that the offering of a sacrifice to God is not only a duty that is implicit but a need that is common to the race.

The Importance of Point of View

Perhaps the most widely discussed of all the difficulties with holy scripture is the difference between our point of view as westerners and the point of view of the easterners who wrote the Bible. Books and books have been written on this subject, so it is presumptuous to expect a few lines will dispose of it, but it has nevertheless been our experience that this difficulty never loomed large for very long, perhaps because children have great simplicity and will see and accept an explanation of something that might tie the adults in knots.

We have tried throughout the book to consider these so-called difficulties as we meet them in the text. Briefly, the point is this. When we say this is the history of our salvation we do not mean this history is written like the history books we are accustomed to read. There is no strict marshalling of dates, no analysis of events, no scientific method, no mathematical precision—

whether in the listing of populations, armies, genealogies or years of a lifetime. This history is written with the focus on the divine reality; our writer (writers, really, for scripture was written by many men) was not only a poet but a mystic as well, and he says things not as an historian says them but as poets and mystics say them. Yet it tells God's story perfectly and as God wished it told, for he was a fully accredited—inspired—writer.

For example, we might have written the first chapter of Genesis this way: "Nothing is known of how the world was created but it is the divine revelation that God created it." Neither our author nor his forefathers from whom he got his story told of creation this way, but rather preserved the divine revelation by clothing it in a story—which in itself had become a sacred tradition. Was this naïve? Hardly. It is the way Orientals teach, the way children learn (and these things were meant to be taught to ordinary people—not scientists and scholars), and to try teaching in the abstract terms of matter, atoms and aeons would have been foolish. Suffice it to say, they never gave it a thought.

Perhaps a comparison might be found in the way Our Lord taught. Was it childish of Him to teach of the Mystical Body and its members in terms of a leaven that a woman buries in three measures of flour until it gives its life to the whole? Of course not. He was talking not to the theologians but to His own people, who learned much better this way. Does this mean there are conflicts between scientists and the authors of Genesis, between theologians and Our Lord speaking in parables? Not at all. One chooses what is suitable to one's audience and teaches in one's customary style. And Our Lord was an Oriental too.

All of this is far too simple, of course, but the purpose of this book is not to explore these difficulties further. It is enough, we feel, to be pointed in the right direction—understanding that we must read the Old Testament with respect for the style in which it is written, and we must be gracious about adopting the authors' methods of thinking and seeing in place of our own. Despite the momentary twinge of disappointment to find that the account of creation is a story (as one delightful mother put it ruefully, "Oh dear, you've robbed me of the fairy tale") we will discover that our new understanding provides us with infinitely more. It was the father of the same family who said, "Well, frankly, *I'm* relieved."

We might go on to point out the magnificent contribution of the Old Testament to the teaching of Christian doctrine, but this has been developed as fully as possible throughout the book (a list of doctrines with related scripture texts has been appended) and now, surely, it is time to get on with our reading.

·II·

BEGINNINGS

Genesis

"In the beginning God created the heavens and the earth . . ."
That is how the Old Testament begins, but that is not how the
story of God and man begins. There is elsewhere in the Bible
a passage that begins before creation, and we ought really to read
this as our prologue to the scriptures. Unlike some stories, the
Bible will only make sense to us if we know first what happens at
both the beginning and the end, and no one has summed up both
the beginning and the end better than St. John in the first chapter
of his Gospel.

Here is where a child wants to start, although he may not say
so. It answers the first question of all: "Who made God?" It
answers the little girl of nine who sat beside me in a plane not
long ago and in the middle of her delightful chatter about ladies
and giants and poems and stories said, "Lots of times I ask myself,
what is life all about? What are we here for, anyway?"

"In the beginning was the Word, and the Word was with
God, and the Word was God." (John 1:1) This is God, knowing
Himself, filled with love—the Trinity. Before any created thing,
always, says St. John, there was God.

"All things were made through him, and without him was
made nothing that has been made." (John 1:3) This is God,
making.

"In him was life, and the life was the light of men." (John

1:4) And there we are with God's life in us—the state of grace. Giving us His life would make us like Himself so we could live with Him forever. That was the original plan before ever an atom was created. But man let God's life go.

Even so, God would have him. He chose a people from among all the peoples of the earth and made them His own with miracles and promises, and finally He came to them as Christ. To those who receive Him, He gives His life as He planned in the beginning. This is what life is all about. This is what we are here for—to live God's life forever, to become the sons of God.

Now back to how it all happened.

Creation

Genesis means *beginnings,* and this is precisely what the first book tells. The book is divided into two parts. The first eleven chapters tell of creation, the fall, sacrifice, the effect of sin, its punishment, and vaguely promises that some day all this will be set to rights. None of it was written by eyewitnesses, since there were no eyewitnesses left to write it down (and anyway, God was the only eyewitness to creation). It is not a scientific account since its writers were not scientists. Nor was it a verbatim transcription of something God dictated from heaven, since that is not how He inspired them. Rather, it tells truths which God inspired these men to put in writing after long years of handing them down as oral tradition, and it tells them in the manner that was characteristic of the writers and their culture. What manner was this? It was the manner of Oriental peoples who had as their background all the lore and imagery of the ancient Middle East and whose literary style gives evidence of these riches.

If we could forget for a moment that this is the holy Bible we are talking about and take a fresh look at the story of creation, we would find much we have seen before: a luscious garden with marvelous flowers, birds and animals, fishes swimming, rivers flowing, two mysterious trees set in the center of the garden, a hero and a heroine—and an evil one. It almost sounds like a story out of the *Arabian Nights.* Small wonder—its writers were blood brothers to the authors of the *Arabian Nights*; they wrote out of the same tradition.

Of course it would have been enough to say, "God made the world." It would be true—but a little dull. Instead, read how they did say it, lingering over the details—sun, moon, stars, light, dark, winged creatures, fish in the sea and green things growing on the land. What a beautiful way to teach the lesson about creation.

But our junior high school science scholars may protest. They have learned that it took billions of years to make the world and the Bible says six days. The answer is right under our noses. Genesis does not propose to tell *how* God made the world but *that* He made it. When we walk through the pasture in the spring and find the first cowslips and say "Look what God made," do we mean that God came down in the pasture, stood there, picked up some clay, modeled petals and leaves, blew life into them, and there—cowslips?

"Of course not!" And our children laugh.

Then we can enjoy the way the story of creation is told in the Bible because the writers were not really so unlike ourselves after all. I don't care how much chlorophyl is in a cowslip—but I am very glad God made it. In the same way they didn't know or care how many billions of years it took the earth's crust to cool before plants and people could live on it, but they were anxious that people know and be glad that God made it.

Adam and Eve

More than one writer contributed his account to Genesis, which explains why there are two stories of the creation of man, each with a different emphasis. The first tells that God made man superior to all the creatures of the earth, while the second account tells that God made woman, a mate for man, like him, and that they existed in a state of innocence. This is the creation of marriage and, when God blessed them to make them fruitful, the family. There is no other way now that God creates man except with the help of parents. It makes man very much like God to be a creator with Him; it crowns his dignity. Not only can he live God's life but he has a share in God's power. Here in principal are the truths we need to explore with our children about marriage and family life, sex, dating and romantic love.

Was it a tree and a fruit that were the means of their fall? We do not know. Does it matter? They disobeyed in some way. The garden, the tree, the evil serpent—figures out of the East— ornament brilliantly the story of the Fall. First there was blessed abundance, peace and a sacred charge, then the assault of pride which destroys integrity and innocence. The horizon is far away before recorded history, the trappings are Oriental, the story is true.

The scene with the serpent gives us the first hint of how this book is going to end. Here is the promise, the first of the prophecies. But first it is interesting to learn why a *serpent*. One after another of our children have objected to the judgment against snakes found in Genesis, for they know from their knowledge of nature that snakes are important and kill many pests. At the time this text was being written, the authors wished to choose an image with which to clothe Satan which would suggest to their people all that was abominable. Now among the pagan idols of the Near East, there were many serpent gods supposedly gifted with powers of magic, whose rites were accompanied by the most vile practices. What better symbol for the person of evil himself? It was the author's own association of the serpent with evil that gave such relish to his wording of God's curse of the serpent in the garden (all junior Audubon members please note).

When the author wrote of the woman and her seed in Genesis 3:15, he had, of course, only Eve and her children in mind, never dreaming of Christ and Mary. Yet they are there, as we can now see. And when in 3:17 God spoke of the consequences of sin to both man and the lovely earth He had created for him, there is the seed of every misery and unhappiness man would ever suffer. How much is hidden in this sacred text which even its writers did not perceive. This is the meaning of "inspired," that the truths of scripture come from God and that the text is truly alive, an abyss out of which God continues to speak.

Cain and Abel

The story of Cain and Abel teaches many things but principally that man is prone to sin now and must be on guard. It tells of sacrifice, both worthy and unworthy, and it charges man with the obligation to care about his brother.

The lesson about sin is clear enough in Genesis 4:7. God says to Cain: "Its [sin's] desire is for you, but you must master it." Why does God hate sin? "Because it hurts God?" "Because it sends us to hell?" Actually it hurts us, not God, and we, sinning, send ourselves to hell, but here is not the place to explore that. God hates sin because it separates man from God, and the story of Cain gives a perfect example.

Adam would have offered sacrifice had there been no fall, and so would his sons—sacrifice to adore God, thank Him, ask His help. Since sin, he also offers sacrifice to show he is sorry. In the story of the two brothers we find an illustration of sacrifice offered worthily and unworthily. The tale has a profound application to our own manner of offering ourselves with the sacrifice of Jesus crucified. In this sacrifice, of course, our Victim *is* acceptable to God but the spiritual riches gained for ourselves and all men are determined by the attitude we show God in offering Him both Christ and self. Cain obviously did not fulfill the requirements of a sincere sacrifice—did not admit that praise was due, did not think it necessary to thank God, did not think he needed God's help in the future, and was not sorry for his sins.

His murder of his brother, his crude rejoinder to God, "Am I my brother's keeper?" (Gen 4:9) is a frightful demonstration of the effect of sin on both man and his world. Sin without repentance breeds more sin, and far from satisfying man's passions only increases them. It creates a world that disacknowledges the Fatherhood of God and cares not for the suffering of its brothers. Even preschool children can gain a profound understanding of God, His love, sin and why sin is evil, with the help of this story.

Adam, Eve, Cain, Abel—these are all good Hebrew names and reveal to us that this story was put down centuries after it happened, as do "keeper of flocks," and "tiller of the soil"—works that appeared very late in the history of man. But this does not rob the story of its validity. These shadowy firsts did appear, long before human memory could recall. Our authors simply clothed them in personalities for us.

With all this to ponder, it is easy to see how the Fathers of the Church saw Abel as a type of Christ Who would also offer an acceptable sacrifice and be murdered by His brothers; and in this first account of sacrifice we see a faint outline of the Mass.

We omit the long genealogy of Adam in chapter 5 for family reading, but in passing it is interesting to learn that the scholars consider the ages of the patriarchs to be symbolic, not literal.

Noe

The story of Noe[1] and the ark, the parade of animals, the flood, the rainbow at the end, reads like a nursery tale, and no

[1] Noah is the more commonly used form. Noe appears in Catholic translations.

wonder. It is a story from the nursery time of the world. Its point is to tell how God hates sin and punishes wickedness, and just as we teach a small child of right and wrong in the simplest possible way, this tale has put its lesson in the simplest possible form. That God is described as "regretting" that He made man, as "being grieved to the heart," (Gen 6:5-8) is simply a device of the writer who, no theologian, set down God's hatred of sin in terms of human emotion. He writes as a Hebrew with a knowledge of God, right and wrong, virtue and sin, reward and punishment: that man has a conscience and that his evil is blameworthy is his firm conviction. But God is merciful as well as just, he declares, as the rainbow after the flood reminds man forever.

Noe, a descendent of Adam, is like all the good men who serve God faithfully and is the second type of Christ to appear in the Old Testament. As Noe is said to have renewed the race with his own progeny, so Christ renews God's life in mankind with His own life in Baptism. The ark reminds us of the Church, for in it the men of good will are protected from the dangers of a fallen world, kept strong and safe by the power of the Mass and the sacraments.

Was there a flood? There is evidence of many deluges in the Near East in ancient times, although accounts vary and have been colored by the men who handed them down. None of these floods, however, covered any extensive area; each one was confined to a village or countryside. All these deluge stories are told from a religious point of view. The gods were angry at man's sins, and to the inhabitants of a village, it seemed that the entire world was coming to an end; certainly *their* world was at an end. The biblical storyteller took over the flood story for his own religious motive, telling the story under the inspiration of the Holy Spirit and, finding two accounts of the event among his own traditions, he used both in his story. Neither the two variations nor the naïveté of his historical-archeological conclusions is too important. The point of the tale was not to make a weather report but to teach God's attitude toward both good and evil men.

This introduction to the history of the redemption shows the state to which man had fallen, the crudity of his behavior, the dullness of his conscience, the confusion of his values. But soon, with the choice of Abraham, we will see God start all over again. The thread of relationship between Noe and Abraham runs through Sem, son of Noe, whose sons would be called the Semites and who would count among their descendents Christ Himself.

We find our next significant clue in the Lord's mystery story in the account of Noe's innocent drunkenness (Gen 9:18-27) and the disrespect of Ham. Centuries would pass before the curse of Ham's son Chanaan would be realized, when the sons of Sem would inherit "the land of Chanaan."

We omit chapter 10, another genealogy, for family reading,

Babel

In the account of Babel, we have the last commentary on the sins of men before the curtain goes up on the story of redemption. This time we see the divisiveness of pride. Lawlessness and lust are bad enough, but to set one's self up as independent of God makes for the worst havoc of all. Since we are familiar with the style of the accounts read so far, it is easy to grasp the point of this tale about the confusion of mankind as it determined to be a race of "self-made men." That there were other languages before this we know, so the origin of languages is not the point. That all men could not have been at Babel we also know, so we cannot consider this the starting point for the migration of peoples. Rather, it is a little jewel, hard-cut and sparkling, which shows the futility of men trying to create unity without God, a good meditation for all the men, parties and peoples trying to do exactly this these days. A frequently made observation about Babel, disunity and reunion is that Pentecost was the undoing of Babel.

Several children in my catechism class answered a test question on Babel this way in their own words: "The story of Babel teaches that men cannot reach heaven without the help of God." At first glance it seemed oversimplified—but it isn't really. All the things men substitute for heaven are merely a sign of their longing for God, even when they don't know it.

Abraham

Although we need not read aloud the long list of names in the genealogy of Sem (Gen 11:10-26), we will find at its end the name of Abram (Abraham) and his appearance brings us to the second part of Genesis. Ages separate the second part from the first, where we read of how things came to be. Now the focus sharpens and we see God choose one man, Abraham, faithful and obedient, with whom He will begin to undo the havoc wrought by Adam, unfaithful and disobedient.

Abraham came out of the Chaldees from the city of Ur, a land

and a city as real as New York City today. He was a semi-nomad, a tent dweller, whose father Thare had worshipped idols (Jos 24:2) and whose country's culture, laws, tradition and worship would mold the religion of the Hebrews with many of its forms and rituals. The journey described in Genesis 12:1-6, coincides with a great historical migration from Ur at the beginning of its decline, and the time of Abraham's appearance in history is roughly 1850 B.C.

It was a tradition of the Hebrews that no one was left who had knowledge of the one true God until Abraham heard His voice. (Gen 12:1-3) Now for the first time since the scene with the serpent in the garden we hear the Lord elaborate on the promise of a redeemer—though this could hardly have been Abraham's understanding of His words: "In you shall all the nations of the earth be blessed." (Gen 12:3) And forth he went into the unknown. Abraham is the epitome of faith and obedience.

The pace of the story is slow and measured, accompanied by the sounds of the East. A Bedouin chieftain moves his tribe and his herds from one pasture to another, stopping to graze them, to water them, to build an altar and worship. A famine drives them across the border into Egypt and knowing the Egyptians to have an eye for beauty, Abraham passes off his wife Sarai as his sister. Although she actually was his half-sister[2] and he might have justified the action because it was essential to God's plan that he be preserved, there is another account of the same kind of incident when Abraham goes to Gerara (Gen 20:1-8), and still another when Isaac goes to Gerara (Gen 26:6-7), and there is a growing scholarly consensus that it actually happened only once—in the Isaac account—but that in the transmission of the story, Abraham's name was substituted.[3]

Melchisedech

Next Lot, a man now with herds and herdsmen, was captured by four warring chiefs, and Abraham pursued them to bring back his nephew and all his possessions. Now enters the majestic figure of Melchisedech, mysterious priest and king who offered bread and

---

[2] Intermarriage, preferable to marriage with outsiders, was common and accepted and assured the purity of the family line.
[3] The substitution was done not to falsify the story but rather to adapt an existing story to another purpose: that God always cares for His own; that men without God (here symbolized by Egyptians) are always dull of perception.

wine in a sacrifice of thanksgiving for Abraham's victory. St. Paul calls Melchisedech a type of Our Lord for his priestly kingship (Heb 7:1-3), and the Church likens him to our own priests. Unlike the Levite priests who were chosen from a special tribe (Num 3:41) with their priesthood a birthright, our own priests are chosen by God out of whatever family He chooses. They appear where He wills, as Melchisedech does in this story, and at their ordination they are reminded: "Thou art a priest forever, according to the order of Melchisedech." (Heb 7:17)

After this Abraham complains a bit, and who is to blame him? His faith was tested not only by incredulity but also by time: years had gone by and nothing had happened. The promise of descendents—was this a manner of speaking? Was it his steward Eliezer whom he would adopt and claim as his heir? In one of the most beautiful scenes in scripture, God tells Abraham to go out of his tent and look up at the stars. "Count them if you can. Thy seed shall outnumber the stars." (Gen 15:5) How was Abraham to know what He meant? But he believed, to the everlasting glory of Israel and ourselves, for we are the adopted sons who are blessed in him. In the Canon of the Mass we call Abraham our father. Pius XI said in Rome one year: "Spiritually we are all Semites." So did St. Paul. (Gal 3:7)

God now made a pact with Abraham and, expressing Himself in a familiar custom, He passed between the pairs of slain animals in the form of a fiery torch to give evidence of His presence and the everlastingness of His promise.

The story of Agar and Ismael is poignant, and Sarai's jealousy is believable. But the arrangement by which all this is worked out is a bit startling, Sarai herself suggesting that Abraham beget the child by her slave woman. We might explain to the children that it was like taking a second wife. Polygamy occurs frequently throughout the stories of the patriarchs and, in the words of Stephen at eleven, "You'd just better explain about all those extra wives or everyone is going to be shocked!"

Actually, this was a provision of the ancient law out of the Chaldees, made in order to protect a man who was otherwise without descendents to whom he could will his possessions. The child of such an issue belonged to the legal "first" wife, and would inherit unless she herself bore a child to supersede it. The people of God were to be taught many new things, the ban against polygamy

among them, but one step at a time. So far no prohibition had
been put on this custom, and we will see later how God permitted
it to serve Him through these early generations of sacred history.

Having promised Himself to be Abraham's God, giving land
and protection to his offspring, God now exacted from Abraham
his part of the bargain. He would have His people mark themselves
with a sign which would perpetually remind them of their promise.
The sign was circumcision. "My covenant shall be in your flesh
as a perpetual covenant." (Gen 17:14) And God changed Abram's
name to Abraham, "father of a multitude."

Christ Himself was marked by this sign and only after the
promise was fulfilled by His redemptive sacrifice did the command
cease to be binding. Then St. Stephen, upbraiding the elders in
the Sanhedrin, called them "stiffnecked and uncircumcised of
heart," (Acts 7:51) which shows us clearly the spirit of circumcision. The mark more than anything else was a sign that one belonged to God; the Jews were His people, He was their God, circumcision was their sign. Christ is the same God and we are His people,
and the mark Baptism makes on us is His sign.

Then God promised at last the longed for son, Isaac, and the
whole idea seemed so ridiculous that Abraham laughed until he
fell over. He was an old man now and though the prospect was
delightful, it was a little hard to believe. With fatherly solicitude
he suggested that Ismael might be a more likely substitute but God
persisted that it would be Isaac. Ismael would be cared for otherwise.

In the relationship between God and Abraham, we find striking images which will nourish our children's notion of God the
Father, too often made a cloud-dwelling ancient with a long white
beard who sits with a black pencil and an account book waiting to
record misdeeds. In the story of the three strangers who came to
visit Abraham, one is identified as the Lord, yet they waited outside the tent for Abraham's offer of hospitality—much as the Lord
waits outside our lives for an invitation from us. Abraham's concern that they enter and rest, bathe their feet, eat a refreshing meal,
speaks of the desire of the eager soul to accommodate itself to the
presence of God. Sometimes the visitation comes in a special grace,
other times the guest is our neighbor in whom we must see Christ;
either way, to welcome the Lord as Abraham did is the only way to
discover Who He really is and to overcome our fear that a too

great involvement in the things of the spirit means a colorless, lacklustre existence.

Because we can see this application, we cannot help wondering if the story is meant as history or allegory. God is pure spirit, He does not sit, bathe, eat. Did this actually happen? The tale was told thus, carefully preserved and handed down as one of the traditions surrounding the beloved Abraham, and if He wished God could appear to sit, bathe and eat. But it is also possible that the people understood it to be a kind of spiritual visitation. Perhaps the answer is that it could be either or both. I walk on the mountain behind our house and when someone asks where I have been, I might say (if they were the kind to understand), "I have been out on the mountain, talking to God." Have I not? This is answer enough, I think.

Sodom and Gomorrha

God knew, of course, what was going on at Sodom and Gomorrha, but the account of His bargaining with Abraham tells even more—that God cares for men, is merciful as well as just, and listens to the pleas of His friends on their behalf. Abraham begged God not to destroy the good in the cities along with the wicked. Say there were fifty just men: would He spare the city for fifty? (Gen 18:23) He would. But suppose only forty-five? God agrees for forty-five. What if thirty? For thirty. Twenty? For twenty. What if only ten? Yes, if only ten. Ardently Abraham begged and generously God agreed. "The Lord departed after he had finished speaking to Abraham; and Abraham returned to his place . . ." (18:33) It sounds like a man who has finished his prayer.

In chapter 19, the story continues with an account of the angels' visit to Lot in Sodom, and we discover for ourselves the wickedness of the Sodomites. The family with young children would be wise to omit verse 8, and its mention of Lot's daughters, as the whole idea is shocking and even when explained serves no purpose. (At the time it would have been thought a superior obligation to protect the guest!) Of the five cities at the end of the Dead Sea, four are known to have been destroyed by some kind of cataclysm and are now presumably sunk under the waters of the sea. The fate of Lot's wife, probably an embellishment from local folklore, is a commentary on those who will not make up their minds to quit evil and turn unreservedly to good, rather like,

"How far can I go without committing sin?" The angels had said, "Do not look behind you, nor stop . . . lest you perish." (19:17) We can imagine her hesitation. "Wait—just one look—to see what will happen." Evidently she was covered with volcanic ash which in time became encrusted with salt from the sea. This tale "is probably the most primitive story that has been used as a source of Genesis," [4] and there is no doubt that it was intended as a morality tale. The cities have become synonyms for wickedness and are quoted throughout history as a measure of vice.

The incest of Lot and his daughters (19:30-38) may be omitted entirely as having no bearing on the story of redemption.

Chapter 20 tells of another king who took Sara to wife after being told that Abraham was her brother, as in the episode in Egypt (12:11-20). For family reading it is much simpler to omit this chapter entirely, as it tends to brake the action and contributes little that is new. Its important point is that the moral law was meant to apply to all, not just God's people. Abimelech, for all he is a pagan, is a good pagan.

Isaac

In chapter 21 at last comes the birth of Isaac. The joy of both Abraham and Sara lives in the text. Although we know both were along in years when the boy was born, the ages given in the text need not be taken literally.

Verses 22-34 tell a little story about a covenant between Abraham and Abimelech (of Gen 20:1-18), and its purpose is to show the importance of covenants between the men of those times, which explains God's choice of this means to bind Himself to His people.

Abraham's Test

Chapter 22:1-19 tells perhaps the most famous of all the stories of Abraham, one that endears him to us forever. It has been suggested that it might be too frightening to tell children, who would be shocked that a father would agree to sacrifice his son. Yet in our experience we have never known this to be the reaction of a child hearing the story within its framework of God's love and Abraham's faith. It shows Abraham's terrible trust, "hoping against hope," St. Paul said. (Rom 4:18) Surely the command to take his dearly beloved son to the mountain and sacrifice him must have pierced

[4] Bruce Vawter, C.M., A Pathway through Genesis (New York: Sheed & Ward, 1959), p. 156.

his heart like a knife. But he had had faith in the promise for years, in the face of insuperable obstacles and ridiculous impossibilities. Faith was a habit with Abraham by now, and like the totally committed man, he asked no questions but proceeded to do as God commanded. The boy's touching question, "Father, you have the fire and the wood, but where is the sheep for the holocaust?" (Gen 22:7) makes us want to weep. One hears the tremolo of the young voice and sees the eager delight on his face. Abraham's heart must have been breaking as he answered, "God himself will provide the sheep for the holocaust, my son." And on they trudged, the boy bent over carrying the load of wood, the father sunk in sadness. The Fathers of the Church point out to us the likeness between these two and two others—God the Father leading His only begotten Son up the hill to sacrifice, the Son carrying wood on His back also.

To be pushed to the very edge and to find God's arms there —this is the discovery of the totally surrendered. Our Lady discovered this after the scandal of Good Friday. All the saints discovered it in their worst humiliations. Abraham already knew it.

Even had he failed to trust in Isaac's rescue, God's command would not have seemed outrageous to Abraham; after all, he had come from a land where the sacrifice of first-born sons was common. God was now forbidding it, but the need to offer sacrifice is inherent in the nature of man and Abraham realized that it was due. This story helps us to realize more keenly the need to offer sacrifice. Perhaps now we might think of "going to Mass" in a new way, as "going to offer sacrifice."

Again Abraham was blessed by God for his fidelity, and all the nations of the earth in him. Verses 20-24 list some of his relatives, among them Rebecca, whom we will meet soon. The death and burial of his darling Sara ends the principal part of Abraham's story.

Isaac and Rebecca

The long twenty-fourth chapter tells the story of Isaac and Rebecca and makes a fine evening's reading. All the elements of romance are here—a colorful cast, changes of setting, a journey, a question, suspense, a climax, rejoicing and a love scene at the end. There is no very lengthy description of Rebecca, but her loveliness permeates the tale like a perfume. Her lithe young body moves

quickly to draw the water for the servant and his camels; with grace
she accepts and wears the jewels he has brought; she speaks easily,
is generous and hospitable. What a beautiful bride! We are so glad
for Isaac, who has become one of our favorites. The celebration of
her engagement is joyous, with gifts, food, guests, music, singing,
until at last she says farewell and with her old nurse and Abraham's
servant begins the journey to her new home. In the evening they
approach the encampment of Isaac who, a little melancholy, walks
in a field. Rebecca slips down from her mount and asks, "Who is
the man coming through the field towards us?" (Gen 24:65) It is
the young master, she is told. Swiftly she veils herself, as is proper
for a bride of the East, and awaits her husband, who takes her to
his tent to make her his wife. And he is "consoled for the loss of
his mother." (Gen 24:67) It is one of the most beautiful of love
stories.

Following the sacrifice story, where Isaac is shown as a type
of Christ, Rebecca next shows us a type of the Church. Now it is
necessary to use caution with this sort of thing lest we let it run
away with us and make the history of salvation no more than a
series of tableaux allegorically presenting various mysteries. But it
is one of the properties of inspiration to lead our minds over these
riches in a way that will illuminate many things we have understood
only feebly before. This is especially helpful with children, for it
gives us illustrations for lessons they would otherwise have to learn
in the most abstract terms. And too, this kind of ruminating on
scripture is prayer. Needless to say, it is good to learn that in the
present matter, St. Ambrose also pointed out the likeness between
Rebecca and the Church.

Perhaps we will not use all of the images and ideas to be found
in the text at one time, but let us consider some of them.

First, Isaac seeks a bride. Take her, instructs his father, from
the people that have already been drawn into the working out of
the promise, not from aliens and strangers. The Church came out
of the Jews—Abraham, Isaac, Jacob, Christ, His mother, the apostles and disciples. (We keep a menorah in our dining room during
Lent and Eastertide to remind us of this, among other things.)

How will this bride be recognized? Let her be drawing water,
said the servant, and let her give him to drink and offer water for
his beasts. This is the mystical function of the Church; to give us
to drink from the waters of eternal life; to refresh even the labors

of men, for they are an extension of God's work. Our Lord spoke to the Samaritan woman at the well of the water of life. "This water . . . shall become a fountain of water, springing up unto life everlasting . . ." (John 4:14)

Rebecca, the bride of the son promised so long, is beautiful and a virgin undefiled. These words are used for both the Church and the Mother of God, spouse of the Holy Spirit.

Would that all Christians responded with as much alacrity as Rebecca's people (and they pagans) who said, "This comes from the Lord; when His will is made known, it is not for us to say Yes or No . . ." (Gen 24:50 Knox)[5]

And Rebecca, returning, saw Isaac, veiled her beauty and went to meet him; he led her to his tent and there she comforted him for the loss of his mother. Here is an echo of the loss at the hands of Eve.

St. Paul says that Christ loves the Church as the bridegroom loves the bride. Perhaps this is the most eloquent of the images, and the most important. For all the talk of tolerance and understanding, there are still bigots and the Church is still spoken of scurrilously, many times within earshot of our children. She is called a political machine, a scheming hierarchy, a priest-ridden laity, an enemy of the state, of freedom, and more foolish things which are nonsense, but what image *do* our children have? What do they see when we speak of the Church? They probably see her in many ways, but let us add this picture of the bride to the store of ideas they have associated with her. It reveals the tenderness of Christ's relation to her with its language of love.

"Remember how Isaac loved Rebecca, how beautiful she was, how she comforted him as his bride? God loves us as tenderly as that, even more. When we have His life in us, we are as beautiful to Him as Rebecca was to Isaac. We *are* the Church, together with Christ, and we are closer to His heart than even Isaac and Rebecca to each other. When you think of the Church and how Christ loves her, think of the sweetness of Isaac's love for Rebecca."

Jacob and Esau

Rebecca was barren until Isaac implored the Lord for her. Then she conceived twin sons who fell to struggling within her.

---

[5] The knowledge of the One God is inserted by the author; still her people assented to the plan immediately.

She turned to the Lord for counsel and He answered that the two sons in her womb represented two peoples and the elder would be overcome by the younger, which was signified at their birth when Jacob, the younger, came clutching the heel of Esau, the elder. Esau, the hunter, was the favorite of Isaac, while Rebecca favored Jacob—understandably enough, knowing the prophecy of the Lord to her.

The Mess of Pottage

Next comes the tale of the birthright and the mess of pottage. Esau, tired and hungry, came home one day to find Jacob making lentil soup and asked him for a bowlful. Now Jacob's reply has been interpreted variously, but I confess that although there may have been craft in it before the end, his first remark strikes me as jesting. One of our boys might jokingly reply to such a request, "I'll give it to you for a million dollars"; Jacob replied, "Sell me first your birthright." To seriously ask for the birthright in such a frivolous, ill-timed way seems inconceivable. Jacob may well have heard from his mother that one day he would obtain his brother's birthright and may have wondered how it would come about, but he hardly seems fool enough to risk its exchange over a bowl of pottage. Esau's reply so surprised him that he asked his oath on it, and when Esau gave his oath even the comment of the author betrays astonishment. "Thus lightly did Esau value his birthright."

We had read this story one night and were enjoying a discussion of it when Philip interrupted.

"What was he cooking?"

"A pot of soup."

"What kind of soup?"

"Lentil soup."

"What are lentils?"

"A kind of beans—dried beans," I replied, becoming a little impatient with the interruption and turning to the others to continue. "Think of it, he sold his birthright, the right to inherit a double share of the family possessions and to *the* position of honor in the family, he sold it for . . ." I groped for a synonym sufficiently insignificant.

Philip interrupted again. "I'd say he sold it for beans."

Exactly.

In chapter 26, God speaks to Isaac and repeats the promise.

The promise runs like a thread through the history of the Jews and is our clue, keeping us from being distracted along the way by too many colorful side issues. At the same time, we must remember that the Hebrews to whom God spoke the promise did not understand all that was implied, but merely that God had chosen them for some future greatness, and that they were His people.

In this chapter we find another episode like the one where Abraham passed off Sara as his sister, but unlike Abraham, Isaac really does lie. Does this mean scripture teaches that the end justifies the means? Not at all. Here it is not teaching but stating what Isaac thought to be the solution to the problem. Not only his life was at stake, but also the existence of the line out of which the promise would be fulfilled, and it seemed expedient to him to insure against the loss of this at all costs. Our judgments of the patriarchs will not be so harsh if we remember that nowhere is it claimed that they were men without any faults. They had faults as numerous as ours, and they had not—as we have—the benefit of Christ's teaching and the strength of the sacraments.

These things need explaining because we are still becoming acquainted with scripture and the point of the story God is telling. As we reread the stories over the years, in the context of the Christian mystery, we will no longer even notice such things as these, because Abraham, Isaac, Jacob and the rest will have become great symbols of patriarchal virtue, great types of faith, obedience, submission.

There follow accounts of events which seem to have no bearing on the promise or redemption, but they testify to the Israelites' tenacious memory for "the precious souvenirs of the early life of the Hebrew forefathers in the land of the promise." [6] We take the same delight in the details of early life in our own colonies, in the New England villages, along the covered wagon trails, on the early frontier in the West.

Isaac Blesses Jacob

In chapter 27, we read of Rebecca's substitution of Jacob for Esau in order that he receive Isaac's blessings, and this is the sleight of hand to end all sleights of hand; a real scandal to the children. I would like to put in a word for Rebecca before she is permanently

[6] Vawter, *op. cit.*, p. 190.

convicted as a villainess. It seems reasonable to suppose that ever since hearing the word of the Lord regarding this son, she considered herself a woman with a God-given mission to maneuver Jacob into position to inherit. She may have gone about it heavy-handedly, but surely, in the excitement of seeing God's prophecy within reach of fulfillment, she must have thought the means justifiable. The supplanting had begun in the womb, had been partially concluded with the handing over of Esau's birthright, and needed only to be brought to completion. I suppose I must admit (seeing the footnote in the CCD translation of Genesis) that both were blameworthy, but I cannot help feeling that Rebecca saw this as her sacred duty.

Whatever side one takes, we can point out how cleverly God got His way, for out of this strange tangle His will was done. Rebecca, right or wrong, was an instrument in the hands of the Lord and her contribution to our redemption was no mean one: she gave us Jacob, the father of the twelve tribes of Israel.

In the Nuptial Mass, the Church prays that the bride be "prudent like Rebecca." Prudence is a virtue that calls for thought and judgment, and then, action. In the two episodes where Rebecca is shown, she is acting—and both times daringly. As a maiden she gave her assent to the plan which removed her far away from her own people, and as a mother she threw herself daringly ("Let the curse be on me!" [Gen 27:13]) into a plan fraught with difficulty. It is traditional to relate the prudence of the Nuptial blessing to the first occasion; wishfully I would like to think that, in view of her good will, it also applied to the second. At any rate, we *can* say that Rebecca was a woman who recognized God's voice and threw herself into His plans. May all brides be like that!

Isaac's final blessing, as Jacob went off to find a wife for himself, puts it all in the proper perspective. "God Almighty bless thee, and make thy posterity thrive and increase, so that a multitude of nations may spring from thee. May he grant to thee, and to thy race after thee, the blessing which he promised to thy grandfather Abraham: possession of the land in which thou dwellest now as a stranger." (Gen 28:3-4 Knox)

Jacob and the Ladder

There are three things to watch for in the story of Jacob: 1) God repeats to Jacob the promise He made to Abraham; 2) God changes Jacob's name to Israel, meaning "one that prevails with God"; and 3) Jacob becomes the father of twelve sons who are to head the twelve tribes of Israel.

With Esau angry because he had been cheated of his birth-right, Rebecca feared for Jacob's life, so she persuaded Isaac to send him off to their relatives in Haran to find a wife. Having chosen Abraham's line from the beginning, God intended that it be kept the blood line of His people.

Jacob started out. He had not been gone long when he stopped one night in a part of the country where the rocks ranged like giant steps in a ladder, and he dreamed he saw a ladder reaching to heaven, on it angels ascending and descending. From the top the Lord leaned down to repeat the promise with words which speak of us also among "all the nations of the earth." (Gen 28:14) Our Lord referred to this episode in His conversation with Nathaniel. (John 1:51) As Jacob saw the angels, so would Nathaniel see "the angels of God ascending and descending upon the Son of Man." God spoke of His Son to St. Catherine of Siena as a bridge which reaches from heaven to earth, "and which constitutes the union which I have made with man." [7] The vision speaks to us of Christ, though not to Jacob; even so it was to him a great sign symbolizing divine protection, and promising that through him the divine will would be worked out. When he awoke, Jacob vowed that if God would prosper his works, then "the Lord shall be my God also." (Gen 28:21)

Jacob and Rachel

The scene at the well where Jacob sees his beloved Rachel for the first time is reminiscent of his parents' romance. Strong, tender-hearted, lonely for his people, he gazes at her with bewilderment and joy, moves the great stone so she may water her sheep, and, weeping, kisses her and makes himself known. When Laban, her father, accepts him into the family circle in an arrangement much like an adoption (evidently he had no sons yet), Jacob asks for Rachel's hand and is told he may have her in return for seven years' work. So Jacob worked seven years to win Rachel, counting them as only a few days—so great was his love.

But God in His justice serves each of us our due, and Jacob

[7] Algar Thorold (trans.), *Dialogue of St. Catherine of Siena* (Westminster, Md.: Newman Press, 1950), p. 75.

found that the Lord of all who permitted him to trick his brother out of his birthright permitted *him* to be tricked in the same way. At the end of seven years, Laban substituted the squint-eyed Lia, and not until the morning light shone full on the bride did Jacob discover the deception. His anguished protest and Laban's curt rejoinder have a familiar ring—rather like the outraged cry of Esau to which Isaac answered: "I have given him my blessing, and on him the blessing will come." (27:33 Knox)

But Rachel would be his if he worked another seven years, and he did, earning Rachel and in time fathering twelve sons and a daughter by his wives and their two maidservants. A careful reading beforehand by the parents will enable them to ease the children through chapter 30 with its intrigues between the wives, their jealousies, the begetting of sons by the maidservants and all the rest. The explanation of polygamy which they heard in the story of Abraham is now readily accepted by them. It was all right for people to do it then; *it isn't now.*

Oddly enough, this complication between the two wives seems like a parable on the soul and its love for God. Jacob is like a man who finally sees the beauty of God and falls in love, and God invites his embrace. Filled with sweetness, all labor for God seems nothing, His love promises so much. Then at the top of his longing, a truth is discovered: it is not the way of the Lord to give the soul all the delights of union with Him until the difficult path of virtue has been followed. A little bitter, the soul suffers purgation, always looking ahead to the joy of union, and a bargain being a bargain, he wins it if he does his part. So say the saints and so says God. The fruitfulness of the two wives is like the fruitfulness of each of the two ways. Although it was his beloved Rachel who bore the sons dearest to Jacob's heart, Joseph and Benjamin, it was Lia, so plain and unattractive—like the practice of the ordinary virtues—who bore Juda, out of whom would come the Promised One. This is only a by-the-way meditation, but it is the kind of thing we find in scripture if we let our minds graze over God's words and feed there.

Jacob Comes Home

At the end of twenty years Jacob was inspired to return to his homeland, and he asked that Laban give him all the lambs and kids born spotted or blotched at the next lambing season. He needed, and had a right to, property to take with him so he could provide for his family. When we read of the breeding of the animals, according to a scheme which would make a geneticist smile but which is part of the ancient story, we may doubt that the arranging of spotted sticks had much to do with it, but we cannot deny that God worked things out to Jacob's advantage. He left rich with flocks, men and maidservants.

The stealth of Jacob's departure may mean that he was bound to Laban under some kind of adoption arrangement; and Rachel's theft of her father's household gods might be explained by the fact that these always went to the eldest or to the son who received the special blessing and double share of property. Perhaps this was an attempt to secure at least a specious right to Laban's goods. At any rate, it does show that she and her family were still pagans.

The hasty departure brought Laban in pursuit, and once again we see the Lord determine to make events suit *Him.* "Take care not to say anything at all to Jacob!" He warned (Gen 31:30); and it was Laban's respect for the God who protected Jacob's race and who, incidentally, had prospered his own affairs under Jacob, that stayed his hand. The excuse Rachel gives for not rising from her saddle presents a trifling difficulty, but this can be translated, for the benefit of little ones listening, as "I am not feeling well." (Gen 31:35)

No sooner had Jacob settled his difficulties with Laban than the memory of Esau's anger posed another problem. His wily plan for pacifying Esau reminds us a little of Our Lord's tale of the steward who used the things of this world to gain him friends and whose tact, He said, we might imitate in our own effort to get to heaven. (Luke 16:1-13) Setting aside for Esau a large number of goats, bucks, ewes, rams, camels, cows, bulls, asses and colts, he dispatched them with their drivers in a veritable procession of gifts designed to calm whatever remained of Esau's wrath. (Gen 32:4-21) We must skip to Genesis 33:1-17 to finish the encounter with Esau. As we might expect, Esau was happy with his gifts, the brothers met and parted peaceably and each went to his own district to live. (Genesis 33:18-20 is thought to be part of the story of the sack of Sichem.)

Jacob Wrestles with the Angel

The struggle between Jacob and the angel (Gen 32:22-31) should be a special evening's reading all by itself. The episode is mysterious and wonderful and a moment of sheer drama, but it needs explanation. Our fourteen-year-old said, the first time around, "I don't think I get the point."

This event seems to be a turning point in the life of Jacob, a conversion. His first meeting with the God of his father is like a commercial transaction compared to this one. True to His word, God had prospered the worldly fortunes of Jacob, but this was never the point of God's choice of the Jews, and now He was making the point. At the same time, He was making a new person of Jacob, one dedicated to God's plan and not his own. Jacob was notably a fighter, a man who did not give in. The wrestling till dawn is marvelously significant and God is pleased with his perseverance; He rewards it by changing his name to Israel, "one who contends with God." The nation coming forth from Jacob would be known as Israel, a nation that struggles with God and is used by Him.

This name signifies the Church, also, and in it, ourselves; and it recalls the pain of our own conversion from "Please give me" to "Let me serve You." It is a figure of the struggle with temptation, with indecision, with wanting to question God's will. Our young adults suffering their own agony of discovery, wrestling with the question of vocation, share an experience like Jacob's as he wrestled. He is one of their friends, and it might help them to pray to him.

If we move on to Genesis 35:1-15 (thought possibly to be another version of the name-changing episode), we will see how profoundly Jacob's attitude was changed, as shown by his concern for the idolatry among his family and servants, and the sweeping purification of all their possessions, from statues and ornaments to a complete change of garments—all meant to be signs of a total change of heart. Then God once more renewed His promise.

The ravishing of Dina in chapter 34, her brothers' treachery, their murder and sack of the town, read like any family scandal, though on a grand scale; and the anguish of Jacob as he decries his sons' crime is all too familiar. The wisdom of the father, his self-discipline, his sense of high purpose under God, none of these could he *make* his sons possess. At best, he could teach and give good example and hope it would "take." However, as we know, it was a long time before they learned.

The account of Jacob's youth and middle years draws to a close with the tragic death of Rachel upon the birth of the youngest son, Benjamin, the dearly beloved. Strangely enough, although the glimpses of Rachel are few, throughout her story there is the haunting sense of her beauty and Jacob's love for her. Holy Church has placed her in the Nuptial Mass also, asking for the bride, "and may she ever follow the pattern of holy women; may she be dear to her husband, like Rachel . . ."

There follows a short account of Jacob's contribution to our redemption, the twelve sons who would found the twelve tribes of Israel; and then the burial of Isaac. We skip chapter 36 for family reading.

Joseph

Joseph is our favorite of all the stories in Genesis. Christopher said recently, "I pretend it's happening to me." It is that kind of story—all excitement, color, suspense, and plots, plots, plots; and it is very beautiful.

Joseph, unlike Abraham, Isaac and Jacob, is not called a patriarch, nor was it from his house and tribe that the Promised One would come. In fact, God did not even speak to Joseph of the promise, yet he was in every way as important as the others. What did Joseph do that made him so important?

First of all, in the story of Joseph we must watch God at work maneuvering. In all his adventures, Joseph was being moved about by God so he would be where he was needed at the time he was needed. One day famine would strike the land of Chanaan and the people of God would be in danger of starvation. Herdsmen, whose wealth is in their flocks, do not stay alive very long after the water dries up, the grasses are parched, and the animals begin to perish. But these people had to survive—God had made a pact with mankind and had chosen these people to work it out.

The second point of the story, for families, is that God leaves men free to make their mistakes or do their evil, and then uses its consequences to work out His own will. So often the family struggles from crisis to crisis, seeming always to be the victim of injustice, bungling, "bad breaks"; but God is able to make good come of all three, and while we don't always see what He is up to,

He is always up to something. We must learn to wait—with faith—like Joseph.

Joseph was born of Rachel, was next to the youngest of Jacob's sons, and was one of his father's two favorites. Naturally his brothers were jealous. This story presents such a true picture of family life at its worst as well as its best—a hodgepodge of loyalty, jealousy, co-operation, bickering, affection, annoyance; and Joseph is so real in it that it is hard to believe the writers of the text did not know him personally. It is a tribute to the love this people had for Joseph, that they handed down this warm, living portrait of him from generation to generation.

Joseph was envied by his brothers and it did not help matters when he told them his grand dreams. Even Jacob chided him for this, but he was thoughtful all the same. He knew God too well to suppose that such things could have no meaning.

So when his father sent him to locate his brothers and their flocks, they concocted a scheme to be rid of him. Dismissing the possibility of murder, they threw him in a dry well and, seeing a caravan approach, on the spur of the moment they sold him to traders from Madian.

One night, during this part of the story, Philip was busy with a cardboard carton, some paper, scissors and paste. By the time we finished our reading and were ready for night prayers—the Psalms that had mention of Joseph and Egypt in them—he had produced a neat little shadow box showing Joseph kneeling in prayer at the bottom of the dry well, throwing himself on the mercy of God. It added much to our prayers.

Joseph in Egypt

At about age sixteen, therefore, Joseph was carried off to Egypt.

Since he is one of the most magnificent types of Christ to be found in scripture, it is not surprising that all this should strike a familiar chord. It is also clear why Joseph, caring for the chosen ones of God in Egypt, is also a type of St. Joseph who cared for Mary and Christ in Egypt.

And Jacob grieved to see the bloody coat, and judged the boy to be eaten by wild beasts.

Chapter 38 tells of Juda's son, Onan, who "spilled his seed

upon the ground," and is best omitted at this time. It is one of the scriptural references to the teaching of the Church about artificial birth control but it has no place in a discussion which includes small children. Juda's traffic with his daughter-in-law adds only to our wonder at the weaknesses of Our Lord's forebearers and the family line He took for Himself, its closets rattling with skeletons. Skip chapter 38.

Joseph's Test

In Egypt, Joseph was bought by Phutiphar, captain of Pharaoh's guard, and so brilliantly did he execute his tasks that the royal captain put him in charge of his entire household. Now Joseph was very handsome (Rachel was his mother), and Phutiphar's wife "cast her eyes on Joseph and said, 'Lie with me.'" (Gen 39:8) How can we read this to small children? Or shall we omit this also?

I think not. It is a beautiful story telling of Joseph's virtue, and it is easily read with a bit of changing. We might have her say, "Come, make love to me," and then interpolate. "Wasn't that too bad? She wanted Joseph to sin against God's law, and offend his master, by making love to her as though he was her husband. Husbands and wives are very loving with one another and this is pleasing to God, but what Phutiphar's wife wanted was very wrong. He wasn't even her husband!"

Joseph's resistance, her trickery, his imprisonment, is a noble tale of love for God and virtue and gives us an example of a man who was in the world but not of it. Joseph had become thoroughly Egyptian in his way of life and work, but his loyalty to the Lord reveals that he was ever the faithful Israelite, obedient to the God of his father.

Joseph and Pharaoh

In prison, Joseph correctly interpreted the dreams of the king's butler and baker, and in time, when the Pharaoh was troubled by dreams, the butler remembered him. Asked by the Pharaoh to explain his dream, Joseph answered that only God could do that, but his inspired interpretation so pleased the king that he had Joseph released and put in charge of the whole land of Egypt, to prepare during the years of plenty for the seven years of famine.

A Visit to the Museum

It is a great help, at this point, for the family to explore at least a little of the history and culture of Egypt where Joseph and the Israelites dwelt. The Pharaohs who ruled at the time of Joseph and his family were not Egyptians but are thought to be the Hyksos kings of the period from 1730 B.C. to 1570 B.C., which would explain their friendliness to the Hebrews. Although this was a period of cultural decline, compared to life on the plains, the monuments, display and ritual of these pagans were the ultimate in elegance. A visit to a museum to see the artifacts and domestic tools of both the rich and the poor, the models of their cities, the decorations on their buildings, the manner of their life, helps us to understand how Joseph lived, and how later the Hebrews on the march to Chanaan could yearn for the glories of Egypt as for paradise itself. No wonder there was moaning and groaning in the desert; the goodies of Egypt included onions, leeks, garlics, melons and cucumbers! We saw all these staples beautifully painted on the wooden crate for a sarcophagus on our visit to the Museum of Fine Arts in Boston, and it helped enormously to create the atmosphere in the story of Joseph in Egypt.

When we looked through books of Egyptian sculpture and painting, we could see that Joseph looked something like this, smooth-shaven, with his hair so, his court clothes so; his furniture, his writing materials, his house, like these. If beautiful to begin with (he had Rebecca for a grandmother), in Egyptian dress he must have been like a god. Pharaoh's daughter surely thanked *her* gods when she was given as wife to Joseph.

Such a colorful story. We have watched our own small boys listen wide-eyed and heard them say, at a pause, "Go on. Go on!" And we remembered that Mary's boy listened to the same story. Did His face look like this?

Joseph's Reunion with His Brothers

When Jacob learned there was grain for sale in Egypt, he said such a funny thing—it sounds like our house: "Why do you stand there looking at one another? . . . Go down to Egypt and buy some." (Gen 42:1-2) And they did, all but Benjamin, whom Jacob kept at home lest some harm befall him. Pretending to suspect them, Joseph sent them back with grain, keeping Simeon as hostage, and told them to return with Benjamin as proof of their good faith. The complications that follow—Joseph's trickery, the revelation of his identity—make a gorgeous tale, but it is when we hear Joseph forgive his brothers for their betrayal of him that we see at last the great figure of Christ outlined for us.

"God sent me down before you to preserve a remnant for you in the land, and to deliver you up in a striking way." (Gen 45:7-8) The author had no thought of Christ, but the image of Joseph, who came down to Egypt to save his brothers, who fed them so they would not die, speaks of Christ, Who came down to save us and Who feeds us so we will not die. This is a beautiful story to tell children preparing for their first Holy Communion, as well as for the family that needs to refresh its understanding of *why* we must receive the Holy Eucharist. We often hear the habitual reception of this sacrament questioned on the grounds that "one gets too used to it." The story of Joseph makes clear the dreadful urgency that we eat this Food, lest we die. The Hebrews would have died, had not Joseph fed them. "Unless you eat the flesh of the Son of Man, and drink his blood, you shall not have life in you." (John 6:54)

There is an odd little commentary on the ways of men in Joseph's words to his brothers as they leave for Chanaan the final time, to bring back Jacob, their father. They had been forgiven, reunited, wined and dined and gifted. They had been promised food and asylum through the years of famine and longer. Yet knowing them well (from experience!), he felt bound to give them a word of advice.

"Do not quarrel on the way." (Gen 45:25)

It sounds just like a family.

Thus it came about that the Israelites began to live in Egypt. When Jacob died, Joseph mourned him and, keeping a promise, took him back and buried him in the land of his fathers. And Joseph himself died in Egypt, rich in years, to rest there until the day his people, leaving at last, would carry his body back with them.

·III·

THE PEOPLE, THE PROPHET
AND
THE LAW—
FROM EGYPT TO SINAI

Exodus

The Flight from Egypt

If you and your family were marooned on a desert island and
allowed only one book of the Old Testament for your instruction,
you would have to choose Exodus. The book of Exodus is like a
mountain peak that towers over the rest of the Old Testament, a
key book enshrining the central point of all salvation history up
to the coming of Christ.

In this book is to be found the heart of the matter, and in it
you would have in type the struggles and defeats and recoveries
of the entire history of God's people, dominated by the figure of
Moses, prophet and man of God, intercessor between God and
His people; and you would have in type the history of the Christian
and his soul's struggles, defeats, and recoveries, dominated by the

figure of Christ, intercessor between the Father and His people.

Thank goodness we do not have to make such a choice; it would be unthinkable to dispense with the rest of the Bible; but this device serves to place Exodus in its relation to the rest—as pole or center. Without this book, the language of the Psalms remains beautiful and poetic but not always intelligible, for the relationship between the Psalmist and God is established in Exodus. Without it, the prophets plead and threaten but do not make much sense because the point of their pleading is the people's forgetfulness of what happened in Exodus. The Law given to us in Exodus is the great measure of deeds through the long story of the Israelites; without it their story would be—and often was, when they forgot it—every man for himself.

Exodus means *going out*, and refers to the Israelites' flight from Egypt. They had enjoyed peace and prosperity for a long time under the Hyksos Pharaohs, who were Semites and aliens like themselves, but with the return to the throne of truly Egyptian kings, their good fortune began to change. The descendents of Jacob were frankly unwanted and the solution to their presence at first seemed to be to convert them into a huge labor force. But this did not discourage their increase, rather, they continued to multiply until finally the Egyptians reduced them to a state of outright slavery. Thus the opening of the book of Exodus finds things vastly different from the last chapter of Genesis.

This is probably one of the easiest of all the books of the Bible for family reading. In addition, it is enormously exciting, and the fact that we already know some of its high points will not spoil it for us.

We found it convenient to read Exodus from a booklet containing both the text, in the new CCD translation, and a commentary, and giving us ample room to make marginal notes and to underline in a way not permissible on the pages of the family Bible.[1]

Moses

Excitement begins at once with the account of Pharaoh's condemnation of the boy babies and brings us in no time to Moses floating safely on the river in his ark of reeds. For a fleeting moment we remember Noe safe on the waters of the flood.

[1] Roland E. Murphy, O. Carm., *The Book of Exodus, Parts 1 and 2 with a Commentary* (New York: Paulist Press), price 50¢.

Already there is a surprise. Moses, the greatest of heroes and prophets, in his youth was far from perfect in virtue and faith. First his murder of the Egyptian worker and later his faint-hearted acceptance of God's call make us wonder that God uses men much like ourselves to accomplish His ends. However much we admire and love Moses, one thing we must admit—he was not a self-made man. Without God, even he could do nothing.

Before going further, it should be remembered that, as with Genesis, Exodus is not history as we would write it. It is the compiled account of oral tradition from three different sources, written down long after the events took place. This accounts for the overlapping of events, repetition, variation in detail, and for seeming discrepancies, none of which alters the mainstream of the story. It is no longer bothersome, for example, to find that two names are given for Moses' father-in-law, Jethro and Raguel; that God is sometimes spoken of as *the Lord*, sometimes as *the angel of the Lord*; or even to discover a certain variation in the way Moses and Aaron command the miracles. As for the repeated instructions about the paschal meal [2]—which make the children fidget—the solution is to read one set of instructions and omit the others. It is also helpful to know that chapters 1-15 are thought to have been put together for reading at a liturgical event when the people were to be reminded of their past and given instruction, and thus take the form of an epic summary of their history. If we were to summarize the high points of our own struggle for liberty for a Fourth of July commemoration, we might do much the same thing.

The Burning Bush

The meeting with God in the burning bush begins Moses' lifelong intimacy with the Lord. The flame that burns without consuming is like God's love, and we find it often in religious art and the liturgy. In Advent we call on Christ with an O antiphon which says: "O Adonai and Leader of the House of Israel, who appeared in the bush to Moses in a flame of fire . . . come and redeem us with an outstretched arm." There is a shrub commonly seen on the streets of our towns in the fall which is called "burning bush," because its scarlet seems a flame that burns without consuming. One cannot see it without remembering Moses. After we had read his story, we bought such a shrub for our own yard and now God

[2] From pasch (pronounced *pask*): passover

speaks to us, too, in this bush, though in a different way. And there is a nice little detail in Exodus 3:5 to tuck away for the time when proper manners and respect for sacred things are of the moment. "Remove the sandals from your feet, for the place where you stand is holy ground." God insists on reverence in sacred places.

The message of the Lord was this, that Moses should go to Egypt and demand that Pharaoh let the people go, and that Moses should lead them to Chanaan, the land of milk and honey. But Moses was afraid. Who was he to accomplish all this? God reassured Moses that He would be with him in all his works. Indeed, Pharaoh would be difficult in the end, but God would smite the Egyptians with wonderful deeds and finally he would let them go.

Hard of Heart?

In Exodus 4:21, God says He will make Pharaoh obstinate, and this bothers children. How can God, Who is so good, want to make a man evil? "I will make him obstinate, harden his heart." Other such words might be better understood to refer to the holy will of God against which these villains ever fling themselves, daring to defy it. If a man wishes to harden his heart with disobedience, God will permit it. Men are free. As we become more familiar with the scriptures, we will find that the biblical writers attribute everything to God, the good as well as the bad, and we will begin to see things from their point of view. Even sin comes under God's control. It never takes Him by surprise, and He can always turn sin to the benefit of the good people.

The Plagues

Next come the ten plagues. The plagues in themselves were natural phenomena visited upon Egypt at different seasons of the year. (I grew up near a body of water which turned brownish red, like blood, every August, from the algae present in it—and filled with jellyfish. Great plagues!) The miraculous to the Israelites was not always or necessarily a suspension of the law of nature, but could include as well unique natural demonstrations of God's power. We often speak the same way ourselves. One boy in our family who keeps pet goats said with wonder at kidding time: "It's a miracle!" Not really—and he knew it; but it was wonderful. What *was* miraculous by the Egyptians' standards, the Israelites', and our own—even at their most scientific, was the control of these phe-

nomena displayed by Moses and Aaron. When we were reading of
the plagues one time, a younger brother continually interrupted
during the story to determine whether the Israelites were protected
after each of the smitings, until finally an older brother stated the
case for him once and for all.

"It was miraculous, don't you see? Where the Egyptians were,
it was dark; where the Israelites were, it was light. Even if the
Egyptians had gone where the Israelites were, it would still have
been dark for them and light for the Israelites." And a rather good
analogy of hardness of heart it was, entirely satisfying to an eight-
year-old who knows that "you can't fool God."

The Passover

In chapter 12, God gives instructions for preparing the paschal
lamb to be eaten in the houses of the Hebrews on the night the
angel of death passes over them (hence "Passover") to reap the
harvest of the first-born of Egypt. The meal, Moses was told, was
to be repeated year after year, age after age—a yearling lamb or
kid, without blemish, roasted, eaten, head, feet, entrails and all,
and not a bone broken. And God meant repeated until the end of
time—as it will be, for Christ has transformed this meal into the
Mass. On Calvary the soldiers forebore to break the legs of Christ,
thinking Him already dead, but "These things came to pass that
Scripture might be fulfilled, 'Not a bone of Him shall you break.'"
(John 19:36)

With hyssop the blood of the victim was to be smeared on the
jambs and lintels of their doors so death should not touch them.
Now, with Christ's death, we too are marked with the blood of the
Lamb; eternal death need not touch us.

This story, said the Lord, is to be told over and over, to the
children and the children's children. It is the answer to the youngest
child's question, "What is the meaning of this night?" asked at
the Jewish family's Seder supper on the Passover. It is the story told
to the Christian children as they commemorate with their family's
paschal supper on Holy Thursday the transforming of this meal into
the Mass and the Holy Eucharist. The liturgy for the Easter vigil
is so filled with the imagery of this story that we cannot understand
the rite if we do not know the story.

Then at midnight cries of anguish arose all over Egypt and
Pharaoh was struck to his knees. "Begone! You will be doing me a

favor!" (Ex 12:32) And God, Who is a Father too, knew Pharaoh's anguish.

The Ransom of the First-born

In chapter 13, the Lord instructs the Hebrews that the first-born male of every womb is thereafter forfeit to Him, each being ransomed lest the people forget the price He exacted for their freedom. Thus the Christ child was taken to the temple to be presented to the Lord and to be ransomed at the time of the purification of His mother. (Luke 2:23) He, Who so loved the Law and those who kept it, became the perfect example of obedience to it. To meditate on the fourth joyful mystery of the Rosary really should take us all the way back to Exodus.

The mysterious thing about scripture is that each time you read it, it seems new. I have heard Christopher, the second time around, genuinely puzzled over the story of Pharaoh.

"Do you think he's *ever* going to let them go?"

And I have heard him, the third time around, shout "Yea!" when at last Pharaoh and his minions were drowned in the sea.

The Word of God for Our Instruction: Baptism

It is the same for grownups, especially if we search deeper each time into the spiritual significance of the scriptures. It explains many things we have not quite grasped before. For example, with respect to Baptism, I had often heard and read that the going down into the waters of Baptism is a sign of death, and the rising out of them a sign of new life. I accepted this symbol but it was never quite real, perhaps because I was too insensitive or too literal, or perhaps because during all the years of growing up Baptism had been taught to me as a washing free from sin, without ever a mention made of the coming of Life.

But Exodus makes it brilliantly clear. The Lord led them out of slavery in Egypt by way of the waters of certain death in the Red Sea[3]—and brought them out safely to show them that their lives as well as their freedom they now owed to Him, their destiny was now bound to Him. This is the most eloquent of all the great types of Baptism and illustrates, in a way we cannot miss, the certainty of our own birth to new life having emerged from the waters

[3] More accurately the Reed Sea, not the great Red Sea of the geography books. Common usage has made Red Sea acceptable.

of this sacrament. Our slavery in Egypt was that time before Baptism when we lived in a domain ruled by the prince of the world. Our freedom now in the life of grace makes it abundantly clear that we belong to Christ. This is what it means to be "the people of God." Could we but realize what it means to be the people of God, we would have our fingers on the wellspring of commitment, for it is the awakening to our redeemed-ness that brings all the talk of dedication and apostolate into focus. God brought His people out of the sea for a reason—to work out the salvation of mankind. This work continues and His people live on in the Church, but too often as His people we do not know this. The Christian obligation has been thought to be "saving our own souls," with no hint that it is connected in any way with the great saving action inaugurated by God on Mount Sinai, which continues to touch the lives of men today, gathering them to Him.

Exodus with its stunning images speaks of all these things. Perhaps with this story God will help us to discover at last who we are, and the work we are supposed to be doing.

The People Complain

Hardly had the people finished dancing to Moses' great canticle of thanksgiving than they began to complain, and nowhere is there a more accurate picture of the short-sightedness of man than in the trials in the desert. Saved from one disaster after another, the Israelites are briefly thankful and then return to doubt, fear and grumbling—a picture of ourselves if ever there was one. As the redeemed we rejoice so little.

But we should be fair to them; they had none of the wisdom of our hindsight, and the desert *was* terrible. To judge them is to judge ourselves. They had been brought out of Egypt a rabble, someone has said, and it remained for God to make them into a nation. Considering the length of their stay in a pagan land, it is remarkable that they remained faithful to the God of their fathers at all. When freedom and the vision of the long-promised land of milk and honey seemed about to materialize, who wouldn't risk his neck? No one had warned them of all these tests! They grumbled at Mara, and Moses begged the Lord and He made the water sweet. They grumbled in the desert of Sin, and Moses spoke with the Lord and He sent manna and quail. With each test they grumbled, blamed the Lord, blamed Moses; and the long bitter slavery in Egypt began to take on a loveliness it had never possessed before. They had had food and shelter *there*.

And poor Moses—we love him so for all he suffered. "What shall I do with this people?" he cried in desperation. (Ex 17:4) I have cried out the same myself. "What shall I do with these children!" Certainly God in His way has cried out the same over me.

The Waters of Grace

All these events in the desert are types of the sacramental life. The water from the barren rock at Meriba, the sweetened water at Mara, are like the waters of sanctifying grace poured out over the people from Christ's side on the Cross. The manna which fed them miraculously throughout their forty years in the desert, strengthening them on their journey to the land of promise, is like the Holy Eucharist which miraculously feeds us as we make our way from earth to heaven. Both Our Lord and St. Paul used Exodus to teach these things.

St. Paul wrote: "I would not have you ignorant, brethren, that our fathers were all under the cloud, and all passed through the sea, and all were baptized in Moses, in the cloud and in the sea. And all ate the same spiritual food, and all drank the same spiritual drink (for they drank from the spiritual rock which followed them, and the rock was Christ). Yet with most of them God was not well pleased . . . Now all these things happened to them as a type, and they were written for our correction." (I Cor 10:1-11)

St. Paul has even snatched an idea from a later rabbinical tradition—that the rock which provided water when Moses struck it continued to follow the Israelites through the desert—to teach that as we make our way through the desert of life, Christ is with us and provides us with the waters of life.

The Bread of Life

Our Lord told the people, "Our Fathers ate the manna in the desert, even as it is written, 'Bread from heaven he gave them to eat' . . . Amen, amen, I say to you, Moses did not give you the bread from heaven, but my Father gives you the true bread from heaven. For the bread of God is that which comes down from heaven and gives life to the world . . . I am the bread of life." (John 6:31-35)

These passages from the New Testament might conclude the family's reading of the waters from the rock, and the manna.

The Lesson of God's Power

Again the Lord showed His might in order to teach a lesson. In the battle with the Amalecites, the victory rested not upon the numbers or arms of the Israelites, but on Moses' ability to keep his hands raised, a sign God had chosen to show that His power was with them. When Moses put his arms down, their men fell back; when he held them up, their men pressed forward. In the end Aaron and Hur had to hold his arms up for him. In this episode, we meet Josue for the first time, the great general whose exploits we will read of later on. Josue is a beautiful figure always, strong, obedient, ever faithful. We must watch for him.

God Makes His Covenant with the People

Finally they reached Sinai and encamped at the foot of the mountain, and Moses alone went up and heard God speak words which, once agreed to by the people, would make them irrevocably His—His people, His nation, His beloved. God bade Moses tell the people:

"You have seen for yourselves how I treated the Egyptians and how I bore you up on eagle wings and brought you here to myself. Therefore, if you hearken to my voice and keep my covenant, you shall be my special possession, dearer to me than all other people, though all the earth is mine. You shall be to me a kingdom of priests, a holy nation." (Ex 19:4-6)

The Israelites answered: "Everything the Lord has said, we will do." And God prepared to become Israel's spouse.

The people were ordered to sanctify themselves, and three days later, when a mighty trumpet blast sounded from the mountain, Moses "led the people out of the camp to meet God." (Ex 19:16) While they waited, Moses ascended alone and received the Commandments[4], and returning to the people he related the words of the Lord and prepared the sacrifice which would ratify the Lord's

[4] When reading the great action of the Theophany, it is wise to skip chapters 21, 22, and 23:1-19 temporarily, returning to read them later.

covenant with His people. With this event, we have arrived at the most significant action of the Old Testament, its height and its heart.

On an altar surrounded by twelve pillars for the twelve tribes of Israel, Moses sacrificed young bulls as a peace offering to the Lord. Taking half the blood, he splashed it on the altar, a symbol of God's partnership in the agreement, and then he read the words of the covenant again to the people, who again answered that they would do the will of the Lord. Then Moses took the remainder of the blood and sprinkled it on the people, binding them to God in a ritual that signified union: now God and Israel were bound together as in a marriage.

Blood is a sign of life; to the Israelites this blood with which they were marked was a sign of the new life they would now lead as the people of God. "This is the blood of the covenant which the Lord has made with you in accordance with all these words of his," said Moses. (Ex 24:8) The plan for redemption, inaugurated at the foot of Mount Sinai, was finally revealed in the words of Christ at the Last Supper: "This is my blood of the new covenant, which is being shed for many." (Mark 14:24)

At long last we understand the many references to our being bathed in the blood of the Lamb. We understand now the choice of Christ's death, a bloody death by crucifixion. Why His "Body and Blood"? I used to wonder as a child, when anything else would have sufficed. It was all part of God's infinite mercy, adapting Himself to the signs men understand. Blood has always been a sign of life. This Blood pouring over us from the sacrifice of Christ is the most glorious of all the signs of Life.

Then God told Moses to ascend the mountain once again and He would give him stone tablets on which were written the Commandments.

The Law

Now we can turn our attention to the Law. The Law as given in the Pentateuch (the first five books of the Bible) in Exodus, Leviticus, Numbers and Deuteronomy, are the Laws which were either given to Moses or grew out of those laws, and therefore it is called "the law of Moses." (As daily life for the Hebrews grew more complicated, additional laws were needed.) In themselves, these laws are not unique for they reflect ideas common to the ancient Near East, but what *is* unique is that they were given by God, not legislated, and they frame the life of the nation which was founded by God and whose destiny was related to the keeping of His Law. The Law is the measure of God's love in the Old Testament; beyond it the Israelites must not go, or they will be lost to Him. Let them break it and already He speaks to them as though He does not know them.

We omit reading most of the laws because they do not make successful family reading. Children soon become bored with the long instructions and prohibitions. Parents might scan this section ahead of time, starting with chapter 21[5], and point out things of special interest. For example, all have heard of the "eye for an eye" law of talion in Exodus 21:23. The point of this law was not to exact rigorous justice, as we have supposed, but to keep men from going beyond the claims of justice. God's concern for the widows, the orphans, the poor, in Exodus 22:20-26, is thought-provoking, and Exodus 23:1-9 shows us many obligations of social justice.

"You shall not boil a kid in its mother's milk," reads Exodus 23:19. Why this? Many of the dietary laws were associated less with hygiene than with pagan ritual. Kid boiled in its mother's milk was part of a menu used at a Chanaanite feast, "The Birth of the Gracious Gods," which also involved obscene fertility rites, and the Lord was determined that His people stay a safe distance from such things. All through Exodus 23:20-33, God instructed the people to have nothing to do with the loathsome Chanaanites.

Liturgical Laws

Seven chapters tell of ritual legislation and give instructions for building the Ark of the Covenant, the Table, the Lampstand, for the making of vestments, and many other things. This material also might be read ahead and then discussed. Much future action will center about these sacred objects. The cherubim to be mounted on the Ark are not the human-like creatures we call by this name, but great winged lions with human faces, seen frequently in the art of Mesopotamia, and other Middle Eastern peoples. The culture of their pagan past molded the worship of the Israelites.

Plainly, God had definite ideas about proper worship. The

[5] Returning to chapter 21, we scan: 21, 22, 23:1-19, 25, 26, 27, 28, 29, 30, 31:1-17.

wealth of rich colors, textures, fine materials, precious stones, scents, rites prescribed in the liturgical laws teach that liturgy and the correct enactment of it demands care and attention.

The Golden Calf

And now comes the puzzle of their idolatry. How could they worship something so crude as a golden calf! Was it really meant to be a statue of God? What was wrong with Aaron, had he taken leave of his senses?

Perhaps it is easier to understand their behavior if we recall that they had recently come out of Egypt where at least one could *see* the gods. How comforting, to be able to see your gods. (God eventually made Himself visible to us in Christ.) After our visit to the Egyptian art in the museum, where we saw beautifully wrought statues of golden gods, half-man, half-beast, we did not wonder that the Israelites began to hanker after some such image of the God who was supposed to be leading them. There is still another possibility. It was a belief among the ancient peoples that the thrones of the gods rested on the backs of bulls. Some scholars feel this was what Aaron had in mind, and that his statement, "This is your God, O Israel . . ." (Ex 32:4) was meant to indicate the invisible God enthroned on the back of the visible beast. The footnote in the CCD translation of Exodus states that the young bull, a symbol of strength, was used by Aaron as a symbol of the strong God Who had led them out of Egypt. As for Moses, they said: "We do not even know what has happened to him." (Ex 32:1) He seemed to have gone off and left them.

None of this justifies them, of course. They were too close to paganism for comfort, and this was precisely why God had warned them not to make graven images as the pagans did.[6] And when they disobeyed His explicit command, they incurred His anger.

Reconciliation

"Go down at once to your people whom you brought out of the land of Egypt," said God to Moses, "your people—whom you

---

[6] This helps us to understand why the use of images in worship was forbidden the Hebrews, and why sacred images are permitted in worship today. Far removed from the mentality and atmosphere of the idol-worshiping pagans, great works of art help to lead man's mind to prayer and contemplation.

brought." (Ex 32:7) Repeatedly God had said that the Israelites' obligation under the covenant was fidelity. Now that they had already been unfaithful, He would destroy them. And now we see Moses interceding and pleading for the sinful people. Never is Moses more like Christ than in his role of intercessor.

Chapter 33 is so tender with God's love for Moses that we seem to be listening to a conversation we were not meant to hear —a conversation between two lovers. Then God renews the tablets of the Law, and after the second vigil on the mountain, Moses descends, his face so radiant with the nearness of God that Aaron and the others are afraid of him.

We skip chapters 35 through 40:33, and complete our reading of Exodus with chapter 40:34-38. The Lord, reconciled with His people once more, dwelt there with them. And "Moses could not enter the Meeting Tent, because the cloud settled down upon it and the glory of the Lord filled the Dwelling." (Ex 40:34-35) When the cloud rose from the Dwelling, the people set out on their journey, and when the cloud did not lift, they stayed—that they might know they were the Lord's and He was with them.

In the story of the Annunciation, St. Luke uses almost the same words about Our Lady, who is called the Ark of the Covenant, for in her womb resided the living Word. "The Holy Spirit shall come upon thee and the power of the Most High shall overshadow thee." (Luke 1:35) It gives us a hint of the riches of scripture for the family to explore in the years to come.

Leviticus

The book of Leviticus takes its name from Levi, son of Jacob, whose tribe was chosen in the days of Moses to act as the official ministers of divine worship and whose priestly role elevated them above the common priesthood of the people, received from the Lord. This book is a collection of laws governing the life of the people, covering almost every conceivable situation: religious, domestic, dietary, hygienic, and others. It is something like our own parish priest's *Rituale*, though much more complicated, and its purpose is to teach the people the ways God wishes them to observe the outward, official cleanliness which will be a symbol of their interior purity of heart and union with the Lord. Its central idea is found in the oft-repeated, "You shall be holy, because I, the Lord, am holy." (Lev 19:1)

We omit the book of Leviticus except for a short little story which tells of God's jealous care for the impeccable performance of the liturgy, and His compassion for human sorrow and heart-ache. The story is told in chapters 9 and 10 (9 can be summarized, 10 read).

Aaron and His Sons

On the octave day of the ordination of Aaron and his sons, two of his sons, during a solemn ceremony, burned incense before the Lord in a manner that had not been authorized. The Lord was angered and sent fire down upon them (perhaps a bolt of lightning) and slew them. Warned by Moses not to leave his priestly post to mourn, Aaron suffered in silence. As the ceremony continued, Moses discovered that the goat of the people's sin offering had not been consumed by the priests and he berated them angrily. And Aaron, bereaved, answered that this terrible misfortune had befallen him today—would the Lord expect him to *eat*?

And Moses understood.

The Journey in the Desert— from Sinai to Jordan (Numbers)

Reading Schedule

The book of Numbers takes its name from the two censuses which number the Hebrews, in fantastically large numbers, not to be taken literally. For a year, the Israelites camped at the foot of Mount Sinai, until God indicated it was time for them to move. Numbers tells of their further journey through the desert on the way to the land of Chanaan. We found the book of Numbers to have somewhat the same effect on several of the children as the

journey through the desert had on the Hebrews, which isn't surprising since it *was* long drawn out. We worked out, therefore, the
following schedule of chapters, devised to eliminate long sighs,
yawns, and candid comments such as, "Aren't they ever going to get
there?"

Summarize:	1	Census
	2	Arrangement of Tribes
	3	Sons of Aaron, the Levites
Read:	6:22-27	Priestly Blessing
Summarize:	7	Offerings of Princes
Read:	9:1-5	Second Passover
Summarize:	10:1-10	Silver Trumpets
Read:	10:11-12; 33-36	Departure from Sinai
	11	Discontent of the People, the Elders, Quail
	12	Jealousy of Aaron and Mariam
	13:1-4; 16-33	The Twelve Scouts
	14	The Revolt
	16:1-11; 16-24; 35; 17:27-28	Rebellion of Core
	16:12-15; 25-34	Rebellion of Dathan and Abi-ram
	17:1-26	Grumbling of People; Aaron's Staff
	20:1-13	Sin of Moses and Aaron
Summarize:	20:14-21	Edom's Refusal
Read:	20:22-29	Death of Aaron
	21:4-9	Bronze Serpent
Summarize:	21:10-35	Journey around Moab, Victory over Sehon, Og
Read:	22; 23:1-8; 11-18; 20-21; 25-30; 24:1-5; 9b-19; 25	Story of Balaam, the Talking Ass; Oracles
	25:1-5	Worship of Baal-Phogor
	27:12-23	Josue to succeed Moses
	32:1-33	Gadites and Rubenites
Summarize:	34	Boundaries of Chanaan
Read:	36:13	Conclusion

What shall we look for in Numbers? Stephen, who is twelve,
commented wryly on something we found.

"Boy, it sure surprises you, the kind of people He came from."

I guess so. Here again we will see the Hebrews, fresh from
slavery in Egypt, complaining, rebelling, sinning, carrying on—all

between miracles. Here again is Moses interceding, and here is the Lord sparing them for Moses' sake. This book tells us something of the spiritual formation of these people, chosen from all the men on the face of the earth to give form and flesh, one day, to Christ. Numbers is the history of their migration to Chanaan, the promised land. In type it is the history of our own spiritual journey through life to our promised land in heaven.

The People Gorge Themselves

No sooner had the Israelites started out than they began to complain once more. Oh, for meat. They had nothing good to eat, no cucumbers, no melons, no onions, no garlic, no leeks like in Egypt—only "this wretched manna," until Moses asked God why He had ever given him the task of leading such a people! If this was all the future held for him, please let him die. So God promised meat, "meat until it comes out your noses!" [7] And a great wind arose and drove inland from the sea flocks of quail which fell on the ground and covered it. The people gorged themselves so rapaciously that some of them died.

Jealousy of Mariam and Aaron

Next, Mariam and Aaron became jealous. "Who does he think he is, the only prophet on the face of the earth?" But the Lord heard them. It was true, He said, that other prophets heard the Lord speak, but in visions and dreams. Moses beheld God face to face. When the Lord was finished thundering, Mariam was white with leprosy. A week's banishment was the price of her cleansing. Mariam's defiance, followed by her punishment, her formal banishment from the community and her re-entry are like a foreshadowing of the sacrament of Penance, the sacrament of restoration to the divine community after serious sin has cut one off.

Exploring the Land

Now the Lord told Moses to send one man from each of the twelve tribes to explore the land of Chanaan, and the men came back with marvelous tales of a land flowing with milk and honey, but one occupied by giants to whom the Israelites would seem as grasshoppers.[8] "Let us go nevertheless; we have the Lord with us,"

[7] The choice of words is the author's, but inspired.
[8] A fantastic exaggeration, although the people were of larger stature.

cried the faithful few. "Never! We will be destroyed!" cried the rest.

Forgetting that God had broken the might of Egypt for them, the people began to cry out that it would be better to die in the desert than to go up to Chanaan and be slaughtered, and the Lord took them at their word. They would prefer to die in the desert? Very well. Not one would live to see the land of promise. Forty days they had spent scouting the land. A year for each day they would now wander in the desert until they had their reward and every member of that generation brought out of the sea had perished. Only Caleb and Josue, "who serve me unreservedly," would live to see the land, together with the children of the rest.

Now like bratty children they changed their tune. Let them go! Let them go! In vain did Moses warn them, it was no good without the Lord's blessing. But off they went and met with defeat, learning once again that they would get nowhere without the Lord's blessing.

The Rebellion of Core

The two rebellion stories which follow are combined in the text and are very confusing. It is easier to read them through as shown on the reading chart—Core's rebellion first, then Dathan and Abiram's.

Core and two hundred and fifty Levites suffered a fine case of jealousy because, although they were permitted to serve at the altar, they could not offer sacrifice as did Aaron and his sons. (It was rather like altar boys wanting to act as priests.) With astonishing boldness, they challenged God's commission of Aaron, and in a holocaust of fire God answered them. Core and his band were consumed.

The Rebellion of Dathan and Abiram

Dathan and Abiram rebelled because Moses, they said, had set himself up as an authority and had failed to provide the land of milk and honey as promised. Imagine forgetting that they had refused to go. In view of the drastic punishment visited upon them and their families ("But that's not fair! It wasn't the children's fault!"), it is helpful to know that the punishment of the families of the guilty men rested upon an ancient Semitic principle of solidarity. All associated with the guilty man partook of his guilt and shared his punishment (rather like Adam and ourselves). Should the man merit, on the other hand, his family shared his merit.

For all this, a modern child's sense of justice is still offended, so it seems important to explore a little further. First of all, these men knew the risk of rebellion; jeopardizing their families was their own free act. If a man today decides to swindle his employer, he does it knowing that the happiness and good name of his family is at stake. We cannot blame God for the sins deliberately committed by men, or their consequences.

If we think of some of the ancient customs still practiced by aboriginal tribes today, we might be better able to see how the ancient customs in the Old Testament which shock us were, nevertheless, reasonable and just to them. For example, there is the custom among certain tribes of cutting off part of a finger as a consolation gift to a grieving family. We may dispute the sense of this, but they believe it to be an appropriate gesture. Even the victim of such mutilation suffers it willingly as a matter of course and would be surprised at our indignation. This is accepted practice among them and they never question it. Among the Semites, the principle of solidarity was not questioned, nor were their customs of war and punishment. We must put ourselves back in their time and see with their minds if we are not to be continually disturbed as we meet these things in their story.

Most serious of all was the fact that the leaders of these families proposed the ultimate in treason—to turn from the leadership of the only man to whom God had given the power to get them to the promised land. Without Moses, the Hebrews would have perished. They had called down death on their own heads, either way.

If all this seems much ado about nothing (the episode is not of key importance), it is justified in order to keep the children's image of God in the Old Testament free of distortion. The God of the Old Testament is not a cruel God, a bitter God, an angry God. He is the same as the God of the New. The difference is in the men (and He took them as He found them) and in the ways it was necessary for Him to show His fierce love for them. He never became a permissive parent. He was raising to their maturity an unruly bunch of children who were always at their best after He had nipped at the calves of their legs with His switch. Left to themselves, they went to their ruination. Parental discipline is a language of love, also, although at times it may sound harsh.

When the people murmured again the next day, blaming Moses for the deaths of the rebels, God declared He would destroy the lot of them. The tender solicitude of Moses bidding Aaron to light his censer and go among the people with an offering of atonement recalls Abraham arguing for the just men of Sodom and Christ lamenting for Jerusalem and wanting to take her under His wings. The scourge of the Lord was checked, but not before many died.

Once again the Lord confirmed His choice of Aaron for the high priesthood in the lovely episode of the blossoming staff; to this day the symbol of Aaron in religious art is the staff with almond blossoms.

The Punishment of Moses

The punishment of Moses is a great puzzle, resolved only when we remember that God is always just and does not judge men wrongly. Moses had seen God face to face. "To whom much is given, much is expected." The explanation we thought best (there are several) is discovered with a careful reading of Numbers 20:7-12. God asked Moses and Aaron to strike the rock and bring forth water for the people and their livestock. Instead of doing it immediately, and allowing the people to renew their faith by seeing the wonder of His power, the two made it an occasion to harangue. I am sorry to say it reminds me of the nagging of parents. When at last he finished talking, Moses struck the rock and water rushed forth—but the Lord angrily revoked their privilege of seeing the people into the land of Chanaan.

The Brazen Serpent

Exile had finally come to an end and preparations were made to move on to Chanaan. Marching again, the people complained again and this time God punished them by sending poisonous serpents. "We have sinned!" they cried. "Pray to the Lord for us!" And the Lord bade Moses make a brass serpent and mount it on a pole. All those bitten by serpents, who looked on it, would recover. St. John tells us in His Gospel that this is also a type of Christ (John 3:14). "And as Moses lifted up the serpent in the desert, even so must the Son of Man be lifted up, that those who believe in him may not perish, but may have life everlasting."

Balaam and the Talking Ass

As the Israelites made their way towards Chanaan, they met increasing resistance from native tribes whose land they would pass through. With the Lord at their side, they battled victoriously the king of Arad, the king of the Amorrites, the king of Basan, until Balac, king of Moab, became fearful of them and called on Balaam, a soothsayer, to put a curse on them. The story of Balaam and his ass is told in a way that is entirely familiar to children—with the rhythm and the ring of the storyteller. Inspired by all means; tradition indeed; and the style has the earmarks of Aladdin and his wonderful lamp. The ass sounds for all the world like our dog Huckleberry, whose behavior is generally accompanied by a running translation of what he is saying, contributed by any one of a half-dozen interpreters in our house.

But even Balaam could not curse the people without the Lord's permission, and in the end he was forced to bless them, to the great consternation of Balac. He did his dirt though, later, when he induced Madianite and Moabite women to lure the Israelites into illicit relations with them, and to sacrifice to their god Baal-Phogor. And the Lord wiped out those traitors who, even as they drew near the land of promise, betrayed the covenant He had made with them.

The Jordan at Last

There at last, on the east side of the Jordan, facing west to the land of Chanaan, ranged the people of the Lord. Forty years had not perfected them, but the Lord deemed it purification enough for the time. They had at least learned (although they would forget it many times) that they were the Lord's and that they could not successfully step outside the frame of their relationship to Him. Either they walked in His ways, or their works would not prosper. They had made their journey to the promised land under the leadership of Moses and no other.

From them we learn this: we too are the Lord's. Either we walk in His ways or our works will not eternally prosper. We make our way to heaven under the leadership of Christ—and no other.

Deuteronomy

The name Deuteronomy, given to the final book of the Pentateuch, means "this second law," and does not really present us with a new second law, but rather with the story and the giving of the Law of Sinai told again in a new way. It is written in the first person singular, as though Moses were speaking, and is a summary and discourse admonishing the people to love the Law and obey it in order to find security in the land God has given them. Since it is a repetition of much that we have previously read, it deserves to be saved for another time when a review of the journey and the Sinai covenant is timely. But by no means must we pass it by forever.

The vigorous style of Deuteronomy makes for easy, exciting reading and the presence of Moses is mysteriously real in the informality of his speech. It is no mere repetition of a familiar story, but an entirely new experience. An example will explain.

"In reply you said to me, 'We have sinned against the Lord. We will go up ourselves and fight, just as the Lord, our God, commanded us.' And each of you girded on his weapons, making light of going into the hill country. But the Lord said to me, 'Warn them: do not go up and fight, lest you be beaten down before your enemies, for I will not be in your midst.' I gave you this warning but you would not listen. . . . On your return you wept before the Lord, but he did not listen to your cry or give ear to you. That is why you had to stay as long as you did at Cades." (Deuteronomy 1:41-46)

We are there, listening in. There is the same fatherly concern in Moses' speech that we find in St. Paul's.

The following passages from Moses' sermons in the book of Deuteronomy, used individually, make splendid additions to family prayer and are easily related to our own lives.

Deut. 4:1-8 Exhortation to obedience
        4:25-31 God's fidelity

Like the other books, Deuteronomy is an arrangement of several compositions and was finally put together after the end of the exile.

·IV·

TAKING POSSESSION
OF THE LAND

Josue

The book of Josue tells of the Israelites' conquest of Chanaan and gives us a condensed version of their great military campaign under the generalship of one of God's favorites—Josue. Scholars tell us it is much condensed, perhaps even a trifle embellished, but we can understand this if we try to imagine writing an account of our own Revolution with its campaigns, victory, the independence of the colonies, all neatly summed up in a few pages, knowing at the same time that there was much more to it. The compilers of this book present Josue's successes in much the same manner, intending to show above all that the Israelites did go into the land, did make it their own, did have the Lord at their side.

Divine Promise of Assistance

The book begins with God promising to be with Josue in everything he does provided he keeps the law on his lips and in his heart, never swerving from it, "then you will successfully attain your goal." (Jos 1:8) Here is the next clue the family should watch for. The first part of the promise had been fulfilled, and the Israelites were to move into the second phase, becoming a settled nation in possession of the land and bringing forth in time the One Who saves the world—but of course all this was still shrouded in mystery. The Hebrews knew they had a unique religion under a wonderfully unique God; they had a sense of their chosenness; but they had only very foggy notions of what God was really up to, and they certainly never dreamed it would all end in God-become-Man. Their obedience to the Law was going to be rewarded by success in their material affairs, and this would become a symbol of their blessedness—until in time they would mistake material success for the end of the affair and then this would be their ruination. Not that God intended to break His promise, but their role in the drama of redemption would be shaped by their obedience to the Law.

There are many lessons in the book of Josue to help the family to a keener appreciation of God's will, even a new abandonment to it, as we see the wisdom of His plans and the great power that sustains men who give themselves to Him. To know the history of the Jews in the Old Testament gives our faith a distance it has never had before, makes us patient and better able to trust.

Rahab and the Spies

Action begins in the best mystery story fashion with a sortie across the river to the city of Jericho by spies who are to explore the land about the city. They had barely taken lodgings in the house of Rahab (spoken of as a harlot, but we can omit this in order to avoid a discussion far afield) when their presence was reported to the king, who sent men to rout them. So famed were the Israelites and their God that even after forty years the story of their escape through the sea was known to their enemies, and God's promise to give them the land of Chanaan struck fear into the hearts of the Chanaanites. Rahab knew this only too well, so she proposed a bargain. She would hide the men and see to their safe return across the Jordan if they would promise to spare her and her family when they returned to take Jericho. The bargain agreed to, she hid them under the flax drying on her roof and sent the king's men elsewhere. The spies returned to Josue safely with a full report and the information that Rahab would hang a red cord in her window by which the Israelites would identify her house and spare its occupants.

Crossing the Jordan

To prove to the people that Josue was His choice to succeed Moses, the Lord now repeated the miraculous passage through the water, this time the Jordan, swollen and swift-running with late rains and the melted snows from Mount Hermon. Josue and the bearers of the Ark march into the river; as soon as the soles of their feet were wet the Lord commanded the waters to hold and the people walked through the river bed dryshod into the land of promise. ". . . the river Jordan turned back its course: the mountains bounded like rams, like little lambs, the hills." (Ps 113:3-4) The words of the Psalm seem to describe an earthquake as the means the Lord used to dam the waters of the Jordan. Whatever the means, the crossing was under God's control, proving to the Hebrews that "you have a living God amongst you," (Jos 3:10), one who keeps His promises.

The faith of these Israelites crossing the Jordan had been nourished for years by the story of how God took their fathers through the Red Sea, and that first passage is a type of Baptism, teaching us the mystery of the new life in us. But it, and the crossing of the Jordan and all the other miracles, are meant to remind us also of the power of God and His desire to bring us through the crises of this life if we will trust Him. During times of family difficulties these great stories of God's care for His people are an important addition to family prayer, for as Christians they are our family tradition too, and they show us that we have the same living God with us.

Up to now, references to crossing the Jordan and "going to cross over into camp ground," have been more familiar to us from the Negro spirituals than from their context in the history of Israel. Now we must admire even more the spirituality of a race whose religious songs have made these events speak in figurative language of the spiritual reality—God's promise first to save us, then lead us to heaven.

The two accounts of the memorial stones in chapter 4 are another example of how the same tradition from two different sources is incorporated into the one story.

None of the children of the Hebrews had been circumcised during the years of wandering in the desert so, some time before entering the promised land, this had to be done. To incapacitate the men at this crucial time (before the attack on Jericho) seems unlikely; perhaps the story was placed here by the writer for its symbolic value, for on the task's completion, God said: "Now I have removed the reproach of Egypt from you." (Jos 5:9) The forty years in the desert are often likened to the forty days of Lent, and the people of the Lord restored to His good graces remind us of ourselves renewed and resurrected with Him at Easter.

The Land of Chanaan

The first meal of the Israelites after the Passover, which concurred with the time of the crossing, was unleavened bread and parched grain taken from the land, and the manna for all time disappeared. Because we have spoken of the manna as a type of the Holy Eucharist during our reading of Exodus and Numbers, it is well to follow to a conclusion this comparison of the marvelous foods, and the conclusion is obvious. They had spent forty years wandering in the desert, they had been tried severely, and they had been fed by God with manna so they might survive and persevere. Now the promise had been realized and the land of milk and honey[1] was theirs. The manna was no longer needed. We shall no longer need the Holy Eucharist, food of our souls during our struggle on earth, when we reach heaven and live with God forever.

The Fall of Jericho

One of the most exquisite irritations to beset parents who start reading holy scripture aloud to their children is the discovery, on looking up from a well-read passage, that no one has been paying attention. Seasoned parents know, of course, that inattention is a barometer of nothing at all. It can mean that a child is paying strict attention, all the while buried in the latest Sears catalogue (which he has fished out from under the library table with his toe during the most exciting passage of Josue), or it can mean that he really *is* paying no attention. By the same token, a look of intense concentration may indicate that he is listening carefully, or it may mean that he is looking intently at you as you read from the holy Bible while thinking that Joe Jones' souped-up, chopped-off

[1] Flocks of sheep and goats on the pastures of Chanaan were the source of milk, and the honey of wild bees was to be found in the trees and even on the ground. (See I Kings 14:25)

Chevvy really hangs. Therefore, it is good to bite one's tongue on any acid remark that may come to mind and wait. Time may prove sarcasm ill-chosen and that the dears really are able, as they insist, to concentrate on two, three and four things at once.

Christopher tricked us this way when we came to Josue 5:13-15. Sitting up straight as a beanpole, he emerged from the Fall-Winter catalogue and was suddenly all attention.

"That's what God said to Moses in the burning bush!"

And sure enough, here was the familiar exhortation, "Remove your sandals."

"Then the 'captain of the host of the Lord' must be the same as 'the angel of the Lord'!" he reasoned. He had acquired an ear for the writers' literary mannerisms.

That Jericho fell is the one thing everybody knows from the book of Josue, and miracle it was, whether by trumpet and earthquake or trumpet and something else. All the inhabitants were slain save Rahab and her family[2] and all precious booty was put into the treasury of the Lord; the rest was burned to the ground.

Of Slaughter and Brutality

With the destruction of Jericho there begins a series of bloody campaigns which one suspects might trouble children, who look for the Word of God to be full of love, not brutality. We will discover in no time of course that this poses no problem for boys, who relish the scenes of brutality, but still an explanation is called for.

First, in the ancient world, war was a bloody and ordinary business and certain brutal customs of war (though not half as brutal as our bombs) were commonly accepted. God chose the Israelites with their polygamy, slavery, wars and all and set them on the long road that led to Christ and perfect love; but it was going to be a hard, slow, human business getting there. Because Josue fought under the aegis of the Lord does not mean that the Lord dictated every turn to the right and the left, every blow of the spear and the staff. Josue was no puppet on a string. He was a man of his times and the Lord accepted him as such. Like our more familiar saints, he was given certain graces, the assurance

---

[2] Rahab went with the Israelites, became a convert, and is numbered in the genealogy of Our Lord. (Matt 1:5) St. James and St. Paul praise her for her faith. (Jas 2:25; Heb 11:31)

of God's help, and left to map his campaigns in the accustomed manner. With God's choice of Josue or any of the other saints of the Old Testament, God did not pour on water and make instant Christians. But they were saints all the same, for their co-operation with Him was wholehearted.

Second, when the wrath of God is visited on certain peoples throughout the scriptures, we may be sure that He has judged them justly in relation to their betrayal of His goodness. Even the pagans had consciences. In chapter 20 of Genesis, we are told the story of a good pagan, Abimelech, who all innocently took Sara to wife and was told by the Lord, "I know you have done this with a sincere heart." (Gen 20:6) But not so the Chanaanites; their religion was abominable and it could easily have seduced the Israelites. It was crucially important that there be no integration of the two peoples or the new religion of the One God could die a-borning.

Therefore, although God could have redeemed us without the Hebrews, He chose to use them, teaching and correcting them with the wise patience of a father who knows that human children cannot master all the lessons at once. If the text implies that the Lord ordered certain people to be ground to bits, we must understand that the authors put together the divine choice of Josue as leader and the customs of the times. In so doing they jumped to many conclusions and put many words into the Lord's mouth.

"But," some child may ask with a worried look, "what if innocent people were killed in the cities?" In a fallen world there is always this mystery—before the redemption or after; whether the innocent are swallowed up by earthquakes, floods, wars; are murdered, cheated, vilified. At the very center of the mystery is God Himself, identifying Himself with all the innocent victims as Christ crucified. Let us remind the children that even then, God was preparing to come down and share every man's suffering and give it a redemptive value.

Defeat and Victory at Hai

Mysteriously now, after their successful beginning, the Israelites were thrown back in defeat at the city of Hai. Had the Lord deserted them? Josue implored an explanation and it was revealed that among them was one who had broken a ban, stolen loot and kept it for himself. Death must be the fate of a man who risked the lives of the people. Achan was found guilty and taken to the desert and stoned. Children will have two practical questions. Why, if the text said he was to be burned, was he stoned? And did his family really die with him?

In answer to the first, perhaps he was stoned and then burned. As for the second, the text does not say they all died with him but the mass punishment of a family was according to the "law of solidarity," already discussed in Numbers.[3] This emphasis on solidarity was a means of teaching the Israelites that as God's family what one did affected all. The relation of the members of the Mystical Body can be seen here in a veiled way—the evil of one becomes the burden of all, and the goodness of one becomes the glory of all.

The strategy of the battle of Hai is told in such detail that boys can map it out on paper, and the ceremony of thanksgiving with its offerings and instructions for the people is like another faint image of the Mass.

Josue Conquers the Land

Chapters 9 through 11 give accounts of Josue's campaigns against the Chanaanites and we read in Josue 10:40-43 and Josue 11:16-20 that the whole country was taken—mountains, desert, foothills, leaving no survivors; "no city made peace with the Israelites, all were taken in battle." (Jos 11:19) But this was not quite so. Many of the individual tribes had still to fight against the remaining inhabitants. How so, this story of blanket conquest?

This account of the generalship of Josue is a kind of literary epic written by men who gazed at these events from hundreds of years away and, out of respect for the great leader, credited the nation as it was at its best and its height to Josue. We might write in a similar way about our own country: "And the United States of America stands, the accomplishment of George Washington and the founders of the Republic." This is pardonable pride, a manner of speaking.

The Sun Miracle

Josue 10:11 tells of Josue's victory over the Amorrites with the help of the Lord, who hurled great hailstones from the sky and killed more of the enemy than the Israelites slew with the

[3] See p. 56.

sword. In 10:12-13, we have a passage from the book of Jashar, a book of patriotic songs (also quoted in II Kings 1:18-27) celebrating Josue's victory and citing his dramatic cry to the sun and the moon to stand still until the battle was won. Various explanations have been offered for this miracle but the one we prefer is the opinion that this is the language of poetry. It is common for any one of us to address the elements in a time of crisis. A housewife, hurrying to gather her washing before the rain, talks aloud to the sky. "Don't rain yet! Don't rain yet! Don't rain, don't rain!" Afterwards she tells of the day's events and says: "And I told it not to rain until I got the wash in, and it didn't!" Verse 11 tells that the Lord won the victory with hailstones. Verses 12 and 13 quote the song, and verses 14 and 15 say this was a day of days, the elements, even the Lord, did what Josue wanted. The footnote in the CCD translation has the opinion that there was a darkness which impeded the enemy's flight until well into the following day, and of course one is free to believe it was a miraculous suspension of the natural order, if one wishes.

Partitioning the Land

The second part of the book of Josue tells of partitioning the land among the twelve tribes. Reading these nine chapters poses a real problem, as we discovered when the lists of names and places put Christopher (a great scripture lover) fast asleep. This portion of the book is of interest to the parents but, since it is so deadly for the children, we substituted making a felt-board map showing the tribal portions. The project took a long evening and the result was well worth our time.

We took our pattern from a map in a favorite book,[4] drawn to scale on brown paper and cut apart at the boundaries. Materials: a piece of scrap plywood from the lumber yard, wool and felt, straight pins and yarn. Covering the board with blue wool gave us background color for the water, and a surface on which to stick the individual pieces. Bright felt made each of the tribal portions, with an initial letter in contrasting color to identify each tribe. A piece of yarn made the Jordan. Straight pins helped to keep the pieces in place and made it possible to change the map to suit further history. As we worked, we reviewed what we had read so

[4] Samuel Terrien, *Lands of the Bible: A Golden Historical Atlas* (New York: Simon & Schuster, 1957), p. 26.

far, marked important places, named the patriarchs, their wives and children, and had an altogether satisfying review of the early history of God's people.

Josue's Farewell

The last part of the book of Josue tells of the return of the three eastern tribes to their places across the Jordan, a slight misunderstanding with them and its resolution, and in the end Josue's final and beautiful plea to his people—words for us as well as the Hebrews. He died at the age of one hundred and ten, we are told, and was buried in the mountain region of Ephraim.

Josue's faith, his purity of motive, the beauty of his spirit, and above all his flawless obedience, make him perhaps not as powerful a figure as Moses, but surely one of the most commanding types of Christ to be found in the scriptures. Added to the figure of the great liberator Moses, there is here the fighter and victor. Like Josue, Christ is our leader in battle, having braved every danger ahead of us. It is behind Him that we make our way to the land of promise. The very name Josue is the Hebrew for the name Jesus.

Judges

With some degree of fear and trembling, I feel compelled to say that in places the book of Judges sounds more like Gilbert and Sullivan than holy writ—fear and trembling for the terrible warnings given to people who treat the scriptures in a frivolous manner, and compulsion when I read the marvelously frivolous comment on Adonibezec minus his thumbs and big toes. (Judg 1:7) Add, to Adonibezec, Eglon of the fat belly, and Sisara of the bashed-in temple, and you understand why in our house Judges has been recommended to the neighbors as "the best."

"You ought to hear the story we read in the Bible last night. This king, see, was so fat that when the Israelites stuck a knife in him, it didn't even show."

"*My* favorite part," said Philip, looking very spiritual, "is Samson, and how he killed a whole messa guys with the jawbone of an ass."

Ah yes, these gory delicacies are not the reason for the book of Judges, but as long as these are the great attraction, only a fool would not be grateful for so easily captured an audience. And we have time on our side. Over the years the big issues in this book will become clearer, and the children will appreciate that its hero stories and moral teaching are a stunning commentary on the way of men with their worldliness, sensuality, repentance, forgiveness and the everlasting mercy of God.

The action of Judges takes place in the history covering the twelfth and eleventh centuries B.C., during a period when the Israelites were struggling to consolidate their possession of Chanaan, to change from nomadic life to agricultural; and were falling into idolatry, abandoning God, repenting and being saved again and again by leaders whom God inspired and whom the people called Judges.

There are twelve Judges, six minor ones whose stories are barely mentioned, and six major ones whose stories appear in some detail—Othoniel, Aod, Debora and Barac, Gedeon, Jephte and Samson. These leaders were inspired by God in times of crisis to lead the people to victory over their enemies, and have been compard to St. Joan of Arc, who was inspired in much the same way. Unlike St. Joan, the Judges were not always morally impeccable, and it is interesting to see that the author has made no effort to gloss over their sins. These men had fearful faults, like ourselves, and their gifts did not set them apart from the need to struggle with temptation, or excuse them from the indulgence of their sensuality. A careful prereading of the text by the parents is important in order to prepare their comments on the scandalous behavior of some of the Judges.

In the first two chapters we read how the Israelites tried to entrench themselves in Chanaan (the tribes are frequently spoken of by their founders' names: Juda, Simeon, etc.). Because of inferior numbers and out-dated methods of war, they were unable to conquer and destroy all the tribes about them, so in time they settled for co-existence, and from this they even went so far as to participate in pagan worship. In chapter 2, the Lord announces

that they will be punished. Since they disobey Him, He will not
persevere with His destruction of their enemies but will let the
enemies overcome them; their sufferings will prove whether they
will keep to the way of the Lord.

Othoniel and Aod

Chapter 3 starts the stories of the Judges. Othoniel is hardly
mentioned. Aod is the left-handed Judge who hid his two-edged
dagger on his right thigh and later sunk it in King Eglon. Samgar,
a minor Judge, slew six hundred Philistines with an ox-goad, and
"he too rescued Israel." (Judg 3:31)

Debora and Barac

Next come Debora, the prophetess, and Barac the Judge. Inspired by God, Debora informed Barac that he was to lead the
attack on the Chanaanites and their iron chariots, but Barac agreed
to go only if she would accompany him. From the canticle of
Debora, one of the oldest Hebrew poems in existence, we learn
that the Lord sent torrential rains to bog down the chariots (which
was terribly clever, we all agreed) and the enemy was routed. Sisara,
the general, fled to the hills and there met his squishy end in the
tent of Jahel the Cinite.

Gedeon

The story of Gedeon is longer and richer in detail. Gedeon
rescued the Israelites from the Madianites, a people who traveled
on camels, ancestors of the modern Bedouins. It was their custom
to descend on the countryside like locusts, destroy the crops and
reduce the Israelites to misery, until at last Israel cried out to the
Lord and He chose Gedeon—a most undistinguished man—to be
leader and save the people. Wanting confirmation of this command, Gedeon offered sacrifice and when he saw it consumed by
heavenly fire, he understood the charge was from God. His first
move was to destroy his father's altar to Baal, and when the terrified
people saw that Baal did not retaliate, they called Gedeon by a
new name—Jerobaal (Let Baal take action). Next, he called on the
men of Manasse, Aser, Zabulon and Nephthali to come and fight
for him. Testing the call from God a final time in order to avoid
presumption, we have the famous scene with the fleece on the
threshing floor.

The Dew on the Fleece

Gedeon requested that the fleece he would lay on the threshing floor be filled with dew in the morning and the floor remain dry; and it was. His second request asked the reverse, that the fleece be dry and the floor wet, and in the morning it was. Now he was sure the mission was to have God's protection.

The Fathers of the Church have seen in this episode a type of Our Lady. As the fleece alone was filled with dew, Mary alone was filled with grace. Again, the dew on the threshing floor the second night spoke to them of the divine life which, after filling Our Lady, was given through her to the waiting world. It is a lovely story to read on the feasts of Our Lady or when the family is working on lessons about Our Lady's role in the scheme of the redemption. It is easy to see why the Fathers gave her the title "the second Eve."

Gedeon's Army

The formation of Gedeon's army is a delightful tale and confirms the fact that these stories are not meant to parade the gifts of the Judges as such, nor their military exploits, but to illustrate the power of God as He rescues His people. Gedeon had too many men conscripted, said the Lord. He would be tempted to attribute his victory to the strength of his forces and not to God. He must send home all those who did not relish danger. So Gedeon gave the men warning of the dangers ahead and two thirds went home! He had got rid of the cowards.

Now, said the Lord, tell them to go to the stream and drink water; choose those who drink out of their hands, lapping like dogs (for they would be alert, watching with their eyes) and dismiss all those who kneel down and put their faces to the stream. Gedeon did, and his army was finally reduced to three hundred men. Then the Lord revealed His plan of attack, which came off successfully, and chapter 8 tells how Gedeon pursued the fleeing kings and captured them.

The Men of Soccoth

The episode at Soccoth is not enormously important, but children will ask an explanation and the principle involved is timely. The people of Soccoth were from the tribe of Gad and they

stood to benefit from any victory over the enemies of Israel. Hospitality was a sacred obligation to the Hebrews, who had so often
called upon the Lord for hospitality—food, shelter, protection—
when they would have otherwise perished. It was little enough to
suffer the stranger who came to their gates, to say nothing of their
blood brothers. That Gedeon, with his exhausted warriors, should
be refused bread when they reached Soccoth was a criminal act and
Gedeon seems to have been inspired by the Lord to punish them.
The episode is repeated with the people of Phanuel as well. The
grinding with thorns and briars is a reference to the manner of
tearing the chaff from the wheat during threshing.

One of the ills of our time is indifference, not only to suffering,
but to the need for graciousness and hospitality towards one another in the name of our common brotherhood. This story offers
the family an opportunity to talk together about this obligation.

Gedeon Retires

With the slaying of the Madianite kings, Gedeon's military
career comes to a close, and in gratitude the Israelites try to make
him king, but he answers, "The Lord must rule over you." (Judg
8:23) We have seen Gedeon, filled with the power of the Lord,
transformed from a rather ordinary, even timid man into a fearless
general who untiringly pursued the enemy of the Lord and destroyed him, thus saving Israel for the task it was destined to per-
form. But in the end when the work of the Lord was accomplished,
the great leader established in his city an ephod, a liturgical object
before which it was possible for him to ascertain the will of God,[5]
and sad to say, the people began to pay idolatrous homage to it.
How much Gedeon was to blame the text does not reveal, only that
"it caused the ruin of Gedeon and his family." (Judg 8:27)

Perhaps the lesson we learn from these last few verses about
Gedeon is that one receives the grace to do what one must do,
but not to do what one must not do—so we had better not try
that.

Gedeon's Son Abimelech

Next comes the miserable Abimelech, son of Gedeon's secondary wife. Fiercely jealous of his half-brothers, Abimelech maneu-
vered his fellow Sichemites to make him their king and then

[5] See p. 82.

marched off to Ephra to murder these very brothers—all but Joatham, the youngest, who escaped. Then Joatham recited a parable to the people of Sichem foretelling their doom. The story speaks of the unseemliness of the noble trees to choose the despised buckthorn for their king, and warns that if this is not done in good faith, the buckthorn will devour the other trees with fire. Joatham explained: if the people of Sichem really thought that in return for all Gedeon (called Jerobaal here) had done for them, it was right for Abimelech to slay his sons, and if they thought such a man suitable to be their king, well and good. But if they had not acted in good faith, they and Abimelech would destroy each other.

Events bore him out. In three years' time the Sichemites had had enough of Abimelech (he did not rule all Israel but only *these* Israelites) and "God put bad feelings between them" (Judg 9:22)—which we understand means that the evil of their own hearts caused the bad feelings. Of a sudden, they wanted revenge for the killing of Gedeon's sons. Violence broke out, Abimelech attacked the people, destroyed them and their city, sowed salt in their fields in revenge—so nothing would grow there—and burned alive the people of the upper city as they hid in the treasury. When a woman pushed a millstone down and crushed his skull, he had his armor bearer run him through before he died so it could not be said he was slain by a woman.

The moral of this tale seems to speak to us about our responsibility in electing the men who govern us. We must weigh carefully the virtues and qualifications of our candidates, not vote solely for sentiment's sake or, as with the Sichemites, because "he is one of our own." If we would vote with integrity, we cannot vote for a man because he is of our color, our religion, our race. Rather, we must cast our vote for the welfare of our country.

Jephte

Next there are brief references to Thola and Jair, two minor Judges, and then comes the story of Jephte. But first the author tells us that the Israelites succumbed once more to pagan worship and were overpowered by the Ammonites, and this time God was so disgusted that He refused to rescue them. But they pleaded and whined until "He grieved over the misery of Israel," (Judg 10:16) and He raised up a man to lead them. This man was Jephte, born to Galaad of a harlot.

Sooner or later the children will ask, "What is a harlot?" and sooner or later we will have to explain.

"Well, in this case it means a woman who is not very good and isn't even Galaad's wife, yet lives with him as though she is his wife and bears him a son."

"Are there harlots now?"

"Yes, there are. It is too bad, because they don't know God well enough to love Him and be good. We will have to pray for all such people to know God better and love Him more."

And firmly return to the story.

The Daughter of Jephte

When the elders of Galaad went to fetch Jephte to be their leader, he was surprised but he agreed to take their cause. Preparing for war, Jephte rashly promised the Lord that, should He grant him success, he would sacrifice the first person to come out of his house on his return home.

Now this was truly a rash vow, not one the Lord would approve nor expect Jephte to keep, for ever since the episode of Abraham and Isaac on the mountain it was more and more clear that human sacrifice was forbidden. That Jephte should make this vow even when the law forbade such killing shows us clearly how dangerously close to the Israelites were the pagan customs of their neighbors. But Jephte thought it a proper vow, and felt it must be scrupulously kept even when, to his sorrow, it was his daughter and only child who came out to greet him. The daughter of Jephte is like a delicate little meadow flower which is crushed before it has a chance to blossom. Trusting her father's integrity, she solemnly agreed that he must keep his vow but asked for two months in the mountains with her friends to "mourn my virginity," which meant she would mourn because she had not lived long enough to marry and bear children.

This was the "self-fulfillment" of the ancient peoples, to have borne children, to have added to the race; and the daughter of Jephte had kept herself chaste in anticipation of marriage and motherhood—so much more natural a reason for chastity than the negative flight from sin. Her story is a beautiful addition to our family discussions of sex and chastity and marriage. The text closes with a sad little reminder that after that time, the Israelite women used to go to mourn the daughter of Jephte four days of the year.

The Shibboleth

After an altercation with the men of Ephraim, Jephte set guards over the fords of the Jordan with instructions to ask every passing man if he were an Ephraimite. All those who said "no" were asked to pronounce the word "Shibboleth." If they said "Sibboleth," they betrayed themselves as Ephraimites, for these people could not pronounce *sh*. This is how the word shibboleth came to be used as a password, or party slogan. Apostolic causes of recent years have bristled with shibboleths. From time to time such words as *lay apostolate, liturgical, rural life,* even *scripture* (!) have been shibboleths—indicating that such a person or group was "way out."

And that is the story of Jephte. Again we see the mercy of God in His promise to protect Israel for the role He had designed for her. Even when they fell, sincere contrition was enough to move His heart to forgiveness. This is true for us too.

Samson

Abeson, Elon and Abdon are mentioned briefly, and finally we come to the last of the Judges, Samson. Samson is the least likable of the Judges and one has to look long and hard before it is possible to appreciate him the way the Israelites did. Samson's parents, however, are entirely lovable and the story of their encounter with the angel is enchanting, reminiscent of the story of Elizabeth and Zachary.

The spirit of the Lord was in Samson from his mother's womb and he was consecrated to God. He was to take no wine or strong drink, have no contact with the dead, nor should a razor touch his head (Judg 13:5), and this tells us that Samson was to be a Nazirite, one who led a mortified life. Both the prophet Samuel and St. John the Baptist were Nazirites.

Samson, unlike the other Judges, did not lead armies against the enemies of God's people but rather sustained a one-man feud with them, and his story is filled with fantastic accounts of his strength. All this strikes us as very odd, to say the least, and the text has one line at the outset which is entirely puzzling. When he insists upon wooing a Philistine wife in spite of his parents' displeasure, we are told: "Now his father and mother did not know that this had been brought about by the Lord, who was providing an opportunity against the Philistines." (Judg 14:4) This is hard to understand until we remember that it was written long after by an author who, telescoping all the efforts against the Philistines from his point of view, saw that every blow delivered against them was part of the will of God.

On the way to marry his Philistine wife, Samson tears a lion to pieces with his bare hands. (Judg 14:6-9) Outwitted by his new wife, he kills thirty Philistines single-handed. (Judg 14:10-20) Furious to find that his in-laws had given his wife away[6] he sets fire to the grain, vineyards and orchards of the Philistines. (Judg 15:1-8) When even the Israelites, out of fear of the Philistines, attempt to hand Samson over to them, we have the grand scene with the jawbone of the ass with which he killed one thousand men. (Judg 15:9-20) And we may read, or omit—as we see fit— the episode in Gaza where Samson visits a harlot, is surrounded by his enemies, and escaping tears down the city gates and carries them off on his shoulders. (Judg 16:1-3)

But at last he meets Delilah and reaps the whirlwind, and here the tragedy of Samson's life is laid bare. Contrary to his words, the source of Samson's strength had not been the length of his hair alone, but the gifts of the Lord bestowed on him at birth which he had pledged for by his life as a Nazirite—a life of supposed mortification. He had failed to observe any of the requirements save one —his hair was still long. We see his final seduction by Delilah as the last of a long list of surrenders to sensuality and inevitably Samson, as any man, became the victim of his own appetites. The story points out a moral for each of us, showing what happens when we betray one after the other of the gifts of the supernatural life.

Blinded, imprisoned, Samson had at long last the merciful opportunity to examine his own failings and make his peace with the Lord. When he was brought forth into the temple of Dagon for

---

[6] "The dissent of his parents, who object to Philistines as uncircumcised, obliges Samson to conduct the negotiations himself and to contract a *sadika* marriage, the wife remaining with her people." *Catholic Commentary on Holy Scriptures* (New York: Thomas Nelson & Sons, 1957), 244 g.

that last great scene, we hear the piteous cry of a man whose soul has been searched. "O Lord God, remember me!" (Judg 16:28)

In the epistle to the Hebrews, St. Paul has summed up the role of the Judges as follows: "Time will fail me if I try to go through all the history of Gedeon, of Barac, of Samson, of Jephte, of David, and Samuel and the prophets. Theirs was the faith which subdued kingdoms, which served the cause of right, which made promises come true. They shut the mouths of lions, they quenched raging fire, swords were drawn on them and they escaped. How strong they became, who till then were weak, and what courage they showed in battle, how they routed invading armies!" (Heb 11:32-34 Knox)

No wonder the Hebrews revered them.

The last part of the book of Judges, chapters 17-21, might very well be omitted without affecting the history of the Judges. These chapters tell of events which happened to the tribes of Dan and Benjamin during the early period of Judges and are episodes unconnected with the rest of the book. There is one particularly horrible episode, the outrage at Gabaa (Judg 19:22-30), like a similar tale in the story of Sodom. Commentaries tell us that according to the values of the time, first consideration was always given to the guest, second to the wife and daughter, third to the secondary wife or concubine; that the virtue of women was not highly prized, nor were women as such. They were easily expendable in times of violence. While this is interesting historically, a discussion of it is not relevant to the story of salvation and it is certain to shock the children. The tale of the secondary wife who was murdered and whose body was cut to pieces is better left untold.

These last chapters of the book of Judges, 17-21, are actually appendices, included because they related events somewhat connected with the times. The chapters are a warning of how brutal men can become. Yet, even in such cases, God remains God and will always be willing to forgive.

·V·

THE PEOPLE
BECOME A KINGDOM

First Samuel (or Kings)

It's a funny thing about children and books. Whatever they are reading, if it's really good in no time they will say, "This is my favorite book." That is how it goes with reading the Bible. We thought Genesis was our favorite until we read Exodus, and we thought Exodus until we read Josue, and Josue until we read Judges, but when we got to the books of Samuel we were sure they were our favorites, for, as a friend said, reading them again after many years, "Not only are they the inspired word of God, but they are such exciting stories!"

There are two books of Samuel.[1] They start with the period when Samuel, both prophet and judge, was raised up by God to lead the people, and the kingdom of Israel was finally established. For purposes of family reading, they are easily divided into sections, each containing a story within a story.

[1] Most Catholic translations of the Bible call these books I and II Kings, after St. Jerome's translation. I and II Samuel is taken from the Hebrew, is found in Jewish and Protestant translations, and will be restored to the CCD translation of these books. References herein to I and II Kings are from the Knox translation, where all four books are called Kings I, II, III and IV.

Samuel's Birth and Dedication

In I Samuel 1-2, we read of Samuel, his parents, Anna and Elcana, the marvelous circumstances of his birth, his dedication to the service of the Lord and his mother's song of thanksgiving. There is something vaguely familiar about these episodes, and small wonder—for God often used the events of their history to prepare His people for the One Who was to come. Seeing this, St. Luke adapted his account of the birth of John the Baptist to the very manner used in the story of Samuel—and we have our answer. Each story opens in the temple, at the time of sacrifice, with child-less couples participating, and each couple has a child dedicated to God's service. To the Jewish catechumens of early Christianity, the Gospel account of John the Baptist was more than a delightful story—it was a great sign, for the prophet Samuel had also introduced a king.

The People Lose the Ark

Chapters 4-7 tell of the struggle with the Philistines and the loss of the Ark of the Covenant, and again we see the weakness and infidelity of God's people. The sons of Heli were bad priests, and for failing to check their wickedness, God punished their father; while the people, losing their first clash of arms, sent for the Ark to be brought into battle as though it were a rabbit's foot. The terror of the Philistines at the sight of the Ark gave far more glory to God than this frantic expedient of the Israelites, and they threw themselves fiercely into battle, fighting so well that they won the day. With this disaster God permitted the people to fall into all manner of worship displeasing to Him, until at long last Samuel conducted them back to the right paths—all of which reminds us that the Lord's admonition to Josue had warned that in proportion to their obedience to the Law would affairs go well with them.

Saul Is Chosen King

Chapters 8-10 tell of the choosing of a king. Samuel had led the Israelites until his old age and then appointed his sons in his stead, but these were unworthy men who took bribes and perverted justice and the people would not have them. Instead they asked Samuel to give them a king. But, protested Samuel, the Lord was their king! To no avail; they wanted a king like other nations. Thus we meet Saul, "a fine figure of a man, none finer in Israel; he was head and shoulders taller than any of his fellow country- men." (I Kings 9:2 Knox) Saul was searching for a herd of asses lost from his father's flocks the day he came to the city of Samuel and consulted the prophet for help.

Mention of consulting the Lord through prophets, seers and ephods appears regularly through the story of God's people, and it is puzzling. Moses in his time was permitted to go into the tent of the Lord and consult Him face to face, but not so the other priests. They consulted God by means of the ephod, and the Urim and Thummin. In Exodus 28:29-30, we read instructions to Aaron concerning the use of a breastpiece in which were kept the Urim and Thummin[2], and in 28:31-35, there is a description of a vest- ment called the ephod. In Judges 8:27, we read of Gedeon's ephod. But what exactly were these things?

The Ephod, the Urim and the Thummin

It seems the ephod was used variously, and in the present case apparently it was a liturgical object containing the Urim and the Thummin. The Urim and Thummin were the sacred lots, possibly like dice or sticks or pebbles, and they were used as we use the faces of a coin, calling them heads and tails. The Yes or No of the Lord was learned by asking God to indicate His answer with one lot or another, then having the priest draw a lot from the pocket of the ephod.

We might explain it to children this way. Say that I have a special apron with a pocket in it and there I keep two buttons, one red and one green. The Lord has promised to make known His will to me by means of the buttons. Suppose that one day a child comes to ask if God will tell whether he should go to a picnic or stay home, because it looks like rain. In prayer I ask the Lord to show His will by having the red button mean Go, and the green mean Stay. Then I put my hand in the pocket, take a button (without looking), and it is green. Stay. My little friend runs off to refuse the invitation and explains, "I cannot go. I have consulted the Lord and His oracle tells me He wants me to stay home, it might rain."

[2] In the Douay translation the Urim and Thummin are referred to as "the rationale of judgment."

It's a good thing there are no such magic aprons or we'd spend all our time consulting buttons.

But getting back to the day they were hunting for donkeys—which, incidentally, were found—there was more important business on hand than that. The Lord had told Samuel that Saul was His choice for king, and after mysteriously inviting Saul to dine and stay the night, Samuel secretly anointed him. "And Samuel took a little vial of oil, and poured it on his head, and kissed him, and said: Behold, the Lord hath anointed thee to be prince over his inheritance, and thou shalt deliver his people out of the hands of their enemies, that are round about them. And this shall be a sign unto thee, that God hath anointed thee to be prince." (I Sam 10:1)

Anointing

This anointing was a "religious rite . . . accompanied by the coming of the Spirit . . . it conferred a grace." It made of the anointed one a consecrated person sharing in the holiness of God —"he was inviolable." [3] These stories of the solemnly anointed kings of Israel can help us to explain better to our children the significance of their own anointing in the sacraments of Baptism and Confirmation. This anointing confers upon us a grace also, in the coming of the Spirit, and makes us consecrated persons sharing in the holiness of God. The holy chrism used in these sacraments is the same oil used by the Church to anoint both kings and priests, and it is significant of our share in both the kingship and priesthood of Christ, making us a royal race, a priestly people. Therefore we share the royal responsibility of sons of the king who are charged to do the will of their father, to carry out his works, to extend his benevolent reign over all the people. We will read later of David's profound respect for Saul even after enmity separated them, and how he executed a man who dared to lay hands upon and slay the anointed king.

Several days after we had read this story and discussed the various aspects of anointing, I was preparing to shampoo my hair and had put oil on it. One child after another, seeing me, stopped and stared and asked, "What have you done to your hair?"

At last Christopher could bear it no longer and he explained. "She's anointed." And so I am.

[3] Roland De Vaux, *Ancient Israel* (New York: McGraw-Hill, 1961), p. 104.

Finally, in 12:18-25, Samuel gives his farewell address to the people before stepping down in deference to Saul, the new king, and he repeats God's warning to both people and king. ". . . follow the guidance of the Lord your God. If you rebel against Him, if you defy His commands, the hand of the Lord will fall heavily on you and your race." (12:15-16 Knox) And to show how angered the Lord had been at their preference for a mortal king, a terrible storm smote the people; but Samuel reassured them. Since they understood their wrong and repented, they must follow the Lord on this new course and "He will do marvelous deeds in your midst." (12:24 Knox) And the old order gave way to the new on the note of *obedience*. This is the clue to watch for as the story of salvation continues to unfold.

There was a flaw in the character of Saul. He was mightily self-willed. The root of his trouble was his failure to surrender entirely to the will of God, and in chapter 13, Samuel, angered that Saul took it upon himself to offer sacrifice before battle instead of waiting for the priest, announced that God would no longer make Saul's line the dynasty to rule Israel. Here Jonathan, son of Saul, young, daring, honorable, makes his appearance for the first time and wins our hearts as he later won the love and devotion of David.

In contrast to his father, Jonathan's faith in the Lord is a dazzling thing, and the adventure in chapter 14 gives us a remarkable study of the two men. The fears and tensions that later drive Saul into murderous frenzies begin to gather here. The impulsive ban on his men, their terror, his fearful scrupulosity, are like symptoms of an illness; while Jonathan's light heart, fearless daring, common sense, describe a soul at peace with the Lord and happy in His command. At the end of the chapter in the account of Saul's family, we encounter the name of Michol, his youngest daughter, whose beauty will one day capture the heart of David and who becomes the first of his several wives.

Saul's Disobedience

Chapter 15 is Saul's undoing, for here he clearly disobeys. We were reading the account of his return from victory over the Amalecites with Saul leading King Agag and the beasts, when Christopher sat up, startled, and said:

"He's disobeying. God told him not to do that. Now something's going to happen. Something always happens to them when they disobey. And something will happen to me if I disobey too."

Yes, we agreed, something always happens when we disobey, but not always the kind of thing that happened to the Israelites. What happens to us usually happens inside. Together with the damage we do to others by our disobedience and the actual trouble it causes, there comes about a weakening in us, and we cannot live God's life as well as before. Our likeness to Christ grows a little less and our love for God gets cooler. In the end the disobediences, added to one another, can lead us to a suffering far worse than the Israelites'—a suffering that could last forever. We must not disobey.

What happened to Saul was this. The Lord sent Samuel to Bethlehem to seek out a shepherd boy and anoint him as future king of Israel, and "the Lord's spirit passed away from Saul," and an evil mood came upon him. (16:14 Knox) Someone at court remembered a boy who played the harp well and might soothe the king's sufferings, and David, son of Jesse the Bethlehemite, a "skillful player, sturdy besides, well-spoken and personable . . . and the Lord is with him" (16:18 Knox) was brought to the royal service and Saul loved him. Whenever Saul was sunk in gloom, David would fetch his harp and play and the evil mood left him.

David and Goliath

Oddly enough, the account of David and Goliath in chapter 17 gives us a completely different story of the meeting of David with the king, which some think indicates there were two traditions held by the Hebrews. Whichever is correct, the story is a classic to which children need no introduction, yet reading it aloud uncovers many new details—accounts of the gifts Jesse sent to the front, the description of Goliath, the reward of riches and the king's daughter to the champion, Eliab's annoyance to find his young brother roaming about the camp, David's misery in the king's armor, and much more. We first read of the size of the Philistines when the Hebrews returned from exploring Chanaan (Num 13:28-33) and even then we suspected some exaggeration. The proportions of Goliath are heroic indeed, yet would it be out of order to wonder if perhaps the story-teller stretched them a bit to emphasize the victory of the Israelite over the Philistine, the Israelites bare-armed against the Philistines and their iron weapons, and the great power of God which was ever responsible for Israel's victories?

This is a fine hero tale to be told not only within the context of salvation history, but as an example of real courage. We have renamed it, for such purposes, "The Boy Who Learned How to Be Brave." A background of wild and lonely hills, fair and stormy skies, prayer and songs of God and His greatness, frame David's adventures with the flocks. Later when David volunteers to fight, he explains to a dubious Saul that while herding his father's flocks he had slain a lion and a bear that came to prey on them. "The Lord who protected me against the lion and the bear will protect me against this Philistine." (17:37 Knox) This is how a man learns to be brave, by praying to the Lord for help and then doing what needs to be done. And, we can show the children, David's prayers and songs are found among the Psalms and they will help us to be brave too. "You have given me the shield of your saving help, your right hand upholds me, your care has made me great . . ." (Ps 17:36 Fides)

David, a Type of Christ

David is not only a forerunner of Christ, Who is called David's Son in the Gospels, but he is a type of Christ, born in Bethlehem, a shepherd who becomes a king, betrayed by those he has loved and trusted, a man of justice, patience and sorrow. There was a side of him that was all too human, but this only proves that his holiness was dearly won—no second nature to him but a victory after struggle. Occasionally David fell, but immediately he asked God's pardon, and in his humility David became a greater man, a holier one.

In David's friendship with Jonathan, which introduces the story of his struggle with Saul, we see two men in almost the same relationship as Christ, the kingly Son of David, and St. John the Baptist, the last of the prophets. In I Samuel 18:1-4, Jonathan, the king's son, gives his very garments to David as though vesting him with his own inheritance, and in 23:16-18 (Knox), Jonathan's words, "Thou art destined to reign over Israel and I to take second place," remind us very much of St. John's "I must decrease that He may increase." (John 3:30) Even in death they remind us of the other two. David mourns Jonathan: "Never woman loved her only son, as I thee," (II Kings 1:26 Knox); and Our Lord said of John the Baptist; "Among those born of woman there is not a greater prophet than John the Baptist." (Luke 7:28) Then on the occasion of

John's death, his disciples took away John's body and buried it and came to tell the news to Jesus. "Jesus, when he heard it, took ship from the place where he was, and withdrew into the desert country, to be alone . . ." (Matt 14:13 Knox)

Saul's Jealousy of David

But we are ahead of our story.

Eagerly and tirelessly David served Saul, but when he returned from slaying the Philistines and Saul heard the women sing, "By Saul's hand a thousand, by David's ten thousand fell," (18:7 Knox) jealousy began to eat at the king and he wondered if this was the man who would supplant him. Twice he tried to pinion David to the wall with a spear as he sang, and twice he tried to have him slain in battle, once offering the price of Michol if he could bring back the foreskins of one hundred Philistines.[3] Again and again he would try to kill David, Jonathan would prevent it, and David would be restored to the king's graces, until finally there was no stemming the hatred in Saul's heart and David was forced to become a fugitive.

David the Outlaw

David's life as the refugee leader of an outlaw band is much less known than his other roles and it reminds us of the guerillas of modern times. Having departed hastily without food or weapons, David arrived at Nobe where Achimelech, the high priest, attended at the tabernacle, and he pretended to be on a royal errand. Could he have bread and a weapon? He had come in haste without them. Achimelech agreed to give David some of the loaves of proposition, and for arms he gave him the sword of Goliath. And David hurried on, until he reached safe shelter in the cave of Odollam. There he rounded up his nephews and all the vagabonds of the countryside until he had organized a force of four hundred men.

When Saul learned of David's encounter with Achimelech, his delusions rose to a mighty crescendo and in a horrible blood bath, eighty-five priests and their wives, children and flocks were destroyed. Only one escaped to take refuge with David and tell him that Saul had slain all the Lord's priests.

[3] This might be read "if you will kill one hundred Philistines." (18:25)

David Spares Saul

The suspense that follows in David's encounters with Saul is as real as any adventure lover could wish. David's noble forbearance when he finds Saul asleep and cuts off the hem of his robe is a tribute to his reverence for the Lord's anointed one, and the anguish of his heart pours out in his speech to Saul begging redress for all the imagined wrongs. The bittersweet humility of his final protest is heartbreaking.

"A fine quarry thou huntest, king of Israel, a fine quarry indeed! A dead dog, a flea, were better worth thy quest." (24:16 Knox) One loves David so.

Saul forgives David at this time and asks him to swear allegiance, and when he does the two part, each to his own fastness. In chapter 26 there is another such story, almost identical, only this time David takes the king's spear and cup. Most important of all is the lesson of David's refusal to take revenge. Unlike Rebecca, David waited to let God work out his dilemma instead of taking matters into his own hands, even though he knew himself to be God's chosen and destined to fill Saul's throne.

David, Abigail and Nabal

We have deliberately skipped chapter 25 in order not to interrupt the two meetings of Saul and David, but now we return to the story of David and the niggardly Nabal. Like a little novel tightwoven with color and characterization, this is the tale of an outlaw chieftain who woos and wins a beautiful lady on the death of her ugly husband.

It was the custom for men of such wealth as Nabal, whose flocks and shepherds were at the mercy of roving brigands, to pay tribute on occasion to the sufferance of these men who might have raided but, in this case, did not. At the time of shearing, large supplies of food were available to celebrate the year's harvest of wool, and what David asked was not out of order. Only an unregenerate miser would have refused him, which apparently describes Nabal, for when finally he heard how his wife had saved him, his flocks and his men by giving David loaves, wine, rams, flour, raisins and figs from his stores, "his heart went dead within him, cold as a stone," and ten days later he died of a stroke. (25:37-38 Knox)

In the course of the story, Abigail speaks of David's reputation for justice and forbearance and even of his pre-eminence in the sight of the Lord and how he has been chosen to be master of all Israel. And at the end of the little tale comes the marriage of David and Abigail.

David Takes Asylum with the Philistines

At last David was forced to take an incredible course. He sought asylum among his people's worst enemy, the Philistines, in order to escape the relentless pursuit of Saul, and there he and his men became a band of mercenaries committed to plunder in return for living in the town of Siceleg. Daily David plundered the towns of the Amalecites, razing the entire countryside in order that no one be left to give witness of him, and daily he told Achis, prince of Geth, that it was his own people he struck. In this way did David deceive the Philistine chief who congratulated himself that such a fierce warrior was now committed to a lifetime of service in Philistia, so savagely had he hurt his brethren.

Saul and the Witch of Endor

With the massing of the Philistines to the north, Saul finally gave up his chase of David and turned his attention to war. Samuel had died and all Israel mourned him, and Saul faced the greatest struggle of his military career alone, without help of priest or prophet. He had alienated Samuel by his disobedience; he had slain all the priests; now when he consulted the Lord no answer came. In desperation he took himself to the witch of Endor, despite his own edict that all such spiritualists be considered unlawful, and he asked the woman to call up the spirit of Samuel. The prophet, appearing, repeated the dreadful sentence, "The Lord has forsaken thee." (28:16 Knox) David would inherit the kingdom, and the very day following, Saul and his sons would join Samuel in the land of the dead.

Here Christopher interrupted. "Say, if she could talk to the dead, could she talk to God?"

"Well, they could all talk to God in prayer, but Saul was able to talk to Him in a special way until God took His spirit from him."

"Could she see the people she talked to—the dead?"

"I guess she could. Saul appeared to be seeing Samuel."

"Do you suppose if she could talk to God, she could *see* God?" His face was alight and he rolled back on the couch with his heels in the air. "Golly—I can't wait to see God!"

And of such are the delights of the family that reads holy scripture.

The Death of Saul and Jonathan

The great final battle of Saul's tragedy began and David was saved from opposing his own people on the battlefield only because the Philistine chiefs did not trust him. Such a man? With such a reputation? Ah, no. And they were wise. David's arch protests are indeed suspicious.

Returning to Siceleg, he found the Amalecites had burned the town to the ground and had taken off with the women and children. David's own men "came near to stoning him, so sore were their hearts at the loss of son and daughter." (30:6 Knox) But counseled by the Lord, David gave chase and rescued all, taking sheep and cattle for his booty, and on his return sent presents of spoils to the elders of the neighboring towns of Juda. The time was soon coming for his return.

The death of Saul by his own hand and the slaying of his sons, including the beloved Jonathan, close the first book of Samuel. The first act of what had promised to be a regal drama of victory ended in disaster, with the Israelites scattered into the interior and the Philistines triumphant. They had asked for a king to lead them in war like other nations and make them victorious, and God had given them their king. But their greatness still lay in their election to be the people of God, working with Him to establish a kingdom not of this world, and in this Saul had failed completely through lack of faith and obedience. To another man would fall the role of showing forth the image of the King to come.

Second Samuel

The second book of Samuel tells the story of David's rise to power, and begins with an account of Saul's death which contradicts the story told in the last chapter of I Samuel, but is probably a fiction contrived by the Amalecite who, it seems likely, was a looter and a liar. David's outrage at the report of the Amalecite and how he had him slain for his deed show, as we have said, the significance attached to the anointed one.

David's lament for Saul and Jonathan is one of the most famous of Hebrew poems and is full of that language which seemed to spill out of him so easily, words that praise and mourn, that speak to the mountains and the dew and the created things almost in their own tongue. "Mountains of Gelboe, never dew, never rain fall upon you . . . on thy heights, Gelboe, Jonathan lies slain . . ." (II Kings 1:17-27 Knox) St. Paul was like this. He spilled out torrents of words as easily as David and his mind darted in the same way to the kinship between men and things, each of them being a child of God.

David is Anointed King

Now David took counsel of the Lord and was told to remove to Hebron with his wives and children and followers. There at last he was anointed king by the men of his own tribe, over Juda alone, to be sure, but the prophecy of the Lord was beginning to be fulfilled. One lone son named Isboseth was left of Saul's line, and a grandson by Jonathan, a little lame boy named Miphiboseth. Abner, general of the armies of Saul, had Isboseth crowned king over the rest of Israel but he was a king in name only, for Abner ruled from behind the throne. In an exchange of arms between the two factions, Abner slew the brother of David's general, Joab, and incurred his promise of vengeance—and all the while the Philistines smiled to see the men of Israel fighting among themselves, forgetful of the archenemy in possession of so much of their land.

When Abner saw that the ascendancy of David was inevitable, he went to David on the pretext of a quarrel with Isboseth over one of Saul's wives[4] and offered to rally Israel to his command, recalling the promise of the Lord that he would rule the land. On his return after plotting this coup, Abner was ambushed by Joab and murdered in the blood vengeance considered due to the family of

---

[4] The cause of the quarrel can be omitted, substituting: "Then Abner and Isboseth had a quarrel." (II Sam 3:6-11) It is explained thus: the heir to the king was heir to his wives and when Abner took one of Saul's wives, Isboseth threw it in his face, hinting that Abner really considered *himself* king.

a slain warrior. But David did not consider it rightfully due; his curse of Joab[5], his grief over the betrayal of Abner, his condemnation of vengeance (and who had better right to condemn it after having foregone it so many times?) endeared him more than ever to the hearts of the people and more than ever they longed to make David their king.

Still bloodshed was not finished. To David's further grief, Isboseth was now murdered by two Benjaminites, and so angered was David by this that he had them horribly slain and displayed over the public reservoir in Hebron. David's capacity for pity, tenderness, trust, and forgiveness, and at the same time this anger that was so violent and bloody, makes him irresistible, for it shows us a picture of all that is both good and brutal in ourselves. Forgiving, he forgave almost foolishly; sorrowing, he was inconsolable; loving, he was heartbreakingly tender; and angry, he was vicious.

At last the tribes rallied to David at Hebron and in one voice claimed him their king, and there in the Lord's presence he made a covenant with them. They anointed him king of Israel at the age of thirty years, and he would reign for the following forty years.

David Makes Jerusalem His Capital

In chapter 5, we read of the capture of Jebus, or Jerusalem, an event which may have taken place later in the history of his reign but which the editors of the sacred books put here (if so) in order to symbolize more clearly the union of the north and south under David. Because of its height and strategic position, and because it had no part in the history of any of the tribes, this site proposed itself to David as ideal for a capital to which he might bring the Ark and, from time to time, the people, in the spirit of unity before the Lord. The effort to de-emphasize tribal divisions and mold Israel into one community under God was David's greatest accomplishment and makes him like that Son of his Who was to come to mold all men into a divine community and lead them to a heavenly Jerusalem.

So difficult were the natural cliffs and battlements that surrounded Jerusalem that its inhabitants scoffed at the idea of cap-

---

[5] David's curse is another passage to be omitted, substituting: "And David cursed Joab's family, asking God to punish them." (II Sam 3:29) Such curses were so stereotyped, as is the case with certain expressions today, that they were not always meant literally.

ture, saying they left only their blind and lame to defend the town. But David had spent many years in the vicinity herding his father's sheep outside of Bethlehem, and he must have known about the tunnel between the spring of water and the city. With little effort the place was taken and thus Jerusalem became the heart of Israel, its royal palace affectionately called after its king who had been a shepherd—David's Keep. Now David had no doubt that the Lord blessed his reign.

It followed that the Philistines began to be alarmed. Never inclined to underestimate either the temperament or genius of David, they determined to attack before he grew any stronger. But with the help of the Lord, David twice threw them back in defeat, beginning a series of victories which are reflected in the blessing of Jacob (Gen 49:8-12) and would have their end in total conquest.

> "Juda, your brothers shall praise you;
>   your hand shall be on the neck of your enemies;
>   the sons of your father shall bow down to you.
> A lion's whelp is Juda;
>   from the prey you have gone up, my son.
> He crouches and couches as a lion;
>   as a lioness, and who will disturb him?"

These words reach all the way to Christ.

David Brings the Ark to Jerusalem

The story of how David brought the Ark to Jerusalem is told in chapter 6 and it contains a puzzle that needs explanation.

"What did Oza do that was so terrible?" asked one of the older boys, as we read how Oza was struck dead by the Lord. "He was just trying to keep the Ark from falling off the wagon." (II Kings 6:6-8 Knox)

The people of God had yet to profoundly understand that an infinite difference separated the majesty and holiness of their God from the degraded deities of their pagan neighbors. Familiarity does breed contempt—at least the wrong kind of familiarity—and if the revelation of God was to be handed down the centuries to all mankind by the Israelites, they would have to hold it in the kind of awe which would preclude its being distorted, profaned, dissipated or disregarded. Oza had been party to the arrangements for transporting the Ark. Were they makeshift? His gesture to catch the

Ark as it tumbled apparently betrayed an irreverence which provoked the Lord's anger and so filled David with dread that he postponed taking it to Jerusalem and sent it instead to the house of Obededom, a Levite, of the priestly caste.

This story reminds us that for all our own familiarity with God—and He does want us to be most intimate with Him—we must not forget His transcendent majesty, for He is the One Who made all things out of nothing, the uncreated Word. The great virtue Fear of the Lord helps us to love God with awe and reverence so that we avoid sin, not merely for fear of God's wrath but because we see Who God is and the sweet reasonableness of being subject to Him.

David Dances before the Ark

When at last the time was right, David brought the Ark to Jerusalem with great ceremony and sacrifices, with dancing and trumpets and all the people rejoicing. And Michol, watching David from her window as he danced in the street before the Ark clad only in the linen ephod, despised him for cavorting in front of the people, as graceless, she said, as a common mountebank! David's reply reveals that he understood well now the majesty of the Lord and the littleness of earthly kings.

"Nay, before his coming play the mountebank I will; humble myself I will in my own esteem . . ." The text continues, "And Michol, that was daughter to king Saul, never bore child again to the day of her death." (II Kings 6:16-23 Knox) Which means that David's love for Michol died that day when she refused to enter into his joy in the Lord, and never again did he go to her as husband, never again beget in her a child.

We need not discuss this in detail with the smaller children but it is something to make the older children thoughtful, for during all the years of training for marriage, the family tries to make clear to them the importance of choosing a mate who will share not only love and passion and common interests, but also the service of God in the same religion. Here is an ancient tale that shows us the tragedy of a husband who was in love with God and a wife who was not. How bitter and cold had grown the heart of David's first love Michol, the bride of his youth for whose hand he had slain one hundred Philistines. And the cause of their differences was the failure to share together profoundly the joys of their religion.

David Wishes to Build a Temple

As David pondered the difference between his own house of cedar and the tent of skins which sheltered the Ark, it came to him that he might build a more suitable dwelling for Yahweh⁶ but the Lord spoke to him through the prophet Nathan and said *no*. David would have a son who would one day build a house to do the Lord honor. Then in words which apply at times to Solomon, at times to Christ, at times to both, God assured David that his line would endure forever, his throne remain forever unshaken. The promise given to Abraham and to Moses was narrowed down to a descendent born to the house of David, One who would reach beyond David's dynasty and beyond the survival of human descendents. Christ, true son of David, true royal heir, would also be true God and eternal King. His reign would be forever. And David cried out to the Lord, "No words can thy servant David find; such divine mercy thou showest him." (II Kings 7:20 Knox) Then he proceeded to sing a canticle of thanksgiving unsurpassed. Ah—David was *never* at a loss for words.

David and Miphiboseth

In chapters 8 and 10 we read of further conquests, of how David spread Israel's boundaries, of how he amassed her wealth. And in chapter 9 we read the touching story of David and Miphiboseth, the crippled son of Jonathan, sole heir to the lands of Saul. Miphiboseth asked David, wonderingly, why he should concern himself with "a man such as I, no better than a dead dog?" (9:8 Knox) But David would show him kindness in memory of Jonathan —although ordinarily the conqueror put to death the heirs of the deposed king—and he had him come to Jerusalem to live in his house and ever after eat at the king's table. "Miphiboseth . . . a lame man, lame of either foot." (9:13)

We finished our reading one afternoon with this story and we sat silent for a while, and thought and thought. I said, "David was wonderful, wasn't he? So strong and so brave and fierce, and then so gentle and tender."

* *Yahweh* (He is), the manner in which Israel addressed the Lord. Translated by the Septuagint writers by the Greek word *Kyrios*.

And Christopher looked off at the hills behind our house almost as though he would see him there, and said:

"David was everything."

You should understand that Christopher's middle name is David.

David and Bethsabee

But now we come to a David we did not dream existed. The next chapter in his story is shameful and tragic and teaches us the lesson of man's weakness.

In the spring kings went to war, but David had got over his enthusiasm for fighting and he was tired of battles. There came a spring when David sent Joab off with the army to lay waste to the Ammonites while he stayed at home. One day he was walking on the roof of his palace when he saw, on the roof opposite, a beautiful woman taking her bath. He inquired and found she was Bethsabee, wife of Urias the Hethite, one of his most valiant officers. He sent for her, "she came, he mated with her," and she went back home. "Then finding she had conceived, she sent news of her conception to David." [7] (II Kings 11:1-5 Knox)

This poses a delicate problem with respect to children. We have omitted some passages treating of the sins of the flesh because they made no important contribution to the history of salvation and, while prudishness is to be avoided, distraction with such novelties is a waste of time. But here is a passage in the story of David which is enormously important, for it has served over the centuries as the classic example of how even a man who loves God with all his heart can sin most grievously if he is not always on guard against his passions.

Barely finished vowing his everlasting love and gratitude to God for all His favors, David commits adultery and seems to have forgotten the Lord entirely. We cannot possibly omit the story of David's sin without distorting the whole picture.

However, we can prepare our audience with a little warning. "And now, I am sorry to say, David does something very sinful, and this story is a warning to us never to forget that temptation comes to everyone, even such great men as David, and we have to be on guard." The language of the scriptural story is blunt for children but substitution is not difficult. For example where it reads; "she

[7] Death by stoning was the punishment for an adulteress.

came and he mated with her," we can substitute, "and she came and he made love to her as though she were his wife." Our tone of voice adds regret and sorrow and, if it seems necessary, we can add something like, "O dear, isn't that too bad."

In our family, we have read this story to children between the years of 8 and 17 without any difficulty, explaining Bethsabee's conception by saying that she discovered she was going to have a child and David was its father. The older children who understand about conception and the union of the married needed no further explanation. The youngest, understanding that babies have fathers *and* mothers, and understanding in a wholesomely vague way that the love-making of the husband and the wife has much to do with this, did not question any of it but was sorry to see that David had done this wrong thing with someone who was not his wife, because now the baby wouldn't have his father with him.

David's Plot to Kill Urias

More shocking is David's wicked plan for getting rid of Urias, and again we carefully reword the part where David tries to get Urias drunk so he will go home and make love to his wife and think, in time, that the child she has conceived is his own. If this is perceived by the older children, well and good; if it is missed, fine too. The emphasis can be shifted if we stress the virtue of Urias, who denies himself the comforts of his home and the company of his wife for the sake of his fellow soldiers in the field.

With devilish cunning, David works out his plan for the murder of Urias, it is carried out, and David takes Bethsabee for his wife. There is condemnation enough in II Kings 11:27 (Knox): "But meanwhile David's act had earned the Lord's displeasure."

Nathan's Parable

Nathan's parable is not difficult for children and it is good for them to have a try at figuring it out before we read the ominous, "Thou art the man." (II Kings 12:6 Knox) There follow David's remorse, God's forgiveness, and the warning of the anguish that lies ahead for him. That he had sorrow for his sin and was forgiven, that he bore the evils to come with humility and patience is even more important than that he sinned, and perhaps the most important lesson of all to be pointed out to the children is related to the sacrament of penance.

David and the Sacrament of Penance

David took God at His word. When sin is forgiven, it is forgiven. He wasted no time constantly reviewing it, scrupulously doubting the Lord's forgiveness, hanging back from further service of the Lord out of a wrong sense of unworthiness. Who is not unworthy? Yet the Lord uses the unworthy, even the sinners, to accomplish His ends. If we do not understand this about David, some of the things he will say later on, and in the Psalms, will puzzle us. This story ought to have a place in any extensive lesson on penance and confession for it emphasizes so beautifully that even the gravest sin, truly repented, is forgivable. And one can take up where one left off in the service of God.

David and the Sixth and Ninth Commandments

This story helps us to teach another, most difficult lesson—the one on the sixth and ninth commandments. The story of David's sin should not be picked out of context and used arbitrarily without taking great care to describe also the true grandeur of the man, but when we are reading this book of the Bible we can easily point out that these were the commandments David broke and this story explains precisely what it means to commit adultery and "covet thy neighbor's wife." This same sin makes the headlines frequently and the displeasure of God as recorded in scripture, the remorse of the great David, give much weight to our own disapproval of the scandalous behaviour of some of our contemporaries.

We might omit entirely the last few verses of chapter 12:26-31, as they have no real bearing on the story of salvation.

Chapters 13 and 14, with the exception of II Samuel 14:25-27, a description of Absalom, we omit also. The story of the rape of Tamar and Absalom's blood vengeance is truly frightful and of no real value for children. This is not to say that the writers of scripture had no good reason for putting it in. Never ones to gloss over the defects of their people, they recorded these scandals as salutary warnings, possessing great value as moral lessons for adult readers.

Absolam's Rebellion

Culling from these same chapters, however, we discover that David was certainly an overpermissive parent and Absalom no little spoiled. That he should have got out of hand would surprise no one. It is worth while to generalize a bit to the children about this, pointing out before we begin reading that in the past David had not punished him as he deserved, had indulged him past all common sense and it is no wonder he grew up to be a willful, disrespectful son, a schemer and a rebel.

We read the story of Absalom's rebellion on a warm, sunny day, out on a rocky terrace, with the children in half-hearted submission because plainly it would be much more to the point to go swimming. But it *is* a story, and the murmuring died at once. No one suggested leaving before it was done. We told them to watch for events and people who would recall another story, one they know well, for this tale belonged with the other and would help them appreciate the other much better.

Absalom, the indulged princeling, conceived a plan for seizing the power from his father. Every morning he would go to the city gate where all business was transacted and legal cases heard, and there he would seek out the men from the northern half of the country, called the *Israelites* in contrast to those from the southern half called the *Judaeans*. Craftily he would listen to their pleadings, account them just, then sigh and say: "A pity the king has not appointed anyone to hear your cause; would that I could be appointed judge in the land." (II Sam 15:4-5) And he would give them his hand, kiss them fraternally, and thus "he stole away the hearts of the Israelites." (15:6 Knox) Absalom was a crooked politician.

Next he took a trip to the north and sent agents throughout all the tribes there telling them to mass at Hebron, that Absalom claimed the crown and planned to make war on his father.

David is Betrayed

When David heard this, he decided to leave Jerusalem in order to spare the city bloodshed. He went forth with loyal followers, crossed the stream of Cedron, stopped to tell the priests to return the Ark to the city where it belonged, and proceeded (a pause here and a long look is very effective) up the mount of Olives, weeping as he climbed.

"Oh, I know! Our Lord. He was betrayed too and he went up the mount of Olives. David is like Our Lord here!" Now everyone was alert.

Betrayal after betrayal followed. David learned that Achitophel, his counselor, had gone over to Absalom. Siba, servant of Miphi-

boseth whom he had befriended, arrived to say that the crippled
heir of Saul had gone over to Absalom also, hoping that in the end
the Israelites (among them the tribe of Benjamin, his grandfather's
line) would restore him to the throne as the survivor of the original
monarch. At Bahurim, David was assaulted by Semei, another
Benjaminite, who cursed him and threw stones and dirt upon him
until Abisai, the warrior, asked leave to slay him. In anger David
cried out, "Why the son of my own body is conspiring against my
life; why may not yonder Benjaminite do as much!" (16:11 Knox)
To read of the anguish of David illuminates vividly the passion of
Christ, for this is one of the most strikingly drawn of all the images
of Christ.

David and Christ

The two great tragedies move in the same direction, although
there is an abyss infinitely wide between the two men; but the first
prepares us for the second. The earthly king was betrayed and descended into the valley of death grieving over his sinful son. The
Divine King is betrayed and descends into the arms of death in
grief for His lost brothers. As the crucified Christ arose from His
death to reign triumphantly forever, before him David, king of the
earthly Jerusalem, arose from his grief and sat once more in the
gates so that his followers could have comfort in his royal presence.

The story is filled with marvelous characterizations and rich
detail; it rings with notes which sound like the answer in a great
fugue on the Passion of Christ. Without it we would miss the
significance of many references in David's Psalms, and we found
in our family that it added much to our penetration of the Sorrow-
ful mysteries of the Rosary.

Here too we see the growing rancor between the Judaeans and
the Israelites which will erupt one day in earnest, until finally the
people of God, having lost their perspective, will substitute earthly
power for election in God's plan and will be dispersed in slavery
to a foreign power. Chapter 20 ends with a list of David's ministers,
and it is amazing how familiar we have become with some of the
names, unfamiliar to us before except for their appearance now
and then in a crossword puzzle.

Chapters 21 through 24 at the end of II Samuel are an appendix and may be omitted if it seems advisable. (The David nar-

rative continues with III Kings.) These tell of subsequent events which are not necessary to the main stream of the story.

Chapter 21 tells of a famine which is attributed to a crime of Saul, with retribution made quite horribly by handing over seven of his descendents for execution, evidently in the spirit of blood vengeance customary to the time. Mention is made of war with the Philistines, and the aging David, growing weary on the battle-field, is admonished once and for all by his men not to risk his life in battle again. "Such a light as his must not be lost to Israel." (II Kings 21:18 Knox)

David's Song of Thanksgiving

Chapter 22 is a song of thanksgiving sung by David for his victory over the Philistines and all his past successes. It is a magnificent canticle and might be used as concluding prayer for an evening's reading. Called "David's last Psalm," it is actually Psalm 17, with a few changes, but to read it in the context of David's life gives it an extemporaneous quality, as though we see him and hear him sing it.

In verses 21-26, we find the emphasis is that of a man who, having sinned, has made his peace with the Lord and speaks now of innocence restored and hope in God's help for the future. If this is not explained, these verses can be very puzzling. I had wondered for years whether his memory had failed when he wrote this; what of his adultery?

"To humble folk thou wilt bring deliverance; the proud, with their haughty looks, thou wilt bring down to earth. Thou, Lord, art the lamp of my hope; thou Lord, dost shine on the darkness about me. In thy strength I shall run well girded; in the strength of my God I will leap over a wall." (II Kings 22:28-30 Knox)

When we read these lines, we see that they are indeed the words of a man who has known sin, and in sorrow has been renewed.

David Takes a Census

Chapter 23 is a list of David's heroes and their exploits, and chapter 24 tells of David's census, taken against the wishes of both God and his commanders, and of his punishment. Some opinions hold that in an attempt to create solidarity at home, David took the census as preparation for a campaign abroad; others see this as an act of tyranny which could ultimately transform the people into the servants of the state.

The two books of Samuel can hardly be surpassed for action, excitement, or messianic significance, and the story of David is the story of Israel's star rising to its ascendancy. Soon we will see her begin her decline, all because she mistook prosperity for blessedness, and luxuriating in it her people grew confused and her conscience weak. David's early life and reign show us the last of Israel's frontier and now we will follow her through the perils of success. If only we could learn a lesson from it. The confusion of values which led to the decline of the Israelites was not peculiar to them. It afflicts all nations, all men. These people would lose all David had won for them because they would forget that their greatness lay in the fact that they were the people of God and existed as a nation only to be instrumental in the working out of the redemption.

This is the reason for our existence, too. The name of the sickness which, nurtured on too much ease and prosperity, sapped the strength and reason and faith of Israel, is secularism—to forget that the reason for man's existence is God, that God is his end. This afflicts us too. We will see it slowly strangle these people in the books that follow.

·VI·

THE BREAKUP
OF THE
KINGDOM

Third Kings

The story of Solomon, which comes next, is neither as long nor as exciting as the story of David and if we are to take any stock of Stephen's comment, it bears cutting.

"I think if you left out that part about the lands he ruled and the description of the temple, and the long prayer he prayed in the temple, kids wouldn't get bored. You could say something about his territories without reading it all, and you could say about the temple, 'And then he built a beautiful temple,' and you could tell about the prayer without reading it, and that would be better."

A word to the wise is sufficient. When in doubt about this sort of thing, consult the nearest eleven-year-old scripture man (and he does love the Bible, so his comment is not prejudiced). He made another important contribution. I had asked, "If there is so much in it that is boring, why wouldn't it be better just to read Bible stories instead of the scriptures?"

"Oh no, that wouldn't be the same," he said. "This is the word of God. There's lots of difference between reading in a Bible story,

'And then God said they should do this and do that,' and hearing
God say it in His own words."

Needless to say, I was grateful to hear this, because even though
the words of God in scripture have been filtered through the minds
and pens of the writers, they *are* inspired words and they say what
God wanted said, and it is far more exciting to hear them read
right out of God's own book. If his comment "It is the word of
God" smacks of parental instruction, why not? It had been said
enough times. The only difference between a child's knowing and
not knowing something is that someone has said it to him.

The first chapter of III Kings begins with David's old age and
the pretty Abisag who slept with him to keep him warm. The story
is entirely innocent but it is best omitted for the sake of whatever
bungled version the little ones might later tell. This could occasion
ribaldry from older, wiser listeners and we don't want that. We can
read, "And now David had grown old and chill with age," and skip
to verse 5 and Adonias, badly spoiled and never checked or challenged by his doting father.

Solomon Anointed King

Things being no different then than now, spoiled children
acted the same way, and we find that Adonias, like Absalom before
him, had planned to usurp the throne. Informed of this by Nathan
and Bethsabee, David had Solomon anointed immediately and set
upon the throne in his stead. Adonias fled to the altar for asylum
until Solomon would grant him protection, which he did for as
long as Adonias would prove loyal; let him plot mischief and he
would die for it.

The Death of David

Now it was time for David to die, but first he charged Solomon
with obedience to the Lord God, promising that all would go well
for him and his race if he would obey. Next he left recommenda-
tions for the strictest justice to be meted out to his enemies, the
first among them his nephew Joab, general of his army. Twice Joab
had slain valiant leaders of the Israelites, first Abner and then
Amasa (did David know it was Joab who had run Absalom
through?), but his last defection to the side of Adonias had outrun
the king's mercy. "Do not allow those grey hairs to find a peaceful
end," (III Kings 2:7 Knox) was his advice to Solomon. He was to

watch Semei, the Benjaminite who had cursed David on his journey out of Jerusalem so long before, and punish him—for the oath that bound David to suffer him to live did not bind Solomon.

In due time the three were executed, Adonias for trying to trick Solomon into giving him power,[1] Joab for the blood-guilt his murders had brought on the house of David, and Semei for failing to stay in Jerusalem according to his agreement. Abiathar the priest, who had defected with Adonias and Joab, was stripped of his priesthood as the Lord had promised long before when the chief priest Heli, in the time of Samuel, had failed to correct and punish his evil sons. Over and over in the Old Testament, as in our own times, the failure of parents to correct children has always ended in disaster. (I Sam 2:30-32)

Solomon's Wisdom

Chapter 3 tells the most familiar of all the stories of Solomon, first his request that the Lord give him wisdom, and second his judgment on the women with the baby. That this king should ask wisdom rather than power and wealth and glory was entirely unique and so pleased God that He promised Solomon the latter as a reward for the purity of his intention—reminding him that he must always be obedient to the path of the Lord.

It was no idle warning. From here on the struggle between obedience and the lure of the world will plague the kings of Israel until their downfall. It is a lesson Our Lord was to teach to us. "No man can serve two masters; for either he will hate the one and love the other, or else he will stand by the one and despise the other. You cannot serve God and mammon." (Matt 6:24)

Chapter 4 can be nicely condensed starting with 4:1, "And all the tribes of Israel were under king Solomon's rule," and skipping to 4:20, "So Juda and Israel, countless in number as the sand by the sea, ate, drank and were merry." The land, divided in two parts but ruled by one king, was prosperous. The rest of the chapter up to verse 29 can be summarized, telling of the supplies needed for the royal household and Solomon's great renown. In 4:32-34 we read perhaps the most endearing of all the descriptions of

---

[1] As previously explained, to take one of the late king's wives was tantamount to taking his seat on the throne. This was precisely the kind of mischief (2:13-22) that Solomon had warned Adonias would be punished by death. This was the cause of the quarrel between Isboseth and Abner. (II Kings 3:8)

Solomon. He was a man who knew three thousand stories, had made up one thousand and five songs, could tell of all the trees that were, and of the birds and animals, fish and all creeping things. Parts II and V of the book of Proverbs are ascribed to Solomon and some of his songs are found in the book of Psalms. Solomon must have been marvelous company not only for the members of the royal court and his guests, but for his children and grandchildren as well.

The Building of the Temple

Chapters 5, 6 and 7 tell of the building of the temple and are things which Stephen is sure most children would find "kind of boring," so it is wiser for the parents to go over this ahead of time and tell about the temple. In *Lands of the Bible*[2], there is a simplified description of the temple together with a page of illustrations which do much to give us an accurate idea of its appearance. It is not known exactly what the temple looked like, but having been constructed by Phoenician builders it is safe to say it must have been something like their own shrines (a number of which have been restored in modern times). The cherubim guarding the Ark of the Covenant were not angels but great beasts, like lions with human faces and mighty wings, and the sea of bronze was nothing else but a giant wash basin for the purification of the priests, with the smaller basins for the purifying of the victims. Scholars complain that the text describing the temple is confused and inexact, but still the sense of its elegance is there; and the description of the materials, the care and the genius that went into its making.

Solomon's Prayer

With the dedication of the temple and Solomon's great prayer for his people, Jerusalem actually became the center of worship for all Israel. Even after David had chosen the site, captured it, built his city there, and brought the Ark to it, the old places of worship had continued to draw the people; but now Jerusalem became the earthly dwelling place of the Lord and, for all time, the symbol of His eternal dwelling place in heaven.

Long-winded or not, Solomon's prayer is too great to pass over entirely. There is petition for protection, justice, forgiveness, for rain, food, for relief from pestilence and blight, rust and mildew,

[2] Terrien, *op. cit.*, p. 42.

locust and plague, for strangers, for warriors, for prisoners, for all the people.

"Hast thou not set them apart, among all the peoples of the world, to be thy coveted possession? Was not this thy promise, given through thy servant Moses when thou didst rescue our fathers from Egypt, O Lord our God?" (III Kings 8:53 Knox) He concluded with a final admonition to the poeple. "Wholly be our hearts given to the Lord our God, ready (as we are ready this day) to live by his laws and keep true to his commandments." (8:61 Knox)

These are like the beseeching prayers in the Good Friday liturgy and the Collects of the votive Masses. The conditions of fruitful prayer are for us, as for the Israelites, the faithful love and service of God.

Solomon's Infidelity

How is it possible that a king who loved God so ardently and had built so great a monument to His glory could fall to the very depths of infidelity? In this lies the great moral of Solomon's story. The Lord Himself, accepting Solomon's tribute, heard his prayer and promised "never a day but my eyes shall be watching, my heart attentive here . . ." (9:3 Knox), but He had a warning for him too. "But if you and your children are content to turn your backs on me, following me no more, neglecting the commands and observances I have enjoined on you, betaking yourselves to the service and worship of alien gods, then I will sweep Israel away from the land I gave them, and this temple which I have hallowed as the shrine of my name, shall be thrust away out of my sight." (9:6-7 Knox)

There is not the slightest doubt that Solomon would have answered, "Never, Lord God, never! I will never forsake thee!"

But he did. What could have come between Solomon and God?

Chapters 9, 10 and 11 continue the long list of things that Solomon did, things that Solomon possessed, until finally *things* came between Solomon and God. He built, in addition to the temple, towns, fortresses, palaces, cities, stables for his war horses, stables for his horse trading; he built docks, a fleet of ships, mines, logging camps. He traded for spices, gold and silver, precious stones, sandalwood, ivory, peacocks, apes, for clothes, cedars,

armor, horses, mules. He ate from golden plates and drank from
golden cups, he sat on an ivory throne. And Solomon had seven
hundred wives and three hundred concubines.[3] Many were women
of alien religion. "It was of such races that the Lord had warned
Israel, You must not mate with them, or let them mate with
your daughters; no question but they will beguile your hearts into
the worship of their own gods." (11:2 Knox)

And thus, trapped by his power (even the Pharaoh of Egypt
had given him his daughter for a wife), becoming a victim of his
own glory, indulging every appetite, at first restrainedly but gradu-
ally surrendering self-discipline, the historians of the Jews write
soberly: "So, an old man now, he was enticed by women into the
worship of alien gods, and his heart was not true to the Lord, his
own God, like his father David's before him." (11:4 Knox)

What is it we learn, almost as one learns a limerick? "The
fear of the Lord is the beginning of Wisdom." (Prov 1:7) And
Solomon, who was given such wisdom that all the world respected
it, lost it because he no longer feared the Lord. Nowhere does it
say that, like his father, Solomon grieved for his sin. Let us hope
that he did.

The Death of Solomon

Chapter 11 brings us to the end of Solomon and the beginning of the dissolution of the kingdom. Jeroboam was given Israel,
the northern kingdom of ten tribes, and Juda was left for Solomon's son Roboam.

Solomon was forty years on the throne; the years of Israel's
greatest glory. Under Solomon she was a power to be reckoned with;
she commanded respect among the nations and the great ones of
the world made their way to her gates. But it was not for this
that the Lord made Israel into a nation. She had been chosen
to work with the Lord as He prepared to bring forth the One who
would save the world, and in this, under Solomon, she failed.

The Lilies of the Field

Once Our Lord was reproving His disciples for their great concern with worldly cares.

[3] As we read first in the story of Abraham and the patriarchs, God tolerated
multiple wives among the Israelites for a long time. Among the wives there
were different ranks and some translations refer to those of lower rank as
concubines.

"See how the lilies grow; they neither toil nor spin, yet I say to you that not even Solomon in all his glory was arrayed like one of these. But if God so clothes the grass which today is alive in the field and tomorrow is thrown into the oven, how much more you, O you of little faith!

"And as for you, do not seek what you shall eat, or what you shall drink; and do not exalt yourselves (for after all these things the nations of the world seek); but your Father knows that you need these things. But seek first the kingdom of God, and all these things shall be given you besides.

"Do not be afraid, little flock, for it has pleased your Father to give you the kingdom. Sell what you have, give alms. Make for yourselves purses that do not grow old, a treasure unfailing in heaven, where neither thief draws near nor moth destroys. For where your treasure is, there your heart will also be." (Luke 12:27-34)

That was Solomon's terrible mistake. His heart was with his worldly treasure.

After the death of Solomon, one last attempt was made by Jeroboam to unite the kingdom. Taking himself to Sichem where Solomon's son Roboam had gone to be crowned king, Jeroboam asked that the people be relieved of the terrible burden of forced work and heavy taxation; he would lead the ten tribes of the north to submission and faithful service, should this be done. But Roboam foolishly listened to the advice of the young men of his court instead of the counsel of the elders, roared out his defiance and lost the northern kingdom for all time.

On the felt-board map we had made to show the distribution of tribes at the time of Josue, we removed the tribal divisions and divided the kingdom into Israel and Juda.

The Kingdom of Israel in the North

Alas for Jeroboam, who might have proved himself a worthy leader. He sealed the doom of the north by setting up two golden calves as symbols[4] of the God Who brought their fathers out of Egypt, and led the people into idolatry. He set up altars at Dan and Bethel (where Jacob had seen the angels) lest the people return to Jerusalem to worship, and worse yet he set apart priests

---

[4] As Aaron had said in Exodus 32:4.

to offer sacrifice who were not of the tribe of Levi. It was not long before the wrath of the Lord was upon him.

On one of the new feast days, Jeroboam was standing before the altar of sacrifice when a prophet appeared to warn him that Josias, of the house of David, would one day destroy the altar and burn on it the bones of the very priests who offered sacrifice there.[5] To prove this word of the Lord, the altar straightaway fell apart and Jeroboam's arm became withered. And there follows the strange story of this prophet who, having delivered his message, disobeyed the Lord and was punished. It is not an important episode, but children are puzzled by the tale and it gives us an opportunity to show them how even the prophets of God had to be tested.

Even so, Jeroboam would not mend his ways until his son fell sick unto death. His story ends with a dramatic pronouncement by the prophet Ahias that God will abandon Israel "for the guilt of Jeroboam that taught Israel to sin." (III Kings 14:16 Knox)

The Southern Kingdom of Juda

Meanwhile, in the south Roboam ruled Juda, and affairs there went much as affairs in Israel, with the added disaster that the temple was plundered by the king of Egypt. When these kings died, they were succeeded by their sons, Nadab in Israel, and Abiam in Juda.

Abiam was every bit as sinful as his father Roboam, but for the sake of David who ever did the Lord's will, "nor ever swerving, while life lasted, from his decrees, except in the matter of Urias the Hethite," (15:5 Knox) the Lord allowed the dynasty to endure in order to bring forth a son who would cleanse Jerusalem of idolatry. With Abiam's death, his son Asa was king, and he attacked these evils with such vigor that he deprived even the queen mother of her rank for worshiping idols.

Asa's story continues with an account of his struggle with Nadab's successor (having had no relations with Nadab during his short reign). He died an honorable old man and was laid to rest in David's Keep.

In Israel, Nadab, everywhere as sinful as his father, was overwhelmed by Baasa, who followed the tradition of idolatrous worship. The prophet Jehu warned Baasa of the Lord's punishment for his deeds and Baasa, enraged, ordered Jehu's death.

[5] We will read of this in IV Kings 23:15-18.

Ela, Baasa's son, followed him to the throne and was struck down in the midst of an orgy by Zambri, commander of his cavalry, who made himself king and brought to fulfillment the prophecy of Baasa's destruction. But when the news of Zambri's succession reached the army of Israel, they rose up and denounced him, choosing their own general Amri for their king. Hearing this, Zambri retired to the palace and burned it over his head, reaping the same punishment as his predecessors.

It was Amri who bought the hill of Samaria and built the city which would earn its everlasting fame in Our Lord's story of love of neighbor. (Luke 10:30-37) None of its exploits as capital of the northern kingdom would reach as far. Amri's reign was far more vigorous and prosperous than the few verses in III Kings reveal and the best the scribes can say for him is that he defied the Lord's will "more recklessly than any king before him." (16:26 Knox) He spawned Achab, who outdid even his father and carved his niche in history by marrying a Phoenician wife named Jezabel who cut a bloody path through Israel before she came to her end.

At this point, someone may sigh wearily and say, "Why hop from king to king like this, tangling with names we will never remember? Why not just skip these chapters and say, 'Then Israel and Juda had a long list of kings, most of them wicked, who called down the wrath of the Lord'?"

We asked the children, hinting for our answer. "What was a king supposed to give his people in the way of behavior?"

"Good example?"

Exactly, and the Lord's condemnation was always the same; He punished Israel's kings because "they taught Israel to sin." They led a nation born of a covenant with God Himself, created to be His helpmate in the redeeming of mankind, step by step to the edge of the pit. Now and then a good king rose up but the task of sweeping entirely clean a country littered with pagan shrines and soiled with pagan practices, was all but impossible. And when it came time for punishment, the Lord let it fall with a heavy hand. It was the only way to purify them.

The God of the Old Testament

Sometimes we hear people say, "But the God of the Old Testament was so harsh, not like the God of the New." Yet what do we find Our Lord saying of those who lead His people into sin? "But whoever causes one of these little ones who believe in me to sin, it were better for him to have a great millstone hung around his neck and to be drowned in the depths of the sea." (Matt 18:6) They sound like the same God.

Stephen reflected on all this after we had finished our reading one time and then said, "Remember the boy in *Treasure on the Hill,* whose father was teaching him all the sharp tricks of trading? It's sort of like that, isn't it?" [6]

Yes, it is, for goodness is never a personal matter alone. There are so many others for whom we are responsible.

There is still another marvel to be pointed out. Despite all this, a remnant would survive—survive the betrayals, the idolatry, survive being conquered and exiled. For they were God's people and He had promised that out of them would come the blessing for all nations Whom we know is Christ. No other people in history has survived so total a disaster. Even the mighty powers that conquered them have disappeared but not the people of God. They live on now in Christ, in the Church, the new Israel, with the same role as the Israel of old. They exist in order to give themselves to God in the work of restoring divine life to all men everywhere. Perhaps Our Lord was thinking of the past as well as the future when He said of the Church: "And the gates of hell shall not prevail against it." (Matt 16:18) Time and again Israel's wicked kings had dragged her right to the very gates of hell.

Elias, the Prophet

Now we come to the story of Elias, one of the best loved saints of the Old Testament. Inspired by the Lord, Elias went to Achab and told him a drought would afflict the land as punishment for leading the people to worship Baal. Next, the Lord sent Elias on retreat to the valley of the Kerith where the river provided him with water and the ravens with food. This story reminds us of St. Paul the Hermit and St. Antony of the desert, Elias' spiritual sons many centuries later. For years a raven daily brought Antony half a loaf of bread at his oasis hidden in the cave, but when Paul arrived for a visit the Lord increased the rations and sent the

---

[6] Marie Killelea, *Treasure on the Hill,* illus. by Lauren Ford (New York: Dodd Mead, 1960). A beautifully written and illustrated life of Our Lord for the family.

raven with a whole loaf.[7] Elias reminds us of John the Baptist too, who also went to the desert to be alone in prayer before his public ministry.

The Widow of Sarephta

Elias remained in the desert until even the river dried up and then the Lord bade him go to Sarephta, a village on the coast of Phoenicia, and seek out a widow there who would care for him. Elias met the woman at the city gate, asked for food and water, and although she had barely enough for herself and her son, she graciously prepared a meal for the prophet from her meager store. As a reward for her generosity ever after that her jar of flour was never empty nor did her cruet lack for oil.

(There is a game to play when the family is taking a ride, doing the dishes, or sitting around the cook-out fire after the hamburgers are eaten, called *Where Am I?* Bible-reading families can hide in Bible stories and we have someone in our house who made herself small enough to hide in the jar of flour that belonged to the widow of Sarephta.)

Then a dreadful thing happened. The widow's son became sick unto death and in her anguish she wished Elias had never come. His presence only called God's attention to her sins, she said, and how deserving she was of punishment. Elias raising her boy to life is one of the most marvelous passages of all and it brings with it a torrent of rich associations. It has been said many times that the Old Testament prepares us for the New and this episode is a perfect example. So many stories come to mind: the centurion and his sick servant (Luke 7:1-10); the widow of Naim (Luke 7:11-17); the daughter of Jairus (Mark 5:21-43); and the most splendid story of all, the raising of Lazarus (John 11:1-44). No wonder the people thought Our Lord was Elias.

Elias and the Prophets of Baal

Another great tale is Elias' triumph over the prophets of Baal, when he challenged them to a contest before the god Baal and the Lord God of Israel on top of Mount Carmel. So magnificently did he undo the four hundred and fifty prophets of Baal that the people put them all to death. And he is entirely amusing when

[7] A delightful commentary on the nature of the raven, who is one of God's scavengers and picks up food and carries it away.

he proposes that Baal may not hear their prayers because, per-
chance, he is talking, abroad on a journey, or sleeping and needs
awakening (18:27).

But these had been Jezabel's prophets, and now Jezabel, burning with rage, warned Elias that she would get even. Her threat
so frightened Elias that he turned and ran off to the desert, and
there, weary of the struggle, depressed because for all his victory
he was once more at the mercy of the vicious queen, he longed
to die. The situation has a terrible likeness to Our Lord's position
after the great triumph with Lazarus, the triumphal procession on
Palm Sunday, and the return of the rulers to their evil plots.

But the Lord would still use Elias. Again He fed him miraculously, led him on a journey of forty days and forty nights and
brought him to Mount Horeb—the famous Sinai, God's own
mountain. There the Lord spoke to Elias as He had once spoken
to Moses, but this time in the gentle breeze. Let him not be discouraged, but do the work set before him. All would not be lost.
In the end a remnant would be left who had not bent their knees
before Baal. It is an encounter to encourage dedicated souls everywhere who, like Elias, weary of the struggle, see no results, seem
to be fighting a losing battle.

Once more Elias started out to do the Lord's bidding, and
met Eliseus, who was to be his successor, and as a sign of this laid
his mantle on the younger man's shoulders.

The last three chapters of III Kings tell again of Achab's
adventures in war, trickery and murder. It is thought that chapter
20 belongs chronologically before the time of Achab's capitulation
to Jezabel's religion, for it speaks of the Lord's prophets, and
Achab's behavior seems to be above reproach. Having received
victory twice from the Lord (the point of this tale), it was not
Achab's place to let the captive king go free; he should have consulted the Lord. His rebuke at the hand of the prophet is
reminiscent of Nathan rebuking David with a parable, and the
effect of the rebuke, making him a "sullen man, an ill man to
cross," (20:43 Knox) may account for the onset of Jezabel's campaign against the prophets of the Lord.

Naboth and the Vineyard

In chapter 21 there is a story that seems to be clothed in the
language of the Gospel parables. It is certain that when Our Lord

sought images and terms and situations for His own stories, He had at hand a long association with the stories in scripture which were also familiar to His audience. At any rate, this story was fact, not fiction, and involved an innocent man, his inheritance of a vineyard, the king's jealousy and the plot by the queen to murder the man and get his land. Here is a marvelous picture of Jezabel's character and personality entirely dominating the king. Again we meet Elias speaking words that are appropriate to all times. "Thou art a slave. Thou hast enslaved thyself to defiance of the Lord's will." (22:20 Knox)

In chapter 22, Achab consults *his* prophets for counsel, men who evidently had survived the pogrom, bowed their knees to Baal, and literally become false prophets. In 22:15, Michea the Lord's true prophet, bitterly mocks them by repeating their words with great sarcasm. The end for Achab finally came and he was followed by his son Ozochias, in Israel, while Josaphat, son of Asa, became king of Juda. Josaphat was good, following the example of his father Asa, while Ozochias was bad "following the example of his own father and mother." (22:53 Knox)

Things have changed that little. The patterns set by parents, whether the ancient kings of Juda and Israel or parents of the twentieth century, mold the children. And the false gods, whether Baal, golden calves, forest shrines to forest deities, or the gods of money, fame, power, and pleasure—seduce the people.

·VII·

THE END
AND
CAPTIVITY

It was a warm summer day when we read the story of Elias'
ascension in the golden chariot, and three of the Newlands were
listening up in a tree. There are disadvantages if you are reading
to a flock of boys in a tree, but advantages if you are one of
them, for a lifetime of remembering Elias heard from a perch in
a sugar maple should give one a marvelous sense of the affair,
and families with trees that can be climbed and sat in ought to
try at least one scripture reading this way. It's lots of fun.

They finally came down because a mother robin protested.

"Scripture or no scripture," she said, "I have heard the word
of the Lord and am sitting on eggs and I'll thank you to get out!"
And no one blamed her.

Fourth Kings

It was not until the story of Elias in the fourth book of Kings
that we really began to understand about the prophets. At first,
like everyone else, we thought they existed to foretell the coming of
Christ and that seemed reason enough. We had no idea they had

anything to do with *us*. But miracles and predictions of the future were not the important work of the prophets; rather their function was to remind the people that the Lord had chosen them as His own, had given them a Law and a work to do with Him, and to point out that they had lost interest in it. The prophets warned the people that the consequence of infidelity was punishment; it had followed as the night the day in the time of Adam, Noe and Moses, and it would in their own times as well. Like witnesses in a courtroom, the prophets appeared throughout the history of God's people, especially during the reigns of the kings, to testify to the truth about man's relation to God—from the ninth century Elias, Eliseus and the bands of prophetic disciples; and from the eighth to the sixth century the "writing prophets," starting with Amos.

This role of witness was handed down by Christ to His followers and we see it carried on in the Acts of the Apostles where the apostles preached and taught in the same way. And we are meant to carry on the work in our own times, showing forth and speaking of the truths which govern God's relation to man and of Christ Who helps us to live them. It is this speaking of the Word of the Lord that gives *prophet* and *prophecy* their meaning, and by Confirmation, the sacrament which enables us to mature as Christians, we are able to be prophets, and even martyrs.

Now the idea that we are meant to be witnesses is not really news, although we may never have connected the prophets with it, but apparently a new approach to it is needed, for it is still not tremendously important to very many people. How to make it come alive? The focus we want can be found in sacred scripture with the help of the prophets—whose genius was not only to goad the kings of Israel but to goad all the rest of us as well. With Elias and Eliseus and the men whose words have become the prophetic books of the Bible, we can begin to explore the meaning of the role of prophecy in the history of salvation—and in our own lives today.

The Ascension of Elias

Elias and Eliseus had made their way to the Jordan, crossed it dry-shod like Josue, when suddenly, with the appearance of a flaming chariot, Elias went up into a whirlwind as Eliseus cried out in farewell, "Israel's chariot and charioteer!" (IV Kings 2:12

Knox) He was a man whose strength had been equal to an army because God's power acted in his words.

The inevitable question is, "Did he *really* go up in a whirlwind?"

Usually this comes from the older members of the family and not the little ones who never even think to question it. The answer is simply that these words of the inspired text have been accepted down the centuries quite literally, but if you wish to think of it as Eliseus' way of seeing it, you are quite free to do so. Tobias and his family saw an angel in the form of a man, and the Lord Himself once appeared to Abraham as three men, so it is not at all impossible. Elias was carried off in the teeth of a storm and even the searching parties sent out later found no trace of him.

Two questions remain. "I thought Our Lord was to go before us to heaven, in glory, and be there to welcome the saints of the Old Testament?" The story of Elias does not pretend to know where Elias went, whether to heaven, to a place of waiting, or where.

"What about his body?" And the answer can only be, "Who knows?" We do not. It is understood that when Our Lord said Elias had returned in John the Baptist, He meant John had the spirit of Elias (Matt 17:9-13). We will just have to wait for this answer until eternity.

On the Passover in Jewish households, the cup of Elijah (Elias) is always filled with wine and put in the center of the Seder table to remind the family of the possibility of his return. How graciously they plan to welcome him. Our Lord said John the Baptist has already come in the spirit of Elias and has announced the arrival of the Messiah.

The episode in IV Kings 2:23-25, where the boys were torn to pieces by bears for calling Eliseus "Baldy" (the prophets were probably tonsured), shocks children and wants a moment's discussing. Such disrespect to a man of God, a parent or any older person was a very serious offense and Eliseus would rightly condemn it. That the bears attacked the boys was not necessarily the fate called down on them by the prophet, but possibly the consequence of having taken foolish risks with their own safety in the wilds.

The tales of Eliseus continue in the third chapter with the rebellion of Moab. Subdued by Israel for years, this state observed the growing weakness of Israel's kings and struck out for self-government. The kings of Juda and Israel and the vassal king of Edom went to give battle but alas, a water shortage threatened and a call went out for Eliseus who, consulting the Lord, learned that He would send both water and victory. The optical illusion which won the day for Israel illustrates how God used natural phenomena to serve Him in a seemingly miraculous way. The Bible states that Israel left when the people witnessed the child sacrifice by the Moabite King. An ancient Moabite inscription explains that the Moabites, inspired by the desperate act of their king, raced out of their besieged city and in furious battle drove the Israelites away.

The Multiplication of Oil

The story of the woman whose sons were to be taken in bondage for her debts and how Eliseus managed the increase of oil is a reminder of the goodness of Christ, Who provides us with His own redeeming grace that we may ever more escape bondage for our sins.

Eliseus Restores a Life

The story of the woman of Sunam, whose son Eliseus raised from the dead, brings Our Lord very close again. Certainly the Israelites did not see this resemblance to Christ, but we cannot help recognizing it. When we see His likeness again and again in the figures of the prophets—saving, healing, providing—we see that the God of the Old Testament is the same as the God of the New. Even the story of the poisoned broth (4:38-41) speaks of Christ, Who makes bitterness sweet for those who love Him, and when we got to the multiplication of barley loaves (4:42-44), Christopher could no longer be silent.

"That's just like Our Lord's miracle. He had loaves left over too!" (Mark 6:43) See how the people of Christ's time had been prepared to recognize Him.

Naaman the Leper

Still the stories come. Next is Naaman, the Syrian, commander of the king's army, who had leprosy. It was a little Israelite slave, captured in a border raid, who told him of Eliseus, and with the king's introduction and gifts the soldier made his way to Samaria to find the prophet. Told to bathe seven times in the Jordan, Naaman was cured and became a worshiper of the One God— Who is the God of all men, not just the Israelites. Our Lord reminded the people of this the day He spoke in the synagogue and they rejected Him as an impostor. (Luke 4:27)

The epilogue to the story of Naaman shows us the sorry contrast between the humble new convert and the crafty Israelite servant, Giezi, who contrived to waylay Naaman and get at least some of the riches which Eliseus had refused to accept.

As we finished reading of his punishment—leprosy which made him white as snow—Stephen said, "I guess there were some bad Popes too, weren't there?"

And, sad to say, there were. We explained that not every man is tempted to make commerce of the Lord's favors, but for those who do the price comes high. For a while they may seem to prosper, but Psalm 72 reminds us that it is prospering in eternity that counts.

Eliseus Escapes the King of Syria

Next there is a neat little tale about retrieving an ax head, and then a delicious triumph over the king of Syria.

The king of Syria was forever casting eyes on Israel and attempting battle with her, but at each ambush he was anticipated, for the Lord through Eliseus told the king of Israel to beware. Finally this enemy ruler demanded to know how this could be, and when his advisors said Eliseus was probably the culprit, the king sent a company of warriors to Dothain to take him.

The servant of Eliseus saw the array of soldiers about the city the next morning and ran to his master in terror. "Do not be afraid," said the prophet, "we have more on our side than they on theirs." (6:16 Knox) And he prayed to the Lord that the servant's eyes would be opened. They were, and he saw a glorious sight. All about Eliseus on the mountainside there was a host with flaming horses and chariots.

We stopped a moment in our reading. "Do you remember the night St. Peter cut off the ear of the servant of the high priest? What did Our Lord say?" Ah yes, they remembered: He said His Father could, if He wished, summon legions of angels to defend Him. (Matt 26:53) Here in the story of Eliseus we catch a glimpse of the legions of angels.

Then Eliseus prayed that the Syrians would become confused. Going out, he told them they sought the prophet in the wrong city. Samaria was their goal. So off they went to Samaria and right into the hands of the king of Israel, who not only forebore to slay them but gave the whole affair its marvelously comic finale by feasting the soldiers and sending them back to their master. "And Israel was rid," says the scribe with a sigh, "for a while, of freebooters from Syria." (6:23 Knox)

Another tale at the expense of the Syrians follows, and once again two relatively unimportant details will need to be either omitted or explained. Samaria was so long besieged this time that men would pay eighty pieces of silver for an ass' head or five for a pint of droppings. In other words, even the crudest supplies were sky-high. In 6:26-30, there is mention of cannibalism which might well upset children, so it could be omitted, or the woman's complaint to the king be reworded to speak merely of hunger. This is not the only mention of cannibalism in the Old Testament.

The king's reply indicates that this time he did not thank Eliseus for his advice. This time Eliseus would be the scapegoat. However, chapter 7 finishes the story with the undoing of the Syrians, the vindication of Eliseus and the grim and grisly end to a courtier who loftily doubted Eliseus when he prophesied victory.

In chapter 8 we meet again the mother of the boy whom Eliseus raised from the dead, and her reappearance in the story bears witness to the wonders wrought by the prophet.

The Fulfillment of a Prophecy

Now we come to the fulfillment of the prophecy concerning the end of Benadad, king of Syria, and the anointing of Hazael as the future king and scourge of Israel. Eliseus, inheriting the mantle of Elias, inherited his work also, and to him fell the task of anointing Hazael. Eliseus' answer to the king that he would recover his health seems to mean that his concurrent ill health would not be the cause of his death; nor was it. On learning that he was to reign as king of Syria, Hazael smothered Benadad with a wet cloth and succeeded him to the throne. We must watch Hazael closely from now on, for we will see the increase of Syrian attacks with his appearance on the scene, and together with it the stirring of rebellion among peoples long subject to Israel and Juda.

Little by little the land will be chewed away from the Israelites right under their feet.

Two Kings Named Joram

Our very next reading tells us how, with two kings named Joram, one ruling in Juda and one in Israel (the former married into the latter's family), the breaking away proceeded. The Edomites again renounced their allegiance to Juda and although in the end they were driven back, Edom was never more subject to Juda. Nor was Joram of Juda any improvement over the kings who had gone before him. The only reason the Lord did not destroy him was that He had promised to keep the lamp of David's line unquenched forever.

Ochozias succeeded Joram in Juda and his visit to his relatives in the court at Israel is the occasion of the fulfillment of a prediction against the house of the late king Achab. (III Kings 21:21)

Jehu Is Anointed King

Sending one of his disciples to Ramoth-Galaad, Eliseus bade him seek out Jehu from among the officers of the army and anoint him, revealing to him the prophecy of the Lord. He was to be king over the Lord's people in Israel and to avenge the deaths of the prophets slain by Achab's wicked wife Jezabel. All Achab's line was to be wiped out, including Jezabel, who still survived her husband.

Now Jehu did the Lord's will but, as we have seen in the story of the Judges, to give a man charge did not mean that God took over his personality or transformed him into a saint. Jehu was a violent, bloodthirsty man and few could have relished more the work of vengeance, but the truth is that he went much too far. To a point, he is praised for his obedience; yet the Lord did not reward him as He might, for in spite of his bloody courage he lacked the zeal to destroy the hill shrines and the golden calves set up before the Lord. The text says that "Jehu was too careless to follow the law of Israel's God with his whole heart." (IV Kings 10:31 Knox)

But again we are ahead of ourselves. Jehu went out to his fellow officers, advised them of his status, and they immediately acknowledged him as king. "Let no man leave here," he said, "lest the court be alerted to what has happened," (9:16 Knox) and he mounted his chariot and set out for Jezrahel where king Joram of Israel lay sick with king Ochozias visiting him, and where Jezabel, Joram's mother, resided in her palace. Unsuspecting, Joram and Ochozias rode out to greet Jehu and the pogrom began. Jehu first slew Joram with an arrow and bade the soldiers deposit his body on the vineyard of Naboth, whom Jezabel had murdered in order that her husband could possess his land. Next, Ochozias was wounded and was pursued as far as Mageddo where he also died. The finale to the story of Jezabel begins with her concern for her make-up (she blackened her eyebrows and braided her hair) and ends when she is thrown into the street and trampled on by horses. Nothing remained of this vicious queen except her skull, her feet and the tips of her fingers. As the prophet had foretold, her body became the food of dogs.

However, in Samaria, Achab still had seventy male descendents. Jehu sent a letter to the chiefs there bidding them choose one heir to set upon the throne, then array themselves around him and prepare for battle. But, said the chiefs of Samaria, who were they to oppose a man who had killed the kings of both Israel and Juda? Better that they give him allegiance and do his bidding. Then chop off the heads of the seventy princes, bade Jehu, and send them in a basket in twenty-four hours. And it was done.

Making his way to Samaria, Jehu fell in with some of the members of Ochozias' line and had them slain also, forty-two in all, whose throats were cut beside the pool by a shepherd's lodging. And when he arrived in Samaria, he supervised the mopping-up. All Achab's household that was left in Samaria was destroyed to a man.

Jehu Destroys the Temple of Baal

Even bloodier things lay ahead. Jehu now announced a general assembly of all who honored Baal. All must come to the temple of Baal for ceremonies. Jehu and his officials robed themselves as priests, and guards were alerted to carefully eliminate any of the Lord's servants whom curiosity or carelessness had lured into the crowd. The temple was packed; not another man could wedge in. When the sacrifices were over, Jehu's men made their exit and soldiers entered and put to death all who were inside, took the statue of Baal and destroyed it, and leveled the temple to the ground. Its site became a public privy.

Even so, Jehu did not abolish the hill shrines. When we read over and over that the kings of Israel and Juda taught Israel to sin, it is this infidelity of heart, this perpetuation of hill shrines, that the scribes have in mind. For other crimes the kings were also to blame—moral evils, injustices, and more—but the principal sin was their betrayal of the covenant God had made with them: "If you hearken to my voice and keep my covenant, you shall be my special possession, dearer to me than all other people, though all the earth is mine." (Exodus 19:5) On this hung the entire relation of God to His people. The story of Jehu ends with foreboding: "It was in his days that the Lord began to grow aweary of Israel; and Hazael struck at all their frontiers." (IV Kings 10:32)

Joas, King of Juda

We turn once more to events in Juda. On the death of Ochozias, his mother schemed to murder oll the princes of the royal house so that she could reign as queen. But one small boy, Joas, was rescued by his aunt and hidden away to await the day of vindication. In Joas' seventh year, Joiada, the high priest, gave orders that the boy be brought forth, anointed in the temple and set on the throne as the rightful king of Juda. And Athalia, the wicked queen, was murdered. Chapter 11 tells the story of Joas who, as long as the high priest was his advisor, obeyed the Lord's will. To his credit, he saw to the badly needed repairs in the temple and announced that all sacrificial offerings would henceforth be used for this purpose until the temple was restored to its proper dignity, but he had not the courage to destroy the hill shrines. And Hazael, tool of the Lord, continued to attack the Lord's people. Closer and closer to the city he came until even Joas paid him tribute out of the temple treasure to stay the sacking of Jerusalem.

Joachas, King of Israel

Chapter 13 brings us to Joachas, son of Jehu, and his desperation in the path of Hazael. Nothing was left of the army of Israel but fifty horsemen, ten chariots and ten thousand foot soldiers, where there had been two thousand chariots before. The king of

Syria had swept away his opposition "like chaff on the threshing floor." (13:8) When Joachas died he was succeeded by his son, another Joas.

The Death of Eliseus

Now we have two kings named Joas, one in Israel and one in Juda, and the story of the king of Israel leads us finally to the death of Eliseus. Desperate because Eliseus was about to die and because Israel was at bay before Syria, Joas went to visit the prophet and addressed him in the same words used of Elias: "Israel's chariot and charioteer!" Eliseus bade him fetch a bow and shoot one of his arrows out the window toward the east. Providence would help him defeat the Syrians, promised Eliseus, and bade him continue to shoot. But Joas halted after shooting only three arrows, and Eliseus cried out in anger. He had betrayed the gift of the Lord and three victories, no more, would he win against Hazael of Syria.

It was during a year of war and bloodshed that Eliseus died, and not long after his burial another funeral procession made its way through the neighborhood of his grave. Suddenly, a band of guerillas threatened to attack the mourners, who threw the corpse into the first grave at hand (perhaps a cave in the hillside) and ran away. No sooner had the corpse of the dead man touched the bones in the grave than he came to life and rose to his feet. It had been the grave of Eliseus.

How beautifully the story of Eliseus brings us face to face with Christ. The prophets of Israel were channels of grace to God's people, instruments of the voice of God. Their mission was to lead the people back to their life with God. Like a sign of the One Who was to give men divine Life, the very bones of the prophet restored the dead man.

Jeroboam II of Israel

With chapter 14, new kings and complications come thick and fast. Amasias, son of king Joas of Juda, came to the throne in Jerusalem and only half-heartedly obeyed the Lord's will.

"He too," I started to read, and was interrupted by a chorus: "left the hill shrines standing!" The family was alert to the great sin of the kings.

One detail in the story of Amasias is a puzzle. He put his father's murderers to death but not their children, in obedience to the law.

"But I thought whole families were destroyed for the guilt of the father. In Moses' time they were. How come?"

In early times, the principle of solidarity dictated that the guilt or merit of one member of the family was shared by the others. However, "a world which consisted merely of family groups . . . passed . . . and in its place there arose a society divided into king and subjects, employers and workmen, rich and poor . . . The feeling of solidarity grew weaker and the individual person began to emerge from the family group . . . A member of a clan had a right of appeal from the judgment of his clan to the king himself." [1]

Amasias challenged Joas of Israel to a trial of strength and was roundly beaten. Murdered finally, he was succeeded by his son Azarias who, just to make it difficult, is called Ozias in the books of Paralipomena, Amos, Osee, Zacharias and Isaia. The latter name was the popular version, the former was used in the Annals of the Kings.

It was during the fifteenth year of Amasias in Juda that Jeroboam II came to reign in Israel, and although there is hardly a hint of it in the short account of his life, it was a long and prosperous reign. This bore out the prophecy of Jona (14:25), a mysterious person about whom nothing is known. Most important of all, it was during the reign of Jeroboam II that the prophets Amos and Osee cried out their warnings from the Lord. Although their names are not mentioned in the account of this period (IV Kings), their speeches were later written down and became the books of Amos and Osee.

The Prophet Amos

Since Amos entered the story of Israel at this point, we now turn to the book of Amos. These books of the prophets can be used for spiritual reading at any time, but first of all they should be

[1] Roland De Vaux, *Ancient Israel* (New York: McGraw-Hill, 1961), p. 23.

placed in their historical context, where they have both spiritual and historical meaning.

How much of the book to read depends entirely upon the audience. Adults will enjoy reading and savoring the entire message of the prophets. Children, however, are easily tired by the repetition of ideas (though rich in their variations) and the lack of action. We have found it wisest to choose from these writings key passages which identify the prophet, his time, the situation in which he lived; and give his message, trusting that when they grow up the children will want to go back and read more by themselves. Our own choices were made to suit our combination of children; other families might prefer to choose other passages.

(We read Amos from a pamphlet instead of our family Bible, so we could mark the selected passages with a pencil. The text of Amos, Osee and Michea are presented in the one pamphlet, together with a commentary, in an extremely readable format.)[2]

We chose the following passages from the book of Amos:

Amos 1:1 Who is Amos?
      7:1-17 Three visions and Amasia's protest
      2:6-16 Israel's crimes
      3:1-2 The Lord's condemnation
      3:14-15 An end to the hill shrines
      4:1-5 "You cows of Basan"
      4:6-13 "You returned to me not"
      5:21-27 Hypocritical sacrifices
      9:8b-15 Restoration

The book of Amos is arranged by speeches rather than events, so after reading 1:1, which tells us the who, when and where of Amos, we turn to 7:1-17 to read three of four visions by which God spelled out the fate of Israel. When this was heard abroad, the high priest Amasia bade Amos begone to Juda where he belonged; there let him earn his keep by prophesying. And Amos' reply that he is not a prophet means that he does not belong to that class of professional prophets who do earn their keep this way. He has heard the word of the Lord while tending his sheep. (Am 7:14-15)

In 2:6-16 and 3:1-2, we read Amos' stirring condemnation of Israel. Her injustices are listed, the favors of the past are recalled,

[2] Marcian Strange, O.S.B., *The Books of Amos, Osee and Michea* (New York: Paulist Press), price 50¢.

the doom ahead is described. The Lord cries out like a wounded lover. "You alone have I favored, more than all the families of the earth!"

We skip to 3:14-15, where the Lord predicts an end to the hill shrines and the sumptuous apartments of the rich. In 4:1-5, Amos speaks of the ladies of Samaria as "you cows of Basan," in the plain speech of a countryman. In 4:6-13, the Lord tells through Amos how He tried to bring the people to heel with smitings and misfortune, "yet you returned to me not." In 5:21-27, the Lord rages at their hypocritical sacrifices, their songs to honor Him, the music of their harps. If they would offer Him something, let it be justice and goodness in an unfailing stream.

Here Stephen blurted out, quite vehemently, "They deserved it—every bit! He brought them out of slavery in Egypt and they forgot all about Him!"

Yes—but we see ourselves in this, too. He has brought us out of our own Egypt by way of Baptism. He has lifted us out of sin with the sacrament of Penance, yet we easily forget Him too.

In 9:8b-15, the Lord suddenly gentles his voice and speaks softly.

"But I will not destroy the house of Jacob completely." And we read that Israel will be restored and the fallen house of David will be raised up. These verses have both an historical and a messianic meaning and the children will guess at what the Lord is hinting.

"I know, Jesus."

Yes, Jesus. He will be the great blessing that will go on forever. The prophet speaks of both the restoration after exile for the Jews, and—although he did not understand it—that restoration by redemption of divine life to the children of men. Christ is the means of our restoration, our everlasting blessing.

Amos speaks to us as well as to the Israelites, of infidelity and injustice and the need to worship with a heart that is true. We read it in the context of the history of Israel, and we meditate on the message it has for us today.

The Prophet Osee

A contemporary of Amos was the prophet Osee, who heard the word of the Lord in the days of Ozias, Joatham, Achaz, Ezechias, kings of Juda, and Jeroboam II, king of Israel. (Osee 1:1)

Osee's message is much the same as Amos' but it is not as suitable for reading with young children because of the device he has used to represent Israel's infidelities. Part autobiography, part symbolism, this story weaves together Osee's experience with an adulterous wife whom he nevertheless loves and wants, and God's experience with unfaithful Israel. Here we begin to hear Israel spoken of as a harlot, prostitute, adulteress. The relation between God and His people has been one of love, a wedding of the people to God. Yahweh is Israel's spouse; thus the decrial of the spouse's infidelity in the terms of human love.

Osee writes that in time his wife sickened of her lovers and was welcomed back to her husband again. This is to be the future of Israel too. However, these images of infidelity in love and marriage, while stirring to grown-ups, are inappropriate for children, and it seems wiser to explain that Osee says what Amos says, generally speaking, and when they grow up they will enjoy reading him by themselves.

A few exceptions prove the rule. In Osee 8:7, we find something familiar from long use, yet rarely identified with its source. "When they sow the wind, they shall reap the whirlwind." And Osee 11:1 gives us a beautiful image of God as Israel's Father, and is used by St. Matthew in his Gospel to show that Christ is the new and perfect Israel. "When Israel was a child I loved him, out of Egypt I called my son." (Matt 2:15)

Osee's use of *Ephraim* for Israel needs explaining. One of the sons of Joseph, Ephraim was adopted by Jacob on his deathbed and therefore was called one of the twelve tribes. Having settled in the north, Ephraim is often used as a synonym for Israel. Osee is also making a pun with the word for it sounds like the Hebrew word for *fruit*.

Back in the fifteenth chapter of IV Kings we find the same old sins. With the death of Amasias in Juda, his son Azarias (Ozias) came to the throne and, like his predecessors, left the hill shrines standing. He ended his days a leper, with his son Joatham taking charge of official business. On his death Joatham became king of Juda and he in turn was succeeded by his son Achaz. Achaz was followed by Ezechias and it was during the reign of these three that the prophet Michea cried out in the name of the Lord to tell both Samaria and Jerusalem they were doomed.

The Prophet Michea

Michea came from Moreseth, a small town near Jerusalem, and we know even less about him than about his contemporaries. His speeches are not arranged chronologically or even with continuity, so it is necessary to hop around a bit.

We chose the following passages from the book of Michea:

The Trial
1:1-7   The crime of Israel
3:1-2; 9-12   Accusations
6:1-5   The Lord presents His case
7:1-4   Condemnation
7:8-9   The hope of the accused

Restoration
4:1-7   Promise of restoration
5:1   The One to come
7:18-20   The faithfulness of God

Chapters 1, 3, 6 and part of 7 are written in the style of an accusation at court. Israel is on trial and God is the witness against her, condemning her in chapter 7. Michea's threat in 3:12 about the destruction of Jerusalem is an example of a prophetic statement which found its mark. Because of it, the capture of Jerusalem in later years was temporarily averted. Like a parent, God first warned His children of punishment should they fail to reform, and if they did reform He held His hand. It is important to point this out, for otherwise the prophets seem to have no function but to hurl thunderbolts.

In 6:3, we find a reproach familiar to us from the Good Friday liturgy. "O my people, what have I done to you, or how have I wearied you? Answer me!"

Throughout chapter 4 we find the promise that one day Israel will be restored. In Michea 4:3, we come to an old friend: "They shall beat their swords into plowshares, and their spears into pruning hooks: one nation shall not raise the sword against another, nor shall they train for war again." Please God.

Chapter 5:1-4 probes even further. We meet the veiled figure of the Messias and, although the prophet did not know this, the Mother of God. (5:2) Every Epiphany the little children in our family have enacted the visit of the Magi at our celebration at home, and their father—disguised as Herod—has annually called on the "scribes" to tell the whereabouts of the newborn king. It is the prophet Michea who identifies His birthplace. "But you, Bethlehem-Ephratha, too small to be among the clans of Juda, from you shall come forth for me one who is to be ruler of Israel." (Mic 5:1)

Michea ends on a note of hope and praise. Who is like this God, removing guilt, pardoning sin, delighting in clemency? (7:18) Long centuries afterward the maiden "who is to give birth" (5:2) would stand at the threshold of her cousin's house and be caught up in the tenderness and power of God's love, the everlastingness of His Word. Out of the reservoir of His words to the prophets of old, so familiar to her, she chose to make her own canticle. From Michea she drew this: "You will show faithfulness to Jacob, and grace to Abraham, as you have sworn to our fathers from the days of old." (Mic 7:20; Luke 1:54-55)

More Bad Kings

At this time a period of great violence set in, perhaps inspired by the injustices about which we have read in Amos and Osee. Jeroboam's son Zacharias reigned for six months and was murdered by Sellum; Sellum reigned for one month and was killed by Menahem; during the ten-year reign of Menahem, Assyria, led by Phul (the Babylonian name given to Theglath-Phalasar) invaded and exacted tribute; he was succeeded by his son Phaceia, who was murdered by Phacee, who was slain and followed by Osee (not the prophet). During the reign of Phacee, Theglath-Phalasar cut a broad swathe into Israel, captured many towns and carried off prisoners. The final doom crept nearer.

Achaz, in Juda, added abomination to abomination by not only keeping the hill shrines but by offering his son in sacrifice by fire after the manner of the Chanaanites, a practice thunderously condemned by God. He was besieged in Jerusalem by the king of Syria and Phacee, king of Israel, and turning to Assyria for help was rescued by Theglath-Phalasar, forming an alliance with him which served momentarily but could hardly have been called healthy. In return for his favors, Theglath-Phalasar exacted various tributes, among them an altar erected in the temple of the Lord to his god Assur. The shade of David must have groaned to see the bronze altar of the temple replaced by this infamous piece of furniture.

Israel Falls

Chapter 17 brings us to the great capture—Israel is taken. In a rage against Osee, who sought help from Egypt, Salamanasar, now king of Assyria, overran the country, besieged Samaria for three years, and at last the city fell. Most of the Israelites were sent off to exile.

Chapter 17:13-23 of IV Kings portrays the infidelity of the men of Israel, "until at last the Lord banished them from his presence, as all the prophets had foretold in his name, and they were carried off from their own country into Assyria . . ." (17:23 Knox)

In an ironic epilogue (17:24-41), the foreign populations who moved into Samaria to take the Israelites' place were forced to learn the worship of the Lord in order, they thought, to placate Him and terminate the plague of lions He sent to show His displeasure. They even found Israelite priests to officiate for them, but it was a hollow and meaningless worship making Yahweh companion to every imported god among them. "This is not to fear the Lord . . . to keep observance and decree, law and command, as the sons of Jacob should." (IV Kings 17:34 Knox)

Thus came the end of the northern kingdom of Israel.

Ezechias, King of Juda

The day after Stephen's twelfth birthday, we were sitting under the big tree in the front yard again continuing our story, and Stephen was admiring his new hatchet. All the boys in this family, on reaching twelve, are allowed to have hatchets in order to join their big brothers on the forest clearance project. Suddenly his face brightened.

"I know," and he brandished the hatchet, "let's cut down the hill shrines!"

I am sorry to say I shrieked. "No you don't! That's a sugar maple tree and it's two hundred years old. Don't you touch it with that hatchet. Just sit still and you'll hear about someone who did cut down the hill shrines."

Hastily we got on with the story.

It is in the story of Ezechias that we finally meet the prophet Isaia. Actually, Isaia had been active in the reigns of Joatham and Achaz (although he is not mentioned with them), but since Osee and Michea were his contemporaries, they seemed to call for acquaintance first. And we found that it worked out nicely to read the story of Ezechias, meet Isaia there, then turn to the book of Isaia and read selected passages from it before continuing with the last of the kings.

Ezechias was the son of Achaz of Juda, and it was he, at last, who cut down the hill shrines.

"At *last*," commented the audience.

Ezechias effected many other reforms as well, and is praised generously for his works. He tried unsuccessfully to defy the king of Assyria, refused to pay tribute, and even set forth on a military venture of his own which came to nothing in the end. Sennacherib, king of Syria, pushed right to the gates of Jerusalem to avenge this audacity and Ezechias, on the advice of Isaia, saw the wisdom of an apology and capitulation to things as they had been. As ransom for the city, he paid all the gold and silver in the temple; even its great golden doors were carted off to Assyria.

This was the rescue of Jerusalem from the destruction previously threatened by Michea (3:12). Long after, when the prophet Jeremia was threatened for warning of ill-fate for the city, he recalled that Ezechias had been warned likewise and his efforts to restore the people to the true worship of Yahweh had lifted God's sentence from the city. (Jer 26:18-19)

But Sennacherib's acquisitiveness was not satisfied. Now he sent envoys to tell the king and the people that although he would not ruin the city, they should surrender to him peaceably and he would transport them to a land of wheat and corn and oil, olives and honey. But the Jerusalemites were unmoved. Ezechias, in despair, consulted Isaia, who reassured him that all would end well, and it did. The king of Assyria was deployed and left, with a parting blasphemy for the Lord, promising to return and subdue the city.

Whereas the Lord had often used pagan kings to chastise His people, this king He would not use because his blasphemies had been too terrible. The Lord's dismissal of the man in the language of Isaia is a mixture of wrath and humor. ". . . and now a ring for thy nose, a twitch of the bridle in thy mouth, and back thou goest by the way thou didst come." (IV Kings 19:28 Knox) So much for Sennacherib. The Lord is Master even of the Assyrians. In the end, He sent an angel to the Assyrian camp and slew 185,-000 warriors (a preposterous number, really), probably by the plague.

The Cure of Ezechias

Next Ezechias fell sick and Isaia came to warn him that his end was near. But Ezechias prayed to the Lord for a longer life and hardly was his prayer uttered than it was granted, together with the promise that in his lifetime he would not see Jerusalem captured. Isaia applied a poultice of figs to the king's ulcer (like a poultice of flaxseed, I suppose), and he recovered. That the recovery was permanent was confirmed by the miracle of the sundial, a stairway on which the shadow cast by the sun was measured by the steps.

The following episode is puzzling unless we understand that chapter 20 should precede the clash with Sennacherib. The Semitic writers, as we have seen, had little concern for chronology and arranged their history to suit their own ideas of what was important. Often, because they were trying to make a specific point, they would take an event out of context and insert it elsewhere. However, we found it no problem to follow the text as it stands and the whole story of Ezechias winds up quite harmoniously as the writers have arranged it.

An envoy from the king of Babylon came with gifts for Ezechias because he was ill. Commentators smile at this; there was more to the visit than bringing goodies to the king. Knowing that this happened before Sennacherib, and right after the death of Sargon, explains everything. The small nations under the dominance of Assyria would have looked to the possibility of a coalition, and this would explain the Babylonian's visit to Juda. Not only that, but it would also explain (and the children raised this question) how Ezechias had any treasures to show. After all, at the end of Sennacherib's siege of Jerusalem, the city was stripped of its treasures, all of them emptied into the sack of the enemy.

At any rate, for Ezechias to show the Babylonian envoy the royal treasure so angered Isaia that, with a roar, he predicted the downfall of Juda to this very nation. Growing from a minor to a major power, Babylon would one day overrun Juda, beat the walls of Jerusalem to the ground and carry her people into slavery. Ezechias was the last of the kings under whom Isaia spoke the word of the Lord. Here seems the place to read from the book of Isaia.[3]

The Prophet Isaia (First)

Unlike Amos the shepherd, Osee the heartsick, Michea the small town dweller, Isaia was a Jerusalemite and a man of parts, well-educated and evidently well-acquainted at court. He had a wife and at least two sons, and he had a great gift not only for prophecy but for words. His language rings with images that are not only Hebrew but typically his own, and his fixed idea was the Messias, the promised One to come from the line of David for whom he was ever longing.

[3] John E. Huesman, S.J., *The Book of Isaia, Part 1 and Part 2 with Commentary* (New York: Paulist Press), price 50¢.

It was not our intention to read the entire first part of Isaia, 1-39, called *first* Isaia.[4] The long prophecies of the destruction of Jerusalem, the end of Juda, the promised Messias, are thrilling for adults but a bit too heavy for children, and we did not want to spoil their enjoyment of Isaia by burdening them with too much. We found the following to be a satisfying choice of texts.

Isaia   6:1-10   Isaia's vision of the Lord and prophetic call
         1:11-20; 3:13-26   The Lord's condemnation of Israel and Juda
         5:1-7   The parable of the vineyard
         5:20-30   Prophecy of destruction
         10:16-22; 11:1-5   Prophecy of the Messias (the remnant to return, the root of Jesse)

Isaia's Call and the Burning Coal

Once again we find the beginning of the book does not give us the opening scene, and we must turn to 6:1-10 to read of Isaia's call. During the reign of Ozias, Isaia saw a vision of the Lord upon His throne surrounded by seraphim singing aloud, "Holy, Holy, Holy." He cried out in alarm that he was unclean and unworthy to see the Lord, and a seraph touched his lips with a burning coal, cleansing them. From this is taken our beautiful prayer before the Gospel, "Cleanse my heart and my lips, almighty God, who cleansed the lips of the prophet Isaia with a burning coal . . ."

The Lord wished to send someone to warn the people against their evil ways and, unlike more reticent prophets, Isaia said, "Here I am; send me." (6:8) Verse 10, "You are to make the heart of this people sluggish . . ." is strange unless we remember that this is a manner of speaking; the people were already sluggish of heart, their ears dull, their eyes closed. The words of Isaia would not only make them more so but would also force them to a final decision for or against God.

The Lord's condemnation of Juda in 1:11 reminds us of the unacceptable sacrifice of Cain, while 1:12-17 has the ring of Our Lord's anger in the temple. 1:18 is the beautiful, "Though your sins be as scarlet, they may become as white as snow."

---

[4] Chapters 40-55, called *second* Isaia, are thought to be written by another author, a member of the Isaian school, and treat of other times.

The Parable of the Vineyard

The parable of the vineyard is one of the most tender of all the love songs of God. Heartbroken, the Lord asks why His vineyard has brought forth only wild grapes? The description of Jerusalem with her broken walls, brambles, briars and drought is haunting and sad, a prophecy in itself. Stephen listened thoughtfully.

"I wonder if it will really happen?"

It did—and it still happens, when we turn away from Him and do not bring forth the fruits of the Spirit.

Prophecy of Destruction

In 5:20-30, we read warnings to the evil and the unjust, the intemperate and the proud; those who call virtue foolishness and turn vice into virtue. We have seen a tiny grass fire catch and race across the dry stubble in a field, just as the prophet describes, and in a matter of moments it becomes impossible to control. So fearful is the rampage of evil in men, once they surrender their vigilance.

The language of 5:26-30 is electrifying. The Lord will give a signal to the nation that is to punish His people. He will whistle to it from the ends of the earth and it will come racing, and roaring, and inundate Juda "with a roaring like that of the sea." (5:30)

The Messias—The Remnant and the Root of Jesse

And in 10:16-22, we read that after the holocaust, a remnant will remain. Perhaps in our house we love this passage because its images are those of the forest, so familiar to us. "And the remnant of the trees in his forest will be so few, like poles set up for signals, that any boy can record them." (10:19) This is a picture of a forest that has been burned.

In 11:1-5, we see what will come from the remnant. "But a shoot shall sprout from the stump of Jesse, and from his roots a bud shall blossom." (11:1) We have seen this too, in our own woods on our own land. A family ought to seek out such a stump just to see how a shoot can spring from it and grow into another tree. One of the O antiphons of the Divine Office for the last days of Advent (December 19) is "O root of Jesse." For years, cutting colored paper symbols of these antiphons has been part of

Advent preparations, but never before has the root of Jesse symbol meant as much to us as since we have read of Jesse and his son David, of the long line of kings, good and bad, that sprang from them, of the longing of Isaia as he stood among his doomed people in his doomed land, looking off into the mist of the future and longing for the promised One. "O Root of Jesse, You stand for an ensign of mankind; before You kings shall keep silence, and to You all nations shall have recourse. Come, save us and do not delay."

In 11:2, we read that the promised One will be filled with the Gifts of the Holy Spirit. This fits beautifully into the lesson on these Gifts which is part of the preparation for Confirmation, where they are explained as virtues belonging first of all to God and made available to us with this great sacrament.

Isaia speaks like a man who is in love. He disappears from our story with the end of the reign of Ezechias.

Manasses Son of Ezechias

With the ascent of Manasses to the throne, the good done by Ezechias was more than undone. Pagan shrines were restored in forest and on hilltop, and even in the temple itself. Philip groaned.

"Not again! Now they'll *never* get rid of them."

There were worse things. Manasses offered human sacrifice and slaughtered so many in Jerusalem that the city brimmed with blood. In II Paralipomenon 33:12, we are told he repented, but the damage was done. Now the Lord proclaimed once and for all that Jerusalem would fall; level with Samaria it would lie, rubbed out as writing is rubbed from a wax tablet.

The writers of the inspired text accord Manasses one small distinction not included in their summaries of the other kings of Juda. They conclude the story of this king by saying in their customary way that all else Manasses did, his history, and—they add unexpectedly—"the record of his crimes," is to be found in the Annals of the kings of Juda. And the days of Juda's end drew nigh.

The Prophet Sophonia

The final chapters of the fourth book of Kings bring us to the end of Juda, the beginning of exile, and the last of the pre-exilic prophets. Josias, the last of the good kings of Juda, came to the throne at the death of his father Amon. In 22:1, we read that he reigned from the age of eight, and it was during his minority that the prophet Sophonia spoke out, warning Juda of the punishment of the Lord but promising, like Isaia, that in the end a remnant would be saved. Sophonia is called a minor prophet like Osee, Amos and Michea, not because he is unimportant but because his book is short.[5]

We read only four short passages from Sophonia.

Soph 1:1-7a The day of the Lord: a day of doom
        1:14-18 The day of the Lord: a day of wrath
        2:13b-15 The desolation of Ninive
        3:12-18 Promise of restoration

The sweeping description in 1:2-6 of how God will wipe away all mankind together with the birds of the sky, the beasts of the field, the fishes of the sea, is a literary device to give emphasis and not meant to be taken exactly. It reminds us of the great Theophany of Exodus 19:16-19, and now that we are better acquainted with Hebrew writing we see that this stirring up of all the elements was a kind of journalistic style to announce the coming of the Lord. This was how they set the scene. No wonder people have had such a hard time with scripture! The Orientals are so uninhibited with their imagery, and we are so restrained.

The "day of the Lord" for Juda would be the time of her correction and punishment and not, as they anticipated, a day of vindication for themselves and ruin for their enemies. Sophonia 1:14-18 describes it as a day of wrath and distress in a passage

---

[5] Edward J. Crowley, C.SS.R., *The Books of Lamentations, Baruch, Sophonia, Nahum and Habacuc, with a Commentary* (New York: Paulist Press), price 50¢.

which has given inspiration to the *Dies Irae*. But Ninive, capital
of Assyria and monument of corruption, would also feel His wrath
even though she had been used many times to chastise the people
of God. Sophonia 2:13b-15 describes the desolation of Ninive,
struck to the ground forever, a lair for wild beasts, a haunt for
screech owls and ravens.

In Sophonia 3:12-13, we find the beginnings of a new idea.
Never were the poor of Israel suggested to be anything but im-
provident or unfortunate, the miserable people of the land. Now
the Lord's prophet speaks of the remnant that will remain as a
"people humble and lowly." In the New Testament, Our Lord will
describe with the Beatitudes the virtues of men who are like Himself, meek and humble of heart, and like Mary, the lowly handmaid of the Lord.

The Prophet Jeremia under Josias

Jeremia was called to be the Lord's prophet in the thirteenth
year of the reign of Josias so we must put him in place also.[6] He
is one of the mightiest of the prophets and his book is very long.
We chose the following passages from Jeremia to accompany the
reign of Josias. (IV Kings 22)

> *Jer* 1:1-10   Jeremia's call
> 1:12-16   Juda will be conquered
> 2:1-3   "You loved me as a bride"
> 2:7-13   The Lord is forsaken by His bride
> 2:30-32   "In vain have I struck your children"
> 3:11-18   The conditions of return
> 4:22; 27-31   The people do not listen

Jeremia was born of a priestly family in the town of Anathoth
just outside of Jerusalem, and unlike Isaia he was a most reluctant
prophet. He lived during the reigns of Josias, Joachas, Joakim,
Joachin and Sedecias. He was viciously persecuted for his prophe-

---

[6] Neal M. Flanagan, O.S.M., *The Book of Jeremia, Parts 1 and 2 with Commentary* (New York: Paulist Press), price 50¢.

cies, plotted against, imprisoned, and finally ended his days in Egypt.

In calling Jeremia (1:1-10), the Lord set forth clearly the role of the prophets. "See, I place my words in your mouth!" (1:9) Then He sent Jeremia a vision in which he saw Juda's conqueror waiting in the north like a boiling cauldron, ready to boil over upon all the people of the land. Juda had disobeyed the Lord and He was going to punish her. (1:13-16)

But it would cost the Lord to punish His people. In 2:1-3, we read of the devotion of Israel [7] in her youth when "you loved me as a bride, following me in the desert." But in 2:7-9, we read "when I brought you into the garden land to eat its goodly fruits, you entered and defiled my land," and the whole of her defection is summed up in words familiar to us in terms of divine grace: "My people . . . have forsaken me, the source of living waters." (2:13) How clearly we can see ourselves in these reproaches to the people.

God had already tried punishing Israel [8] to bring her back to the right path, but it did no good. In 2:30-32 we read, "In vain I struck your children; the correction they did not take." And Juda is even more guilty, for Israel [9] was punished first to give example, but still Juda did not profit. Yet, He will forgive. The conditions of return to God's grace are the same for every man, the price is repentance, "know your guilt," and return—"for I am your master." (3:11-16) No longer, in the time to come, will the Ark of the Covenant be the holiest of their possessions, but Jerusalem herself—now the very Church of Christ—will be the Lord's throne.

His people did not heed God's warnings, so His anger rumbled again: invasion from the north would be the consequence. But even as the prophet shouted his warnings, Juda continued to bedeck herself in purple and gold, shade her eyes with cosmetics and beautify herself in vain. In the end she would fall "exhausted before the slayer." (4:22; 4:27-31)

[7] Here is meant all the people of God, "you clans of the house of Jacob."
[8] Here is meant the northern kingdom of Israel.
[9] *Ibid.*

The Prophet Nahum

It was about this period that the prophet Nahum spoke out, so for a moment we glance at him, not reading his book aloud but putting him in the company of the others. Nahum's prophecy[10] is a savage and triumphant prediction of the fall of Ninive which would finally take place in 612 B.C., a few years before the death of Josias. Nahum proclaims that God's enemies will not triumph forever; that persecutors are eventually cut down. The persecuted people all over the world need a book like this.

Ninive, the capital of Assyria, is flailed as a symbol of all that Juda has hated—idolatry, licentiousness, brutality, foreign domination. It was to this city that the prophet in the story of Jona was sent; no wonder he was hesitant! When Our Lord told the Pharisees that the Ninivites would rise up and condemn them on Judgment Day, He gave a fearful measure for their sin against the Holy Spirit. (Matt 12:41) IV Kings does not mention the fall of Ninive but we know it has taken place when Nabuchodonosor, king of Babylon and conqueror of Assyria, makes his appearance in our story. (IV Kings 24:1)

Josias and the Book of the Law

Now back to the story of Josias told in chapter 22. It was when he was twenty-six years old and during a renovation of the temple that a book of the Law was found—possibly a large part of Deuteronomy. Josias was horrified to discover the extent of the people's disobedience. Sending a delegation of priests to the prophetess Holda, he learned that the Lord intended to punish the people severely for this, but not until his own days were over, for he had consulted the Lord in tears, sincerely weeping for the sins of his people. Chapter 23 tells of the reforms of Josias throughout the land of Juda and even up into Israel, in order to destroy the shrines set up there by Jeroboam I.

[10] See note 5.

The more we read of the horrors that filled the land of promise and its holy temple during the reigns of the wicked kings, the more the children were astounded.

Said one: "I wonder what David would have done if he had known this was going to happen?"

Said another: "If he were alive and those hill shrines were standing, he'd have torn them down."

The first continued: "He had weaknesses but still he was an awful holy man."

And a third soberly observed: "And it was his own son that started those hill shrines."

So it was. It all started with disobedience. It always does. To see disobedience stretch like this from its small beginning to the total chaos at its end is an object lesson hard to duplicate.

After the reforms of Josias, all seemed well for Juda for a while, but the Lord had not changed His mind. When finally Josias met his death in a battle against the Egyptians, the short-lived reforms came to an end and it was clear they were barely skin-deep. Because the hearts of her people were still corrupt, Juda gathered momentum for her final plunge under the last few weak and wicked kings. Joachaz, son of Josias, reigned only three months when he was deposed by the Pharaoh, temporarily in power, and replaced by his brother Eliacim, called Joakim, and under the Pharaoh Joakim "disobeyed the Lord's will after the fashion of his ancestors." (23:37) The people of God had gone the full circle from Pharaoh to Pharaoh; the next enemy would cart them away.

Jeremia in the Days of Joakim

Jeremia had enjoyed peace and quiet during the last years of Josias but the evils of Joakim roused him to speak out again, and for this period we read aloud the following passages.

Jer 7:1-23; 30-34 From a temple sermon—the presumption of the people; abuses in worship, denunciation of human sacrifice

16:19-21 Conversion of the heathen

18; 19 The potter and the potter's flask

20:1-6; 7-13 Jeremia is placed in stocks; his interior suffering and cry of faith

In his temple sermon, Jeremia warns that one does not curry God's favor by merely bowing and scraping in the temple and saying, "This is the temple of the Lord!" Our Lord said, "Not everyone who says to me, Lord, Lord, shall enter the kingdom of heaven." (Matt 7:21) The prophet lists their crimes and asks if they expect to return to the temple with unrepentant hearts and be forgiven. "Has this house which bears my name become in your eyes a den of thieves?" (Jer 7:11) The same holds true for us; even in the sacrament of Penance we are not forgiven our sin if we are not repentant.

He tells how the whole family—mother, father, children—work together to make cakes for "the queen of heaven," Ashtar the goddess of fertility, whose obscene rites have so long seduced the people of God. "Is it I whom they hurt? Is it not rather themselves?" (7:19) In 22-23, he is saying in a typically Hebrew manner that holocausts *alone* were not what God asked of the people when He brought them out of Egypt.

In 7:30-34, there is a furious denunciation of the practice of human sacrifice where children were placed into the arms of the god Thopheth and a roaring fire consumed them. On the mountain hundreds of years before, God had indicated to Abraham that human sacrifice was forbidden; had said of Isaac, "Do not harm the lad." Israel had traveled a long way since then.

In 16:19-21, Jeremia says that one day God will reveal to all the nations of the earth that their idols are false and that He alone is God. We are living now in those times.

Throughout the prophecy of Jeremia there is a rich use of symbols, and we come now to the symbol of the potter's flask. In chapter 18, the Lord tells Jeremia to go to a potter's house and watch him at work. Whenever the potter makes a vessel which is not perfect, he casts it aside, making another to take its place. After explaining this symbol in Jeremia 18, we read Jeremia 19 aloud, in which the prophet is bade by the Lord to buy a potter's flask, take with him some of the priests and the elders, and go to the entrance of the Potsherd Gate overlooking the valley of Ben-Hinnom, where the murderous rites of Thopheth are conducted. There he must smash the flask before the people and tell them that the Lord will smash them the same way because they do not heed his word. This Jeremia does, and the priest Phassur is so enraged that he has him scourged and placed in stocks. (20:1-6) In 7-13, we read Jeremia's prayer of anguish in which he cried out to the Lord, "You have duped me!" (20:7) But in the next breath he asserts his terrible faith. "But the Lord is with me, like a mighty champion!" (20:11) The faith of Jeremia is something to remember in the very dark hours of our lives.

The Prophet Habacuc

Chapter 24 of IV Kings introduces us to Nabuchodonosor who three times invaded Juda and carried away captives and the third time destroyed Jerusalem. It was about the time of the first invasion that the prophet Habacuc appeared. The passages we chose from his short book show us that God, after being queried by the prophet for the severity of His punishments, gives cause for hope—not just hope for the remnant which shall return, but hope for the just man who lives and dies during times of punishment, as just men live and die as victims in our own day. The Hebrews had no knowledge of happiness or sorrow after death until much later in their history; yet here is a prophet who is told by God to have heroic faith in something he hardly understands—and he does. In Habacuc's little book[11] the principle of unswerving trust in God is set forth and his "the just man, because of his faith, shall live," was a favorite reference of St. Paul. (Gal 3:11; Rom 1:17; Heb 10:38) At the end of Habacuc's prayer (canticle), he says that though all conceivable terrors come upon his world from the hand of God, "Yet I will rejoice in the Lord and exult in my saving God. God, my Lord, is my strength . . ." (3:18-19)

> Hab 1:1-4 The prophet complains of God's severity
>   1:5-11 God admits severity
>   1:12-17 Will punishment never cease?
>   2:2-4a God bids patience; "The just man, because of his faith . . ."
>   3:1-2 Prayer for God's intervention
>   3:12-15 Description of God's coming
>   3:16-19 The prophet's faith in salvation

[11] See note 5.

Jeremia and the End of Juda

Chapters 24 and 25 of IV Kings bring the kingdom of Juda to its end. Joakim died and the throne passed to his son Joachin (Jechonia, abbreviated by Jeremia to Conia) whose reign lasted only three months, but long enough for him to disobey the Lord as his father before him. Ignoring the warnings of Jeremia, this king tried to resist Babylon too, was besieged in the city of Jerusalem and was captured. He, his family, his entire retinue, were marched off in the second deportation of prisoners and his uncle Sedecias was chosen to rule in his place.

Again in the reign of Sedecias (Jer 27:2-22), Jeremia begged the people to surrender to Babylon and the purification the Lord had designated for them. To do so was to be saved and to save the holy city. But Sedecias was weak, and although he summoned Jeremia in secret for counsel, he had not the courage to follow his advice in public. In Jeremia 27:2, the Lord tells Jeremia to make a wooden yoke and wear it as a symbol of the yoke He would have the people carry, and in 28:10 the false prophet Anania calls him a liar and breaks the yoke in the presence of the king and court. By thus perverting God's message, Anania forged a yoke of iron for his people and determined the hour of his own death that very year. This tale is easily condensed and told after a pre-reading by the parents, reading aloud only the most dramatic pronouncements.

Chapter 29:4-14 is a letter written by Jeremia to those already captive in Babylon, instructing them how to live during exile. Seventy years (the symbol of a lifetime) they would be in exile and during that time they were to live as the Lord would wish, building houses, planting gardens, marrying wives and begetting families, praying for the city where they were exiled, for on its welfare depended their own. In 12-14, we find something familiar: "when you call . . . when you look . . . when you seek me with all your heart, you will find me . . ." This does not make a New Testament saint out of Jeremia, but rather shows us how filled with the language of the prophets was the mind of Our Lord.

In 31:15, there is a passage that is very familiar. "A voice was heard weeping in Rama, and loud lamentation: Rachel weeping for her children." Where have we read this before? It is used in the Mass of the Holy Innocents. Rachel, the mother of Joseph, the grandmother of the two northern tribes, Ephraim and Manasses, weeps in her tomb for her children, but the Lord says: "Cease . . . they shall return from the enemy's land." (31:16)

And in 31:31-34, we read of the new covenant. Jeremia did not know, but the Blood of Christ would be the sign of the new covenant. "For this is the chalice of My Blood, of the new and everlasting covenant." (Matt 26:28) It would be a covenant made not only with the Jews but with all mankind.

The passages read have been as follows:

Jer 27 Serve Babylon or perish
28 The two yokes
29:1-14 Letter to exiles
31:15-16 Voice of Rachel weeping
31:31-34 New Covenant

The Fall of Jerusalem

The fall of Jerusalem is told in the twenty-fifth chapter of IV Kings, and when we had finished it we turned to Jeremia a last time for his vivid account of the events of those days. Retelling the story is more successful than reading it word for word—with only the most brilliant passages read aloud.

Jer 37 Jeremia in the dungeon
38 Jeremia in the cistern
39, 40 Jerusalem taken, Jeremia freed
42, 43, 44 Jeremia consulted, rebuffed; flight to Egypt

Jeremia 37 tells how Jeremia, after the lifting of the second siege, was unjustly accused of consorting with the enemy and thrown into a dungeon, and in Jeremia 38, we learn that during the last days of the third siege, he was thrown in a cistern and left to starve; but for the charity and courage of Ebed-melech, a Chusite, he would have died there. (We will see the Lord reward the Chusite for his good deed in 39:15-18) Jeremia 39 and 40 tell how the city and all its people were taken at last, but Jeremia was released by Nabuchodonosor and left to do as he wished. Chapters 42, 43 and 44 tell how the survivors consulted the prophet again, only to defy the word of the Lord and march off to Egypt, and how the Lord pursued them with His anger and promised to lead the master of Babylon along their trail to destroy them there.

Jeremia vanishes from history in Egypt, where he has warned

his people one last time to turn back to the Lord, to which they replied: "We will not listen to what you say in the name of the Lord." (44:16) He drops out of sight, a man worn and haggard, hoarse and exhausted, entirely spent after a lifetime of serving the Lord—and his life seemed a total failure. Only a few listened, only a few were saved. They were his people and he had loved them, but they did not love him back. Jeremia was very much like Christ.

We finished the story of Jeremia and sat for a moment, quietly. Stephen climbed down from his favorite place in the tree.

"He was an awfully good prophet," he said. "You can just tell by reading him. And he went through an awful lot to be a prophet."

Yes—and by Confirmation we share with him the role of prophet. Jeremia teaches us much about this role, for he is the very personification of the word *prophet:* to be witness to the Lord.

The Book of Lamentations

The Book of Lamentations is a collection of five dirges, probably written shortly after the fall of Jerusalem. The poet was an eyewitness to those tragic days and poured out his anguished soul in words of beauty and grief. Each chapter is a separate lament. The first, second and fourth chapters are said to be in the form of a funeral dirge and grieve over the lost mother, Jerusalem. The third chapter is an individual lament in which the writer describes his bitter suffering and his hopes that the Lord will one day bring it to an end. Its climax is a prayer for help. The fifth chapter is a communal lament, a whole people speaking to the Lord, again admitting guilt and expressing hope, ending with a prayer for restoration.[12]

The Lamentations are used in the Divine Office for Holy Week and many passages are familiar to us from their association with the Passion of Our Lord. "Come, all you who pass by the way, look and see whether there is any suffering like my suffering." (1:12)

[12] See note 5.

"The Lord has trodden in the wine press virgin daughter Juda." (1:15) And in 2:1, we find an expression familiar to us from the Psalms and from Our Lord's use of it in the Gospels. "The Lord . . . has cast down from heaven to earth the glory of Israel, unmindful of his footstool on the day of his wrath." These short chapters of Lamentations make appropriate additions to family prayer during Lent and Holy Week.

The Book of Baruch

The Book of Baruch tells of the Jews who remained in Babylon after the exile (like Tobias and his family) and adapted themselves to life away from their homeland. Although it is attributed to Baruch, the secretary of Jeremia, the work was probably written long after the time of that great prophet and his scribe. As we have seen before, it was customary to identify a work with the "school" or spirit in which it was written (for example, Second Isaia and the Wisdom Books) and this is evidently the case here.

Baruch shows us that the Jews of the exile kept fast to their religion and the rest of their people by means of letters, alms for sacrifices, the sharing of prayers, the reading of the sacred books, synagogue services and especially their devotion to the Law and the expectations of a Messias. This beautiful poem in praise of Wisdom (Bar 3:9-4:4) might be used at family prayer some evening:

> Yet he who knows all things knows her;
>> he has probed her by his knowledge—
> He who established the earth for all time,
>> and filled it with four-footed beasts;
> He who dismisses the light, and it departs,
>> calls it, and it obeys him trembling;
> Before whom the stars at their posts
>> shine and rejoice;
> When he calls them, they answer, "Here we are!"
>> shining with joy for their Maker. (3:32-35)

In chapters 4:5-37 and 5, the children of Israel are comforted and Jerusalem is told not to mourn as though she will never be restored. "Fear not, my children; call out to God! He who brought this upon you will remember you . . . will, in saving you, bring you back enduring joy!" (4:27-29)

Chapter 6, the Letter of Jeremia warning the people against idolatry, brings to mind the debacle of the people of God at the foot of Mt. Sinai, the endless problem of the hill shrines during the reigns of the bad kings, and, in our own times, the struggle of missionaries everywhere who labor to uproot idolatry and plant in its place the seed of glory. The thoughts revealed in this letter and the style of its composition are so different from Jeremia's that we can't help suspecting that some anonymous writer has placed his work under the patronage of the great prophet.

It paints a tragic and pitiable picture of the peoples of the world who still pay their tributes to gods of wood and gold and silver and do not know the One God. Image after image of ridicule and derision fill the pages and although this letter is not a great piece of writing, it has the power to stir up hearts to the reality of men still living in darkness and not yet alive to God's life. It suggests the answer to the perennial questions, "Why disturb the pagans? Why not leave them alone to worship their gods and let the Christians be content to worship *their* God?" But the pagans were destined to know the God Who made them, to receive His life in them and be like Him, to share His joy for all eternity also. To give such men the fullness of divine life is why the Church has missions. This is exactly what Our Lord was explaining when He said: "Go, therefore, and make disciples of all nations, baptizing them in the name of the Father, and of the Son, and of the Holy Spirit . . ." (Matt 28:19) They are His, and He wants them with Him.

"For like a scarecrow in a cucumber patch, that is no protection, are their wooden, gilded, silvered gods. Just like a thornbush in a garden on which perches every kind of bird, or like a corpse hurled into darkness, are their silvered and gilded wooden gods . . ." (6:69-71) The writer concludes: "The better for the just man who has no idols: he shall be far from disgrace!" (6:72)

Yes—and let the man who knows the One God be sure he pours himself out in prayer and charity for the men who do not.

·VIII·

THE EXILE
AND
RETURN

"Into the exile at last," was the word around our house as we finished the fourth book of Kings and summer drew to a close. "Now to get out."

Indeed, to get out of exile was the next move, and there was great anticipation, but first we had to make the acquaintance of two more prophets, men who played an important role during the years of exile and without whom the Israelites could have been lost. These men were Ezechiel and the writer of Second Isaia.

Just imagine for a moment what might have happened had all the exiled Israelites been left to their own devices during the years in Babylon. They were poor spiritually when they left Juda; seventy years in a pagan land would hardly improve their spirituality, in fact they might have been expected to lose their faith entirely. Modern tyrants move the faithful about for just such reasons.

The Prophet Ezechiel

Into this situation the prophet Ezechiel fits. It was Ezechiel who taught the people during their stay in Babylon, gathering them together in meetings which, we are told, set the pattern for the synagogue later on; and since the synagogue set the pattern for the instruction part of our own Mass, we owe a special debt to Ezechiel. He knew that a strong, living faith in his people was dependent upon regular teaching. Ezechiel rebuked and threatened, instructed and consoled, predicted and explained, and kept alive in the Israelites in exile a consciousness of their election as God's people in spite of the forlorn state of their affairs. "Humanly speaking, had it not been for Ezechiel, the Hebrew religion might have died." [1]

The problem of choosing what to read from his book is not difficult if we hold to our promise of brevity and choose passages which follow the story line. The long section on Jerusalem before its fall is omitted, as we have already left Jerusalem behind us; also the maledictions uttered against the foreign nations are passed by. Of the three sections remaining, we chose the following passages:

> Ezech   1:1-20   Ezechiel's call and vision of God
> 34:1-24   The parable of the shepherds
> 37:1-14   The vision of the dry bones

Ezechiel's Call

It was about five years after he had been sent into exile with the elite of King Joachin's court that Ezechiel had a vision of God resting on the cherubim. In chapter 1, we read of God seated on angelic creatures described in symbols—cherubim with four heads, winged but with human form, resting on wheels which were full of eyes. The four heads—man, lion, eagle and ox—are thought to indicate beings with the intelligence of man, the nobility and domination of the lion, the swiftness of the eagle and the strength of the ox. The wheels signify their constant attendance upon God, Who is all-present and all-seeing. Creatures like these are to be found in the art of the Middle East and can be seen in the Babylonian, Assyrian and Persian collections of any museum, showing us that the mind of Ezechiel, like that of any man, was stored with images from the culture around him.[2]

Above the cherubim, Ezechiel saw a vision of the Lord and he fell on his face before it. A voice told him to go to the Israelites

---

[1] Edward F. Siegman, C.PP.S., *The Book of Ezechiel, Parts 1 and 2 with Commentary* (New York: Paulist Press, 1961), p. 6. Price 50¢.
[2] See New York Metropolitan Museum School Picture sets: No. 7, *Ancient Near East;* No. 12, *Animals that Never Were.* Price 15¢ each. Excellent for home and school bulletin boards, discussions, notebooks, etc.

and give them God's message, and with that Ezechiel saw a scroll symbolic of the word of God which he was told to eat; he did and found it sweet to his taste. Here, in either a vision or symbolic act, Ezechiel illustrates dramatically what the Lord said to Jeremia about the role of the prophet: "See, I place my words in your mouth!" (Jer 1:9)

The Israelites would be difficult, Ezechiel is warned, but the Lord will give him stubbornness to match theirs and he is not to fear their dark looks, for they are a rebellious race and need to be taken in hand (as well we knew, having spent the summer reading the books of Kings).

The Parable of the Shepherds

In Ezechiel 34, we find the parable of the shepherds which brings immediately to mind Our Lord and His love for this figure. Verse 34:11, "I myself will look after and tend my sheep," gives us a glimpse of the longing of the Second Person of the Blessed Trinity as He awaited the moment in time when He would reveal His face and say to His people: "I am the good shepherd and I know mine and mine know me." (John 10:14) Did it dawn on Christ's hearers that this was the voice of the Promised One spoken of by Ezechiel?

Two reproaches are addressed to the people in this parable, one to the priests and leaders who have let their flocks stray while they watched out for their own interests, and the other to the flocks themselves wherein are found both sheep and goats—the just and the unjust (although we confess to loving our goats very much and wishing they had not always to be identified with the culprits). In verse 23, Ezechiel utters a messianic prophecy—his belief that one day a descendent of David will shepherd God's people.

The Vision of the Dry Bones

Whether Ezechiel literally saw a plain strewn with dry bones or had a vision is not clear, but the Lord's message was clear enough —a promise of return to their land for the Israelites, welcome news in the midst of their despair, and beyond that a vague hint of the resurrection of the body on the Last Day. Now we can really appreciate the shouting joy in the spiritual *Dry Bones*, always a family favorite but never one we connected with the prophets or scripture. "To tell the truth," said the father of this family, reflecting back to his college days, "I daresay most people think the whole thing started with Fred Waring." As a prophecy of our own resurrection, *Dry Bones* really deserves a place alongside the *Alleluia* in the family celebration of Easter.

Further than this in Ezechiel we did not read. The plans for rebuilding Jerusalem and the temple, the laws governing religious life, the boundaries and tribal divisions of the New Israel are not suitable for reading aloud and we did not want to spoil the children's friendship with their new favorite. We know he is a favorite from a snatch of overheard conversation.

"You know *Ezechiel*. He's the one that saw the vision of God sitting on the creatures with the heads—and the bones lying in the field. He's great." A kind of ragtag description of Ezechiel, this, but how grand that they think so much of him. There are years ahead to become better acquainted.

Second Isaia

Next we turn to the last half of the book of Isaia, called Second Isaia because it was written a hundred and fifty years after the first part of the book by an anonymous author who lived during the Babylonian exile. Nabuchodonosor had died, and Babylon had reached its zenith and begun its decline with the series of weak kings that followed him. Twelve years before the city fell into the hands of Cyrus the Persian, this Second Isaia spoke the word of the Lord. For ten years he was active, giving us a writing which is unsurpassed for its beauty, its spirit of longing, its vision of the Messias; and in which we will find much that is already familiar through the liturgy and the Gospels. We chose the following passages for reading from Second Isaia.

> *Is* 40:1-5   Promise of salvation
> 45:1-6   Cyrus, the Lord's instrument
> 49:14-18   The Lord's love for Sion
> 51:1-3   Remember, and trust in the Lord
> { 52:13-15   Suffering and triumph of the Servant
> { 53:1-12   of the Lord

In Isaia 40:1-2, the Lord tells the prophet to comfort the people with the promise that their guilt is expiated, their service at an end. The words are familiar to us from the Advent hymn *Drop Down Dew*, where they are applied to our own enslavement after the Fall and mankind's longing for redemption, and to our longing for Christ in His Second Coming. "Be ye comforted, O my people, for most quickly comes thy salvation." [3]

St. John the Baptist

In verses 3-5, we find the familiar words used in the Gospels of Matthew, Mark and Luke to describe John the Baptist. (Luke 3:4-6; Matt 3:1-3; Mark 1:1-4) The image is that of a people preparing to receive their sovereign king. The road is made ready, filled in where low and leveled where high, and the spiritual application is clear, with its admonition to be about the leveling of faults, the filling in of omissions. Road building is such a common sight across our land these days, with giant construction equipment leveling hills and filling in gullies between one great city and another, that we might easily adapt this passage in a way that would spark a quick reflection on these words for our children each time they see a highway construction job.

Cyrus as the Lord's Instrument

In Isaia 45:1-6, when the Lord says He will use Cyrus as His chosen instrument for freeing His people, He again shows that all men have a place in His plan for salvation, all are the object of His desire. He speaks to Cyrus: "It is I who arm you, though you know me not, so that toward the rising and the setting of the sun men may know that there is none besides me." Cyrus would come and liberate Israel and permit her to return to her homeland and rebuild her city. Even now God makes instruments of men who deny Him, who insist they do not know Him.

---

[3] The words about the dew come from Isaia 45:8: "Let justice descend, O heavens, like dew from above . . ."

The Lord's Love for Sion

In Isaia 49:14, Sion (Jerusalem) laments that the Lord has
forsaken her, and the Lord answers that even should a mother forget
the child of her womb, He will never forget her. "See, upon the
palms of my hands I have written your name . . ." (49:16)

Before I could explain that it was an ancient Oriental custom
for the bridegroom to have the name of the bride tattooed upon
his hands, Philip interrupted.

"O yes, the marks of the nails."

And he really wasn't wrong.

The Lord would have Israel trust Him, and in 51:1-3 He bids
His people turn back in memory and recall the faith of Abraham
and Sara, and how Abraham was but one man when He was called
and blessed, and now he is many. This is a reminder for us also,
and one of the rewards of reading the Old Testament is to have
stored away in us these mighty figures of faith and trust for our
inspiration. In our own times of trial, God points to these men of
old to remind us He is ever true to His word.

Portrait of Christ

In 52:13-15 and 53:1-12, we have a portrait of Christ, the
Servant of the Lord. Here at last is the revelation that the Promised
One will take on Himself the sins of men and bear the punishment
for them, winning pardon for all. This passage of Isaia might be
read by the family together or individually for any number of occasions, perhaps especially in preparation for the sacrament of Penance. Its description of His love and the chastisement He bore for
love of us would do much to refresh the springs of remorse and
renew the sincerity of our sometimes rather cut and dried acts of
contrition. It would be a great help to one who had difficulty with
confession, for it possesses the kind of beauty that melts tension
and fear of heart, and it places the emphasis on the generosity and
goodness of Christ.

An Invitation to Grace

Isaia 55:1-2 is like an invitation to Mass, the banquet table
of the Lord. "Come, without paying and without cost, drink wine
and milk! Why spend your money for what is not bread; your

wages for what fails to satisfy? Heed me, and you shall eat well, you shall delight in rich fare."

Passages like this one can be used often in the family, at prayer time or for the celebration of a feast, a vigil, a particular liturgical event. We read them from a point of view beyond the redemption and they are rich with meaning for us; the Israelites could hardly begin to guess the things they say.

Gathering of the Nations

That God's plan is to gather all men to Himself is the message of 56:6-8, and it rounds off beautifully with 66:18-23 at the close of the book. Second Isaia sweeps in its great embrace the entire history of man and God, from abyss to abyss. It is especially appropriate reading in these days when the sense of mission and the desire for unity burn high in so many hearts.

"I come to gather nations of every language; they shall come and see my glory . . . They shall bring all your brethren from all the nations as an offering to the Lord, on horses and in chariots, in carts, upon mules and dromedaries, to Jerusalem, my holy mountain, says the Lord, just as the Israelites bring their offering to the House of the Lord in clean vessels."

First and Second Paralipomena

Before we begin the story of the return from exile, it would be well to explain briefly the First and Second Books of Paralipomena, which follow the books of Kings. Paralipomena (meaning "Chronicles" and sometimes called by this name) is a recapitulation of all sacred history from the creation of the world to the end of the Babylonian captivity. To read these books following Kings would undoubtedly bring forth a loud protest from the children (as was the case with Deuteronomy): "But we've just read that!" So, although there are some passages which are original, it is good to save Paralipomena for another time when we want to read of these events again.

Esdras and Nehemias

The books of Esdras and Nehemias[4] tell of the return from exile and affairs during and after the rebuilding of the temple and Jerusalem. Since the postexilic prophets spoke the word of the Lord during these times also, we will fit them into place as we go along. The schedule for the reading of Esdras and Nehemias, and the passages we chose from the prophets Aggai, Zacharia and Malachia, are as follows:

Esd   1; 2-2, 68-70; 3; 4:1-5; 23-24
Ag   1:1-4, 7-15; 2:1-9
Zach   6:9-14; 8:1-23
Esd   5:2-17; 6
Mal   1:1-3, 6-14; 2:13-16; 3:2-3, 20, 23
Neh   1; 2; 3; 4; 5; 6; 7:1-5
Esd   7; 8:1, 21-36
Neh   8
Esd   9; 10
Neh   9; 10; 13

As Isaia had predicted, Cyrus, king of Persia, captured Babylon and invited the Israelites to return to their land and rebuild the temple of their God. The words of Ezra 1:2-3 make Cyrus sound like a worshiper of the Lord but it is more likely that his invitation was embellished by the authors and that it was simply his policy to send captive peoples home to honor their gods. The Jewish historian of ancient times, Josephus, says Cyrus had read the prediction of his triumph in Second Isaia and was pleased that this God hastened his campaign,[5] but it is not certain whether this is true.

So it came about that clan chiefs of Juda and Benjamin, priests, and Levites set out for Jerusalem to rebuild the Lord's temple. All

---

[4] Sometimes called First and Second Esdras, or Ezra and Nehemia, or First and Second Ezra.
[5] *The Works of Flavius Josephus*, Book XI, Ch. 1.

the treasure stripped from the temple by Nabuchodonosor was returned and gifts to help with the task were contributed by the Jews who elected to stay in Babylon.[6]

The Journey Back

It would be easy to imagine all the exiles clamoring to go back to Juda, but this was hardly true. The candidates were second and third generation Jews who had grown up surrounded by the opulence, sophistication and comfort of Babylon, and many were quite content to stay where they were. This reveals that there was an element of choice in the destiny of the remnant as stump and root and shoot of Jesse, and it would hardly have been possible to choose a more perfect means of selection. Those who burned with the memory of the ancient promise and the desire to be part of its fulfillment responded and returned to Juda by way of a caravan journey of some nine hundred miles, a slow and painful crossing of wild terrain in all kinds of weather, accompanied by pack animals heavily loaded with supplies, and moving through regions of hostile peoples, to a city that had been razed to the ground. See how God narrowed down the remnant.

Chapter 2 of Esdras is a list of names and numbers of those who went back to Juda and which we omit, reading only verses 1-2, and verses 68-70. The names of most interest to us are Sassabasar, Zorobabel and Josue, Sassabasar being the governor appointed by the Persian king, Zorobabel a prince of David's line, and Josue the high priest. Our Lord would be a direct descendent of Zorobabel, who is mentioned in His genealogy in Matthew 1:13.

It is important to understand that the "new" Juda was only a tiny city-state at this time, in size about twenty by twenty-five miles—an island surrounded by suspicious neighbors. These new immigrants were not entirely welcome to the descendents of those Judaeans and Israelites who had stayed in the land, nor to the imported population of the former kingdom of Israel to the north, now quite settled and feeling like natives. Chapter 4 tells how the Samaritans to the north, especially alarmed, offered to help build the temple on the grounds that they too worshiped the same God.

At this point Christopher cut in.

"But it wasn't true worship," he said, "because they had a lot of bad luck after Israel was captured and they got a priest to come

[6] During the exile the people out of Juda had come to be known as Jews.

back and offer sacrifice so they'd have good luck. That wasn't a right kind of worship."

And I for one was amazed. He remembered! It had happened so long ago—books, pages, weeks before. The lesson learned was a story of counterfeit worship by people who used the Lord's altar as a talisman, and because of it this child had been impressed that one of the essential elements of worship is sincerity of heart.

Their offer to help was turned down, but the Samaritans did not let the matter rest. Esdras 4:6-16 is a letter of protest to the court, not written at this time but serving as the type of protest that was made. The compiler of the text is saying, aside, to us: "I haven't a copy of the letter but this is the sort of thing it was," and rather than complicate matters hopelessly for the children by explaining all this, we simply read: "So they sent a letter to the king which went like this . . ." Actually, the letter reproduced here is concerned with the rebuilding of the city walls—a problem to arise later in the days of Nehemias.

A restraining order came and the Israelites timidly halted their work and sank back defeated. The glorious return of God's people to the land of promise had not lived up to expectations. (Chapter 4 can be read beforehand and largely explained.)

The Prophet Aggai

"But God still had his prophets, Aggai and Zacharia . . ." says chapter 5, so we turn now to these prophets. Aggai's words are brief and to the point—a scolding for the people because they sit by and do nothing. With Aggai 1:1-4 and 7-15, the prophet gets the people back to work.[7] In Aggai 2:1-9, he speaks of the comparison between the new temple and the more splendid temple of Solomon and bids them not be disappointed but look ahead: "Greater will be the future glory of this house than the former . . ." (8:2-9) And of course we know that one day Christ will

[7] Carroll Stuhlmueller, C.P., *The Books of Aggai, Zacharia, Malachia, Jona, Joel, Abdia with a Commentary* (New York: Paulist Press), price 50¢.

come, Who will call His own body "this temple," (John 2:19) and whose Mystical Body—like a temple—will be able to contain all the peoples of the world.

First Zacharia

The prophet Zacharia (divided, like Isaia, into two sections thought to have been written at widely separated times) is difficult, and the early chapters are filled with apocalyptic visions which are too complicated for children. So we skip over them to 6:9-14, the coronation of Zorobabel, prince of David's line. Zacharia writes, "Here is a man whose name is Shoot, and where he is he shall sprout, and he shall build the temple of the Lord," (6:12) and we can see the two-fold application—one, to the rebuilding of the temple of Jerusalem; and another most thrilling reference to this prince as one out of whose body came, in time, the sacred Body of the Lord.

Zorobabel was the last of the kings, and with his disappearance the Davidic dynasty dropped out of sight until the appearance of Christ, the King of kings. Following Zorobabel, the ruling power in Juda was administered by the high priests.

We might stop here a moment and help the children observe the lesson God had taught His people about kings. From their first demand for a king to rule and win battles, which gave them Saul, to the inspired leadership of David, to the magnificence and weakness of Solomon, through the kings who brought about Israel's humiliation and downfall, to Zorobabel, the people of God had known kingship in every circumstance. It was a painful way to learn that their greatness was not to be a matter of kings or being like other nations. Being Creator, *God* is King. This is not just a title of courtesy. He *intended* to be the King who would rule in the hearts of men, whose reign would know no boundaries. His realm is everything, everywhere, everyone, as He said when He came. "My kingdom is not of this world." (John 18:36) And the people He chose for the working-out of His plan would be great as long as they were subject to His kingship. This is true of us, too. We must be subject, for He is King. Then we will be able to take a fruitful part in His plan to rule in the hearts of men.

No other history of any people is written like this history of the people of God, with the historical action and then God's opinion of it recorded! If this doesn't teach us the right order of all things and ourselves in relation to God, it seems nothing will.

This history of frustrated kingships gives us the background for the Palm Sunday triumph of Christ entering Jerusalem, and the cries of the people, "Blessed is he who comes in the name of the Lord, the King of Israel!" (John 12:13) And it explains their disappointment, for He failed their expectations. They were still expecting an earthly king.

But we must get back to the book of Esdras. Encouraged by the prophets, the people set about completing the new temple. Again there was opposition, but Cyrus' order was discovered to vindicate them and at last the temple was completed. (Chapters 5 and 6 can be read ahead and greatly condensed.)

The Prophet Malachia

Once again the morale of the community slumped dangerously low. The temple was completed; what next? Time dragged on. Immorality, cruelty, divorce, intermarriage with foreign wives, all manner of abuses cried out for correction. And this time the Lord raised up the prophet Malachia. Through him the Lord complains that He has loved Israel but she has not loved Him back, (Mal 1:1-3). In 6-10, He decries their profanation of the altar of the Lord with unworthy sacrifices. And in 1:11, we find the Mass faintly revealed—a liturgical sacrifice which will be offered to Him one day, binding together all the nations of the earth in the eternal *now* of Christ's sacrifice on Calvary and on the altars of the Lord. "From the rising of the sun to its setting . . . everywhere they bring sacrifice to my name . . ."

In Malachia 3:2-3, we find a prophecy of the Messias which has been familiar for years as the Lesson in the Mass of the feast of the Purification. "He is like a refiner's fire, or like the fuller's lye . . ." (And if you happen to live in a town where there are woolen mills, as we do, you know that the fuller's lye or soap is used to wash the raw wool in a series of baths in order to remove the impurities.) In Malachia 3:23-24, we find the prophecy describing John the Baptist and used by St. Luke (1:17), the one the people recalled when they asked if John was Elias. (Matt 17:12) The single verse 3:20 gives us one of the most beautiful titles of Our Lord to be used throughout the liturgy, the "sun of justice."

Malachia fearlessly accused the people, reminded them who they were and how little cause they had to complain (considering their past behavior), pointed ahead to the first coming of "the messenger of the covenant whom you desire," (3:1) and His second coming (as we see it) on that great day of judgment. The people desperately needed to hope.

Nehemias

Now we come to the Esdras-Nehemias or Nehemias-Esdras difficulty. Making no pretence to be scholars, we simply chose the one out of three possible sequences of events that seemed most workable to us[8] and followed it with our reading. This sequence is based on the theory that the book of Nehemias was written independently of Esdras, was discovered later, was physically inserted in the scriptural account of the period following the book of Esdras —yet tells of events some of which took place before Esdras' arrival in Jerusalem.

Nehemias and Esdras were the great reformers of the postexilic period, and a very clear-cut portrait of each of them emerges from these books. Nehemias was cupbearer to the king of Persia, a position of great trust, when he heard from a relative returned from Jerusalem of the ruin and rubble in the former capital. Nehemias begged the king's permission to go and help rebuild the city. It was given, and the last half of chapter 2 tells of a midnight journey

[8] John Bright, *A History of Israel* (Philadelphia: Westminster Press, 1959), p. 363.

in secret with a few trusted friends to view the destruction. The walls of Jerusalem lay in ruins, charred and blackened by fire. His invitation to the rulers and the people to repair the city is characteristic of Nehemias' approach to everything: "Come, let us build Jerusalem's walls and endure contempt no longer! Up, to the task!" (Neh 2:17-18 Knox) Welcoming this ardent leader, all Jerusalem fell to mending the walls. Skipping through chapter 3 we read of the restoration of gates, walls and towers whose very names show us some of the life of the city: the Shepherds' Gate, the Fishmongers' Gate, the Old Gate, the Valley Gate, the Scavengers' Gate, and so on. The restoration had its enemies, of course, who raged and plotted and connived, but to no avail. They had met their match. Nehemias was not a man to be intimidated.

Next came Nehemias' attack on the injustice of the rich with respect to the poor. Nehemias 5:10-12 is reminiscent of Our Lord's parable of the steward who forgave so many debts. (Luke 16:1-13) For twelve years Nehemias took no salary but labored unceasingly for the Lord, outwitting enemies, ferreting out intrigues, shoring up morale, until, the initial work of restoration completed, he took a census of the population. Nehemias 7:6-69 and chapters 11 and 12 list the population and Nehemias' method for determining who would live in Jerusalem. We can omit these passages.

Esdras

Now we leave Nehemias temporarily to meet Esdras, priest and scribe, filled with love for the Law. Esdras went to Jerusalem to teach the men of Israel the law of God, says chapter 7. A letter from the king permitted him to take with him anyone he wished, gave him monies for the venture and commissioned him to appoint judges and magistrates to try cases and execute the law (all of which can be read beforehand and explained, with the list of companions in Esdras 8:1-20 omitted).

The contrast between Esdras and Nehemias is striking; they are wonderfully complementary in character. Nehemias was a man of courageous action—"On to the fray!" Esdras was a man not naturally fearless but, we might say, theologically courageous. In order to assure a safe arrival, Esdras started his journey with fasting and prayer, explaining: "I would have asked the king for an escort of horsemen to defend us from attack but shame withheld me; had we not boasted in the king's presence that our God graciously protected all who had recourse to him?" (Esdras 8:22 Knox) So they fasted and prayed to win the favor of the Lord and all went well. They arrived in Jerusalem safely, the treasure was turned over to the temple, huge burnt sacrifices were offered in thanksgiving and the royal edict was delivered to the king's officials.

Esdras Reads the Law

Back we turn to Nehemias in chapter 8 to find a description of Esdras reading the Law in front of a great throng of men and women, "with such children as were old enough to understand it." (8:2 Knox)

Which would be at least down to age nine, we learned when Christopher interrupted to say, "*I'd* have gone."

All the people gathered before the Water Gate and there in a pulpit which raised him high enough to be seen by all—even the nine-year-olds—Esdras read from daybreak to noon, beginning with a blessing on the name of the Lord to which the people replied, "Amen, amen."

Explained Philip, "That means *Indeed! Indeed!*"

The people wept so to hear the words of the Law that Nehemias and Esdras and the Levites protested. This was a feast day! Let them go home and celebrate, rejoicing in the Lord, "for in the Lord lies our strength." (8:10 Knox) And they did, building themselves the next day little booths of boughs and vines and celebrating the feast of tabernacles properly for the first time since the days of Josue.

Esdras Grieves over the Intermarriages

But things were far from perfect. Turning back to Esdras, chapters 9 and 10, we read of the grief of Esdras to discover how the Israelites had married with foreign women, women of pagan beliefs. Gathering the people from all over Juda, Esdras accused them of these offenses and bade them put away the foreign wives, some of whom had already borne children. The people stood grief-stricken in the pouring rain lamenting their sin.

"Golly," said Christopher, "all the trouble started when Solomon made shrines for his pagan wives. You'd think they'd remember."

But they didn't. Christopher will learn how seldom men profit by the sins of others—only by their own sin and their own bitter sorrow afterward.

"I don't know," said Stephen, "sounds kind of tough on the wives and children. It wasn't their fault." And as near as we could come to a comparable situation within his ken, with elements of both the legal and the religious, was a man who, once married, took to himself another wife. The law of God does not permit this nor does the law of the state, and he could not take his place within the community of the Church or the civic community until he had put aside the second wife—even if she did have children. It *would* be "tough on the wife and the children." It generally is—*very* tough, to rectify sin. This is not God's fault, because He made the law (precisely to protect people from this sort of tragedy); but man's, who broke it. The law about foreign wives had been made to keep Israel from being weakened by pagan elements and God's work from being thus defeated, which Christopher had observed was exactly what happened with Solomon.

Chapter 10 of Esdras and 9 of Nehemias seem very much alike. In Esdras 10, we find the people, clan by clan, confessing their fault and making arrangements to put away these extra wives. Chapter 9 of Nehemias describes such a situation in greater detail, from the marvelous prayer offered by the priests recalling the story of God's goodness to the Israelites, to the signing of a covenant by all present binding them once more to the Lord in every way—by means of the Law.

This is the event which crowned the work of Esdras and changed the whole idea of Israel. No longer a nation, nor two sister kingdoms, no longer important in the Near East, her temple available to only a fraction of her people, the people of God now found their rallying point and center in the Law.

It was the Law from which Judaism took its life. The Law was the word of God expressing the will of God in terms of all things: worship, morals, justice, family life—everything. To love and obey it was life-giving and to defy it meant death, spiritual death to the individual and annihilation for the people as a people.

This new emphasis on the Law revealed, in part, how the promises that spoke of bringing together all the nations of the earth under One God might be accomplished. This would be the requirement for the gentiles' entry into the community of God's people before the coming of Christ: their love for and obedience to the Law.

Understanding this, we see more clearly what Our Lord meant when He said, "I come not to destroy the Law but to fulfill it." (Matt 5:17) The purpose of the Law was to help the people cling to God, and here was the maker and giver of the Law presenting Himself to them in His sacred Person. Christ was the *end* of the Law.

We close the story of Nehemias and his work in chapter 13 after the reformer had been back to Persia and again returned to Jerusalem. Ever he was about his work, accusing, challenging, rectifying; ever he was guarding Juda's fidelity to the Lord. In verse 26, Nehemias takes note of the wrongs of Solomon marrying his foreign wives, and he concludes in verse 30: "Thus it was mine to rid Israel of the alien-born, to marshal priests and Levites for their due service, to plan the offering of wood at appointed times, and of first-fruits. Not unremembered, my God, be all this, not unrewarded."

Surely Our Lord's greeting to Nehemias when He went to fetch him to heaven must have been, "Well done, good and faithful servant."

The Prophet Abdia

This is the shortest book in the Old Testament, only twenty-one verses—half of which are identical with Jeremia's Oracle against Edom (Jer 49:7-22)—and containing a merciless prediction of the punishment of Edom for its crimes against Israel.[9]

The family will fit this book into the framework of salvation history if we remember that the Edomites were descended from Esau, twin brother to Jacob, and were therefore cousins (button-hole cousins by this time) of the Israelites. Granted a certain animosity between the two families over the transferral of the birth-

[9] See note 7.

right from Esau to Jacob, the latter had tried to make peace with
Esau on his return from Mesopotamia by endowing him with rich
gifts, and in the end the Edomites had done very well for themselves. They had settled in the land south of the Dead Sea, with
east, and with caravan routes from Egypt and Arabia to bring them
mountains to protect them in the west and rich plateaus to the
trade.

But they were a proud and vindictive people and from the
very beginning Edom and Israel had not been able to get along—
not even in their mother's womb! At one time Edom had become
subject to David, and at another time Amasias, king of Juda, had
slain many Edomites in the Valley of the Saltmines and conquered
the rock fortress Jectehel, so it is understandable that when Jerusalem was destroyed in 587 B.C., the Edomites gloated. Catching
fugitive Judaeans in ambush, they triumphantly handed them over
to the Babylonians.

In this prophecy, Abdia cries out that such crimes do not go
unpunished, and this book (dated sometime after 550 B.C. when
the Nabataeans from the desert to the east had already begun to
push Edom out of its mountain fortress) predicts that in the end
Jacob—as foretold to his mother Rebecca—would take precedence
over Esau.

"The house of Jacob shall be a fire, and the house of Joseph
a flame; the house of Esau shall be a stubble." (Ab 18)

One thinks of Job and the inscrutable ways of God. Jacob,
said the Lord long ago, would rule Esau. Whatever the means
employed—whatever the wanderings of the two sons and their descendents, the scraps, the disagreements, the vengeance—Jacob
would rule Esau, and Esau would be punished for trying to make
it otherwise.

One needs to be reminded these days that what the Lord has
said, *shall be*—when all about men seem to surrender so easily to
ease and superficiality, and the gates of hell seem to have a very
good chance of prevailing. But they shall not, in the end. Abdia
reminds Edom that the Lord shall have His way.

The Prophet Joel

At the opening of the book of Joel, the people of God have been plagued by locusts and all the land about them lies in ruins. The scene, it is thought, is probably the temple, with Joel standing in the midst of the people exhorting them to cry to the Lord for the deliverance which will surely come. Joel speaks descriptively, painting a landscape full of woe, peopled by lamenting virgins, mourning priests, wailing husbandmen and vinedressers. Wheat, barley, vine, fig tree, pomegranate, date palm, apple, "all the trees of the field are dried up." (1:12) Then, cries the prophet, let everyone do penance and fall on the mercy of the Lord, for the day of the Lord is coming. (2:11) Joel, speaking to his people in the terms of a contemporary situation, speaks to us as well, and we see his "day of the Lord" not only as the messianic day of Christ's coming but also as the last days—often alluded to in this way by the apocalyptic writers.

He tells men how to prepare themselves for both times: for the coming of Christ in grace, and in judgment. ". . . rend your hearts, not your garments, and return to the Lord your God. For gracious and merciful is he, slow to anger, rich in kindness, and relenting in punishment." (2:12-13)

The passage that follows has been familiar to us for ages as the Lesson in the Ash Wednesday Mass. In it he tells who is to prepare himself—the elders, the children, the infants at the breast, the bridegroom and the bride, the priests and ministers, all—lest in spite of the heritage passed on to them, they be lost and the godless looking on say, "Where is their God?" (2:15-17)

When Joel describes in 2:18-27 the blessings God will rain down upon His repentant people to comfort them, a dozen associations leap to mind; even the words of St. Luke in his first chapter seem to have flown from here. "Fear not . . . exult and rejoice! for the Lord has done great things!" (2:21) And further on, in 3:1-6, we find that the prophet Joel supplied the first biblical text to be quoted in the first sermon of apostolic times. Here are the words used by St. Peter on Pentecost to describe the coming of the Spirit which Joel promised to all the sons and daughters of God. (Acts 2:17-21)

"Then afterward I will pour out my spirit upon all mankind. Your sons and daughters shall prophesy, your old men shall dream dreams, your young men shall see visions; even upon the servants and the handmaids in those days, I will pour out my spirit." (3:1-2)

Once again we are reminded of Confirmation, that sacrament in which the Spirit is poured forth on men of every class and condition—"even upon the servants and the handmaids"—to make them, in the original sense of the word, like prophets who speak the word of God and show it forth in the enlightenment of their own lives.

And finally, in chapter 4 the Lord tells how He will sit in judgment on the nations of the earth when the faithful gather in a heavenly Jerusalem and enjoy the wine and milk of blessedness forever.

The date of this book is after the exile, after the Temple had been rebuilt, even after the re-editing of the earlier sacred books; perhaps about 400 B.C.

Second Zacharia

Second Zacharia is thought to have been written around 300 B.C., shortly after the death of Alexander the Great, and a number of its passages are familiar to us from their use in the Gospels and the Holy Week liturgy.

Chapter 9 begins with a description of how the Lord will afflict the enemies of Israel, and in verse 9 we find a prophecy which was fulfilled to the letter on Palm Sunday. "Rejoice heartily, O daughter of Sion . . . See, your king shall come to you; a just savior he is, meek, and riding on an ass, on a colt, the foal of an ass." We had always been familiar with the story of the Lord riding on the ass and thought it a kind of clue to identify Him as the Messiah, but we had not realized that the ass itself was a symbol of Peace. This meek and lowly One was being identified as the King of Peace, as Zacharia makes clear in the lines that follow. "He shall banish the chariot from Ephraim, and the horse from Jerusalem; the warrior's bow shall be banished and he shall proclaim peace to the nations." (9:10) Riding on a horse was often used as a symbol of War.

In the mysterious allegory of the shepherds (11:4-17), there is the ominous appearance of thirty pieces of silver. " 'If it seems good to you, give me my wages; but if not, let it go.' And they counted out my wages, thirty pieces of silver. But the Lord said to me, 'Throw it in the treasury, the handsome price at which they valued me.' So I took the thirty pieces of silver and threw them into the treasury in the house of the Lord." (12-13) And long after a false shepherd betrayed the Good Shepherd for the same handsome price. (Matt 26:16; 27:3-10)

The language of Second Zacharia is strange and obscure, in fact St. Jerome called it the most mysterious book in the Bible. It is filled with messianic references, but these are illumined only now and then by sudden shafts of light. It is not particularly well suited for reading to children, yet it seems a shame not to pause over some of its images.

The frequent use of "On that day" implies some future messianic day, and we think of Peter and the rock when we read, "On that day I will make Jerusalem a weighty stone for all peoples . . ." (12:3) Here is a beautiful image of the sacrament of Penance: "On that day there shall be open to the house of David and to the inhabitants of Jerusalem, a fountain to purify from sin and uncleanness." (13:1) But the people of God are not to forget the price of the victory: "I will pour out on the house of David and on the inhabitants of Jerusalem a spirit of grace and petition; and they shall look on him whom they have thrust through, and they shall mourn for him as one mourns for an only son, and they shall grieve over him as one grieves over a first-born." (12:10) St. John reminds us of this in his Gospel on the Passion: ". . . and again, in another place Scripture says: 'They shall look at him whom they pierced.' " (John 19:37) From the Song of the Sword, Our Lord Himself chose this line to refer to His abandonment by the apostles at the time of His trial. "Strike the shepherd that the sheep may be dispersed." (13:7b; Mark 14:27)

The last chapter is the mighty battle between good and evil in which the enemy is the prince of darkness, and Jerusalem is the great and victorious figure of Christ.

THE STORY BOOKS

The Book of Ruth

The book of Ruth might be read with several different emphases— as a tale of the beautiful relationship between a mother-in-law and daughter-in-law; as the story of a charmingly arranged marriage; as a vignette showing domestic life and customs in the times of the Judges; or with the emphasis on its relation to the story of salvation which, of course, is where it ought to be. And when we read the book of Ruth and search for its relation to the history of salvation it becomes, as you shall see, a tale of suspense. The story is short (only four chapters), presents no problem when read, and the one or two customs which need explanation are easily dealt with.

Noemi, an Israelite, migrated with her husband Elimelech and their two sons to the land of the Moabites during a time of famine in Bethlehem of Juda. There the two sons of the pair married Moabite women, Ruth and Orpha, and there in time all three men died, leaving the women widows. Since the two younger women were Moabites, Noemi fondly bade them farewell with the suggestion that they return to the homes of their people and there find new husbands and bear children. One of them, Orpha, regretfully went back to her kindred, but Ruth would not go.

"Do not ask me to abandon or forsake you! for wherever you go I will go, wherever you lodge I will lodge, your people shall be my people and your God my God," (Ruth 1:16) said Ruth to

Noemi, and she returned to Bethlehem-Juda with her mother-in-law.

Ruth and Booz

Now there lived in the city of Bethlehem a man named Booz, a relative of Elimelech, and it was to his fields that Ruth went to glean. The law of Moses had made provision in this way for the poor and the widowed, that they might be permitted to glean in the fields at harvest time. So industriously did Ruth glean all the day that Booz took notice of her when he went to inspect his field, and discovering from his servants that she was a Moabite girl who lived with Noemi, he gave instructions that not only should food and water be given to Ruth at mealtime but also that the reapers drop extra barley on purpose that she might glean plentifully. Even more, he spoke to Ruth and encouraged her to do these things.

In the evening when Ruth returned to Noemi with a bushel of grain, the older woman asked where she had gleaned and when she learned that it was in the field of Booz, she revealed to Ruth that the man was a kinsman. Now Noemi saw how this situation might be exploited nicely to assure a life of happiness and bounty for her beloved daughter-in-law. She counseled her to deck herself in her finest clothes, to go to the threshing floor where Booz would be working and to wait until he had finished, had eaten and drunk and had lain down to sleep. Then Ruth was to creep near him and lie down at his feet, drawing his mantle over her.

When darkness had come and all the threshers had gone to sleep, this is what Ruth did, and when Booz awakened in the night he was startled to discover a woman sleeping at his feet. Ruth revealed her identity and asked Booz to spread his cloak over her—in other words, give her the protection by marriage rightfully due from the next of kin. This idea was most attractive to Booz, who had already admired the young woman for her industry and her charm. But, he said, there was one nearer of kin than he who had prior right to wed Ruth. If this man would forego his right, Booz would be happy to take such a virtuous woman for his wife.

The next morning Booz went to the city gates, the place where business was transacted, and there finding the relative in question detained him before ten elders of the city for witnesses and asked if he would like to buy the land belonging to the late Elimelech; his widow Noemi had put it up for sale. Indeed, said the man, he would like to buy the land. Well then, continued Booz, he would have to marry the widow Ruth also so she might have children who could inherit in the name of Noemi's son, her late husband. This he could not afford to do, said the relative, meaning that if he were to buy the land it would be for his own sons' inheritance. He made a suggestion: why did not Booz put in a claim in his stead, buy the land and marry the woman?

Which was exactly what Booz wanted, and the transaction was sworn to in the accustomed manner: the next of kin renounced all right of possession by taking off his sandal (the foot was the symbol of possession, as the head was the symbol of authority) and handing it to Booz in front of the elders.

Thus it came about that Booz acquired Ruth and the land of the widow Noemi. To Ruth and Booz was born a son whom they named Obed and whom Noemi took to her heart as if it were her own.

Where is the suspense?

Verse 17 at the end of the tale reveals to us the significance of this little history.

"They called him Obed. He was the father of Jesse, the father of David."

Now we see why the Jews have always had such great love for Ruth, antecedent to their beloved David. She was a grandmother to the Lord, gracious, humble, obedient, a charming servant of God. We take great pride in her too, for still another reason—like us, she was a gentile and a convert, grafted onto the stock of the One true God.

There is in this book a detail which is especially dear to us, a greeting that is used often in the Mass of the Latin rite. When Booz came from Bethlehem to inspect his fields, he greeted his harvesters with, "The Lord be with you!" No wonder it is said that this book forecasts the calling of the gentiles.

Now about the two points that need explaining. Among the Israelites there were various ways in which the rights of the widowed and the hapless were protected for them by their kin. The claim made by Ruth in this story rests on the principle of *Goel*—the right of a relative to ask a near of kin to redeem his possessions and, in the case of a widow, to marry her in order that the first male descendent might take the late father's name and inherit his possessions. The "levirate" marriage was still another kind, involving the brother of the deceased husband and his obligation to marry the widow and beget a male heir to perpetuate his brother's name and line.

Our Lord's family tree is not complete without the lovely gentile, Ruth.

The Book of Tobias

Tobias is a family book, short and easily read. It tells of a father, mother, son and his bride, of their trials, fidelity and final perseverance under the watchful eye of God. There are action, suspense, color and many delightful details, together with noble instructions on virtue—all of it making enjoyable reading for both parents and children. Tobias is a book we might read on the feast of the Holy Family, the feast of St. Raphael, with the anticipation of an engagement or wedding, or at times when faith is tried and afflictions press heavily. But the book of Tobias does not need an excuse to be read; its riches merit reading at any time.

At the beginning of the book there is a flashback to the boyhood of the elder Tobias, praising him for his fidelity at a time when his fellow Galileans were worshiping before the golden calves set up when Jeroboam I ruled in Israel. Shunning their company, Tobias had remained true to God, made his pilgrimages to Jerusalem at the customary times, paid his tithes and faithfully offered his first fruits. "By such acts as these he showed, even in boyhood, what loyalty he had for the law of God," (Tob 1:8 Knox) says the text, and it shows us that the challenges to the young have always been the same; one must ever choose whether or not to follow the crowd and worship at the popular shrines.

In his manhood Tobias married Anna, a woman of his own tribe, and to them God sent a son whom they named Tobias also. From his infancy they taught him "to fear God and keep clear of every fault." (1:8 Knox)

Tobias in Ninive

But in time Tobias and his family were taken captive during the reign of the Assyrian king Salmanasar and carried off to Ninive, and here again Tobias kept the faith. God rewarded him and Tobias became the confidante of the king who, in turn, permitted him the freedom to go wherever he wished and serve his brethren in captivity as he would. On one such journey, Tobias found a kinsman in dire distress and he loaned the man ten silver talents in return for his bond.

With the death of the king and the ascendancy of his Jew-hating son to the throne, Tobias fell into disfavor for his works of mercy and he was despoiled of all his possessions and sent away with his wife and son. And when, on the death of this king, Tobias once more returned to his good works in the name of the Lord, his friends admonished him for imprudence. "Here was sentence of death passed on thee for such doings of thine; from that sentence thou wast barely reprieved, and art thou back at thy grave-digging?" (2:7-8 Knox) But Tobias feared God more than the king and continued to hide the bodies of the slain in his house until he could bury them.

The history of Tobias is a lesson for the family, teaching them that holiness is not an accident or a matter of temperament but a matter of the will co-operating with God. Our children learn in their catechism lessons on the Holy Spirit that such co-operation bears fruit in the soul, twelve fruits in fact—charity, patience, kindness, goodness, joy, peace, long-suffering, mildness, faith, modesty, continency, and chastity—and the lesson is beautifully illustrated in Tobias. Even though he belongs in the Old Testament, the Holy Spirit was present with God's people in those times also, working in the souls of the just and speaking to them through the Law and the prophets. One of the purposes of the book of Tobias was to teach its readers this very thing.

Tobias is Afflicted

Now it happened that one day Tobias came home weary from burying the dead and he fell asleep in the shade by a wall. As he was sleeping warm droppings from a swallow's nest fell in his eyes and blinded him. Even as he had revered God from his infancy and kept His commands, now Tobias did not let misfortune turn his heart from God but continued to thank Him daily for the gift of life, and when his friends taunted him about his good works and their poor reward, he rebuked them and said that "God has life waiting for us if we will but keep faith in Him," (2:18 Knox) words which would be fulfilled with the coming of Christ. Alas, even Anna complained bitterly. We may sympathize with her because now she had to support them both, but it is too bad that her despair finally drove Tobias to the very edge of hopelessness. Weeping, he accepted his sufferings as just punishment for his sins, and piteously asked the Lord to let him die.

The Maiden Sara

On the same day, in the city of Rages, a maiden named Sara also went on her knees before God, weeping, and asked Him to deliver her from her trials. Seven times Sara had been affianced and seven times her bridegrooms had gone to her bridal chamber only to be slain by a devil called Asmodeus. Accused of murdering them herself, Sara begged God to rid her of suspicion or take her from the earth. Her prayer is a model of trust and deserves to be read by all young women so they will never forget that husbands are God's concern as well as their own. Sara's prayer should be part of every Christian doctrine class on Christian love and marriage.

"Thou, Lord, canst bear me witness that I lusted never after man; still have I guarded my soul from shameful desire, nor kept company with the wanton, nor cast in my lot with the lovers of dalliance. If I consented to take a husband, law of thine was my rule, not lust of mine. It seems I was unworthy of these men's love, or perhaps they of mine; it may be thou wast reserving me for another husband; thy designs are beyond our human reach . . ." But with perseverance and trust, "thou grantest clear weather again; tears and sighs are over, and thou fillest the cup with rejoicing; blessed be thy name . . ." (3:13-23 Knox) No wonder Sara is presented to our brides in the Nuptial Mass as a model of virtue.

That same day the prayers of both Tobias and Sara reached heaven, and the Lord heard them and sent His angel Raphael "to heal them both." (Tob 3:25)

Tobias and His Son

Now Tobias, thinking he was about to die, called his son in order to counsel him, and here we have a model of paternal instruction—the law of God summed up by the life as well as the words of a father who, obedient himself, could justifiably enjoin his son to obedience.

Next, Tobias explained to his son that they were in great need, therefore he was to take the bond of his friend Gabelus of Rages, hire a suitable companion and go to the city to ask for the money back. Going out to search for a companion, young Tobias found a strange youth beside the door, dressed for a journey, and discovering that he also was bound for Rages to visit Gabelus, he introduced him to his father. Neither of them knew that this was Raphael, the angel of the Lord.

The Angel Raphael

In this episode a completely unimportant detail might present a difficulty for scrupulous children, so perhaps a word of warning is necessary. When the angel answers the elder Tobias' inquiry about his identity with, "My name is Azarias and a man of renown, Ananias, was my father," (5:18 Knox) does the angel lie? Hardly. This is simply the traditional device of the mysterious stranger who must disguise Himself until the moment comes for His identity to be revealed. Even our Lord did this. He did not use another name but He kept His identity from the companions on the road to Emmaus until the breaking of the bread because it served the Divine purpose. It is the same with Raphael and his story as told us by the writer of Tobias. It did not serve God's purpose that he be known at this time, so a disguise was necessary.

More important is the personification of the angel, which gives us one of the principal sources of our knowledge of angels. In Tobias' adventure with Raphael the attributes of the angels are set forth in a way that helps us to discard for good all notions that angels are cute, pretty, coy or comic. Raphael is friend, companion, protector, a figure of strength and wisdom. Given bodily form for this task, he displays an angelic prescience and agility which allow us to observe something of the superhuman powers of these marvelous spirits. When the elder Tobias assured his weeping wife that their son would be back, for "the angel of God goes with him," there was more truth in his words than he ever dreamed.

The Journey

Tobias started out with his new friend at his side and his little dog frisking at their heels. They did not stop until they reached a river. Going down to wash his feet, Tobias saw a huge fish swim up as though to attack him and, calling out in fear to his companion, he was bade to catch it by the gills, bring it up on the sand and disembowel it, keeping the heart, liver and gall for remedies.

The angel now informed Tobias that they were approaching the house of Raguel, a kinsman, and there he should ask for the hand of his daughter Sara in marriage. But Tobias had heard of Sara and the seven dead husbands, and he demurred saying that if he too were slain by the demon, his parents would indeed be given a "cheerless passage to the grave." (Tob 6:15) Whereupon Raphael explained the seven mysterious deaths, and just as Sara's prayer should make our daughters mindful of the proper role of human love in marriage, so the angel in this passage speaks not only to young Tobias but to our own sons.

"Heed me well, and thou shalt hear why the fiend has power to hurt some and not others. The fiend has power over such as go about their mating with all thought of God shut out of their hearts and minds, wholly intent on their lust, as if they were horse or mule, brutes without reason. Not such be thy mating . . . take the maid to thyself with the fear of the Lord upon thee, moved rather by the hope of begetting children than by any lust of thine. So in the true line of Abraham, thou shalt have joy in thy fatherhood." (6:16-22 Knox)

And when finally Raphael convinced the father of Sara that no harm would come to Tobias, Raguel rejoiced. "Why then, all those prayers and sighs of mine were not wasted; God has granted them audience, and I doubt not his design in bringing you here . . ." (7:13-14 Knox) How important for the parents as well as for the romantic young to learn this lesson of confidence in God. With confidence in God, parents can desist from pushing their children prematurely into romantic situations, while the young can wait in peace until they are ready for marriage and the right spouse comes along.

Still unfinished was the mission to Gabelus to recover his father's money. Apologizing to the angel for asking yet another favor, Tobias begged his help again, and soon Raphael returned with Gabelus and the money. Joy and feasting followed, with a prophetic blessing by Gabelus which asked that "the name of this thy bride, the names of her parents and thine, be used for an example of blessedness!" (9:10 Knox)

Tobias Returns Home

Finally, to the joy of his parents, Tobias returned home and after giving thanks to God for his journey took out the fish's gall at the angel's instruction and rubbed it on his father's eyes. And the old man's sight was restored. Cried old Tobias: "I thank thee, Lord God of Israel, from thee my chastisement, from thee my deliverance came; I thank thee for eyes that see, and eyes that see Tobias my son!" (11:17 Knox) Before the journey he had said to his son: "Praise God all the while, and ask him to guide thy paths aright; let all thy designs repose in Him." (4:20 Knox) The instruction without the older man's example would not be half so eloquent.

Now Tobias would pay the angel, and in summing up his services we see the numberless ways in which we are aided and assisted by our angels. It was when he tried to press reward on his companion that the angel revealed his identity. He explained that when the elder Tobias had prayed and wept as he hid the dead in his house, it was he, Raphael, who had offered his prayer to the Lord. For his works of mercy, Tobias had won favor with God, but it was necessary to test him with suffering until, for his healing, and for the deliverance of Sara, this same angel was chosen to be God's messenger. "I am Raphael, and my place is among those seven who stand in the presence of the Lord." (12:15 Knox) Then the angel disappeared from their sight and Tobias and his son fell to their faces to give thanks to God. The canticle of Tobias which follows in 13:1-10, is beautifully suited to family prayer.

Tobias the elder lived to be an old man and to see his children's children, as did his son. So fruitful was his life in the service of the Lord that "with joy they buried him," (14:16 Douay) a detail not to be overlooked in the story of a family that loved God with all their hearts.

Is the book of Tobias a literal history or a piece of fiction contrived for the instruction and encouragement of the people of God? Both opinions are held. Whichever it is, the book is inspired and its message is invaluable. We find Our Lord in the New Testament reckoning the value of a life such as Tobias': "Not everyone who says to me, 'Lord, Lord,' shall enter the kingdom of heaven; but he who does the will of my Father in heaven shall enter the kingdom of heaven." (Matt 7:21)

The Book of Judith

The book of Judith is one of the most exciting books of the Old Testament. This is hardly the best reason for reading it but there are times when it seems to be *the* reason to read it, especially in a family with older children whose preoccupation with things vital to them—like old cars and new hairdos—inevitably cuts into the time they feel can be allowed for pondering the sacred truths. That this is so disturbs many parents, and rightly. Therefore we propose that such parents might suggest the book of Judith as the principal part of night prayers some evening, or for several evenings, and see if it doesn't present an important challenge to the young in brand new terms.

Judith teaches the lesson of faith in action, and she gives us an example of prudence, the virtue that is mistress of action.

We have said before that it is necessary to judge the actors and events of the Old Testament within the frame of their own time and moral code and this is especially important when reading Judith, since her final action is the murder of Holofernes. Otherwise our young, who have learned in religion class that prudence has to do with the right choice of means as well as action, may be quite scandalized to see that she lied, deliberately put herself into an occasion of sin for Holofernes and danger for herself, and climaxed the affair with a deed which frankly breaks a commandment. This is how Judith looks if viewed from our side of the New Testament.

But if we consider her story in the setting of God's plan for redemption, we see differently. In the first place, this story is set during a period something like the days of our own Wild West when people lived hard and often seemed oblivious of the delicate details of the moral code. Secondly, the people of God were seriously threatened with death either from parching thirst or by the sword that had been promised first to the dwellers of Bethulia and eventually to all the Israelites. Holofernes was not the first of a long line of villains to present themselves throughout the history of God's people in an attempt to wipe them out and frustrate once and for all the promise of salvation. Not that Holofernes really understood that this was the issue; but the devil did, and it has ever been thus with him—from his attack in the Garden of Paradise to his challenge in world communism. In spite of his variety of names and disguises, he is always the same enemy.

Judith is praised by the writers of scripture, the Fathers of the Church, the saints in their spiritual writings, for her desire to save her people. "Thou hast done manfully, and thy heart hath been strengthened. The hand of the Lord hath strengthened thee, and therefore thou shalt be blessed forever." (Jdt 15:11; used in the Mass of St. Joan) And she is held up to us as a type of Our Lady standing forever between her people and the threat of destruction.

Now to her story. As usual, the text contains passages which can be eliminated or summed up quickly in a few words.

Nabuchodonosor had conquered much of the eastern world and had sent out demands for aid among the peoples of the west— to Carmel and Cedar and Samaria and all the peoples beyond the Jordan as far as Jerusalem. Their refusal to submit angered him, and he vowed to take vengeance. He summoned his chieftains and unfolded a plan to bring them all under his domination. Holofernes, commander-in-chief, was to make war on the western kingdoms and show no mercy to their inhabitants, capturing and razing cities as he went. (The description of his army and campaign in chapters 2 and 3 is especially interesting to boys.)

The Israelites Resist Holofernes

Word of this campaign struck fear into the provinces and many who had resisted once sent word that they would rather be slaves than slain (known currently as "rather be red than dead"); many, but not all. The Israelites, fearful lest they and Jerusalem be destroyed, announced throughout their land that the mountain heights were to be occupied, the villages put in a state of defense; and that provisions were to be stored for a campaign. At the bidding of the high priest, Eliachim, they offered sacrifice, did penance, fasted and prayed to the Lord for deliverance.

When the news of their resistance reached Holofernes, he was enraged. What people were these to refuse him entry as had their neighbors? In answer, Achior, a chief of the Ammonites, told him the history of the people of God. They were a people, he said, who worshiped one God and this God had taken marvelous care of them. Tracing their beginning from the time Abraham came out of Chaldea, Achior told him of their life in Egypt, their enslavement, their release; and pointed out that as long as they were faithful to this God He was with them and they flourished and were victorious. But let them displease Him with sin and this God "that is the enemy of all wrong" (Jdt 5:22 Knox) would abandon them to defeat and loss and let them be borne away as slaves by their conquerors. Said Achior to Holofernes: "Assure thyself; has any guilt of theirs lost them the favour of their God? Then indeed march against them . . . but if fault he has none to find with them, then meet them in battle we may not for he will be their defender and ours the plight for all the world to mock . . ." (5:24-25 Knox)

Holofernes flew into a fury. How dare men worship any god but Nabuchodonosor? Or Achior insinuate that anyone might defeat his armies? To punish him, Holofernes had Achior taken within sight of the mountain town of Bethulia, tied to a tree and left there to be captured by the Israelites and later slain with them. But when the Bethulians found him there, they took him back to the town and hearing his testimony they praised him for his faith in their God, and promised him freedom to live and worship among them.

Holofernes next ordered his troops to march on Bethulia, but when they came upon the springs which fed the town, they cut off the water supply instead and by the end of twenty days its inhabitants were down to meager daily rations. Seeing no deliverance at hand, the Israelites turned to Ozias, their chief, and cried out to surrender rather than die, or if death then quick death by the sword rather than the lingering agony of thirst. Ozias wept and promised that if in five days the Lord did not intervene, they would surrender.

Judith Intervenes

Now comes Judith. It is intriguing to notice the difference between Judith and Esther, another of the great women of the Old Testament about whom we will read next. Both were women of great holiness, but the former—so mature, so strong, so daring —is a striking contrast to the latter—so young, so passive, so timid. We see how marvelously the Lord can work wonders with all kinds of people. The same contrasts are found among the modern saints—for example, St. Margaret Mary, fearful to carry out Our Lord's instructions, and St. Joan, full of courage and daring.

After hearing the declaration of Ozias, Judith summoned two of the elders to her house. "By what right . . . do you put the Lord's goodness to such a test? . . . What, would you set a date to the Lord's mercies, bid him keep tryst with you on a day of your own appointing?" (8:11-13 Knox) And she rebuked them for their little faith, recalling how the Lord tested Abraham, Isaac, Jacob and Moses before them. Her words are good counsel for the family as well as the elders of Bethulia, in times of crisis when endurance runs low and faith needs to be strengthened. Hardly had Judith finished chiding the elders for their fearfulness than she proposed a plan. What it was, she would not reveal, but she exhorted them to pray for her and wait—the Lord would bring Israel relief.

Then Judith returned home, donned sackcloth and ashes and beseeched the Lord to have mercy on His people. When her prayer was done, she put aside these garments and bathed, anointed herself with the finest myrrh, parted and tied her hair, put on the raiment of "happier days," her sandals, bracelet, necklace, ear-ring and finger ring, and the Lord Himself "lent grace to her mien. Manly resolve, not woman's wantonness, was the occasion of her finery and he would enhance her beauty till all beholders should vow there was never woman so fair." (10:4 Knox) She took a bottle of wine, a phial of oil, parched corn, dry figs, bread and cheese, and she and her maidservant set forth on their journey.

Judith Triumphs over Holofernes

Taking herself to the camp of the enemy, Judith passed herself off as a Hebrew woman who had slipped past the sentries in an effort to escape the doom that lay ahead for the city, and when the soldiers took her to their commander all marveled at her great beauty. The story of her sojourn in the enemy camp and her slaying of Holofernes is exciting and colorful and the great triumph at the end when she produces the head of the warrior chieftain for her own people is an unforgettable scene.

The story of Judith is one of risk and danger, bravery and daring, set down in dramatic colors and with its many lessons clearly drawn, but the lesson of prudence is especially appropriate for our times. Judith teaches our young that there is a third dimension to their life in Christ: after prayer and study, there is action.

Judith and the Virtue of Prudence

Before we explore this point, it would be wise for the family to refer to the virtue of prudence as it is treated in the catechism and religious texts. "Prudence disposes us in all circumstances to form right judgments about what we must do or not do."

Because it is sometimes prudent to wait before acting, somehow prudence has almost come to mean inaction, hesitation, overcautiousness, and it seems the last of the virtues to have anything to offer our high-spirited young. This is doubly unfortunate since prudence is the virtue upon which all Catholic action depends, and since it is into action for Christ that the energies of our young people need to be channeled.

How is Judith an example of prudence?

First, we know that prudent action depends upon the existence of the other three moral virtues—fortitude, temperance and justice; and all these virtues are to be found in Judith.

Unquestioningly, she possessed the virtue fortitude, as her story more than amply demonstrates.

Temperance? Remaining unmarried after her widowhood, Judith lived ascetically with her serving maids, "a woman of high repute, the Lord's devout worshiper; no man had a word to say in her dispraise." (8:8 Knox)

Justice? Judith kept none of the spoils of her victory when she returned but celebrated, rather, by freeing the bondmaiden who had accompanied her.

In chapter 9, Judith's prayer before her journey reveals the passion of her love for God and her people, her motive for the deed she planned and the means she would use. "Lift thy hand, as it was lifted up long ago; break power of theirs with power of thine! Helpless may they lie beneath thy vengeance who now think to profane thy holy place, dishonour the very shrine of thy name, violate, at the sword's point, the sanctity of thy altar . . ." (9:11 Knox)

Admittedly she put her life and virtue in danger, but for what cause? "The sword of Holofernes! Lord, if it might be his own pride's undoing! Be the eyes he casts on me a lure to catch himself, the professions of love I make, his death blow! . . . bethink thee, Lord, of thy covenant; grant my lips utterance, my heart firm resolve; so shall thy temple ever remain inviolate, so shall all the Gentiles learn that thou art God, and has none to rival thee." (2:12-19 Knox)

Judith begs not only for her own people but for the enlightenment of the gentiles as well, though she could hardly have understood that her words would one day mean that gentile and Jew alike would be united in Christ.

But prudence is the virtue of action and it is her bold action that crowns Judith's deliberation and decision. Her chiding of the elders reminds us that too often we think of solutions in terms of novenas and miracles—much as they did. "The Lord helps those who help themselves" might be applied to Judith who, with prayer, deliberation and then action helped not only herself but all her people.

The Family, the Christian Vocation and Prudence

The Christian vocation is to work with Christ to the end that all men will come to Him and be united to Him, living His life. It calls for creative action at every level and in every encounter, sometimes daring action, sometimes quiet action, sometimes a waiting action; and for making Christ present in society in order that He may act creatively from within us.

A family discussion after reading the book of Judith might have to do with areas within the family's influence where creative action is needed. As one example, both creative thinking and daring action is needed in order to re-form the social life of young people into wholesome patterns. Parents are needed who will see that the emphasis during the years meant for study and growing up should be on friendship, not romance, on group activities of service to the parish or community, giving the young opportunities to become acquainted in situations which reveal talents and attitudes far more suitable to marriage and homemaking than can be revealed in the highly artificial atmosphere of the dating situation. Young people are needed who are able to resist the panic of the going-steady fever, and who will set examples in self-discipline which others, unequipped to be leaders, will be eager to follow. Christ has bound Himself and His action in our society to His presence in us. If we would have Christ act upon such problems as these, we must search out His will by prayer and deliberation and then, guided by prudence, fit our action to His will.

Is the story of Judith history or fiction? Again, both opinions are held but like others of these story books, it is an inspired writing and has its place among the sacred books because God means us to hear it and learn.

The Book of Esther

The book of Esther is an exciting story with all the elements of the most enchanting of fairy tales: a king, a beautiful queen, a watchful uncle, a villain, a plot and in the end a triumph. Its setting is Persia in the lush palace of an Oriental ruler who is said to be the Xerxes of the history books, and its time is approximately four hundred and eighty years before Christ. It is the tale of a lovely queen who risked her life for her people and who gives us a model of humility, faith and courage. The Jewish celebration of Esther's triumph is called the feast of Purim and occurs about mid-Lent. It dates from the time of Esther and was one of the liturgical feasts celebrated by Our Lord, Our Lady and St. Joseph.

But there is another reason why we love this book, long after we have put aside the child's delight in the triumph of a queen over a villain: Esther is a type of Our Lady. We see Our Lady in this story as from a distance, letting the precise details of the royal favorite in the harem fade away and seeing instead the grandeur of Mary's role as the queen who intercedes for her people. Many parallels are suggested. "I will put enmity between you and the woman . . ." (Gen 3:15) Aman's plot to destroy God's people recalls the ambition of Satan. Assuerus' words to Esther as she

approached him unbidden and fearful in the throne room are used
in the Mass for the feast of Our Lady of Lourdes. "Thou shalt not
die: for this law is not made for thee, but for all the others." (Est
15:13)

These types of Mary to be found in the Old Testament are
not, as we might expect, beyond the comprehension of children.
I remember long ago, when we were reading the book of Esther
for the feast of Purim, hearing Christopher at five remark: "Esther
is like Our Lady because she is a queen too, but the king isn't like
Our Lord." We were delighted, and reminded ourselves that rarely
do we give children credit for their great perception.

The story of Esther is set down twice in the Catholic edition
of the Bible—first according to the Hebrew version of ten chapters;
then in the Greek version of six chapters, both of which were
translated into Latin by St. Jerome and put in this order. Although
each contains identical material there are details in the Greek
version which are not found in the Hebrew—among them the
beautiful prayers—and here alone is the name of God mentioned.
So we have tried to incorporate the riches of both translations in
our reading. The following order of reading is for the full sixteen
chapters:

> *Est* 11:2-12; 12
> 1; 2; 3:1-13
> 13:1-7
> 4:1-8
> 15:1-3
> 4:9-17
> 13:8-18
> 14
> 5:1-2
> 15:4-19
> 5:3-14; 6; 7; 8:1-12
> 16
> 8:13-17; 9; 10

Mordecai's Dream

To begin in the right order we must first turn to chapters 11
and 12. Mordecai, a Jew of the tribe of Benjamin, descended from
those carried off to Babylon and exile, has a prophetic dream which

he does not understand. Two dragons rise up to battle, an innocent nation is about to be oppressed, their prayers to the Lord are heard and they triumph over the tyrants. The story proceeds with an account of how Mordecai betrays the plot of two eunuchs who plan to murder the king and has his name recorded in the royal archives. Next appears Aman, the archvillain who apparently thwarts the king's wishes to have Mordecai rewarded, and begins to nurse a grudge against him and his nation for bringing the chamberlains to their death.

Chapter 1 opens with a marvelous display of pomp. King Assuerus has held a high feast for the lords of his realm in order to show off his wealth and power. The scene has all the splendor of an ancient Persian painting. Canopies of white and green and blue, held with cords of fine linen and purple thread, hang from ivory rings fastened to marble columns; couches of gold and silver rest on floors of malachite and marble; golden cups and vessels hold wine and delicacies; and in the women's quarter Queen Vashti entertains equally splendidly for the ladies.

On the seventh day the king commands Queen Vashti to adorn herself with the royal crown and display her beauty before his guests but she refuses. In a rage, he deposes her and bids maidens be brought from all over the land in order that a new queen might be chosen, warning the wives of the land not to imitate the rebellious Vashti for "a man should be lord and master in his own house, and the whole world must take note of it." (Est 1:22 Knox)

Esther at Court

In this wise, we meet Esther—niece of Mordecai, orphaned as a child and tenderly cherished by her devout uncle. Far and above the most beautiful of all, Esther is made queen and Mordecai takes up residence outside her house in order to watch over her, counseling her to make no mention of her religion or race.

Verses 12-14 in chapter 2 might be omitted for family reading since they treat of the manner in which the concubines visit the king's bedchamber. Once again, if necessary, we can explain polygamy as an ancient Oriental custom tolerated under the Old Law; the king and the maidens were in good faith.

With chapter 3 there begin lessons in courage, fidelity and

trust which parents can use often in the family as they strive to instill these virtues in their children. Mordecai and Esther are inspiring figures to be added to the family's collection of saints and heroes.

It was when the king granted high rank to Aman and gave him precedence over all the nobles of the land that Aman decreed all should bow their knees to reverence him. All but Mordecai obeyed. His refusal is explained in 13:12-15, in his prayer to the Lord. "Thou knowest, who knowest all things, that if I refused proud Aman yonder my greeting, it was no pride of mine, no scorn, no ambition of mine that moved me. For Israel's sake, willingly would I kiss his feet, did not fear withhold me from giving man that reverence which is God's due . . ." His steadfastness is an example as necessary for us as for the ancient Jews.

Now Aman filled with hatred and determined to slay not only Mordecai but all his nation. Carefully deceiving the king, he obtained permission to dispose of them as he pleased, and 13:1-7 reproduces the king's letter pronouncing their doom. The day and the month of their extermination was chosen by lot—and *pur*, the Persian word for *lot* may be the root of the word *Purim*.

When Mordecai heard this, so great was his grief that he tore his garments, put on sackcloth and ashes, and made his way to the gates of the palace to attract the attention of Esther. When the queen heard that her uncle was dressed in this way, she sent a servant with a new garment but Mordecai refused the gift and reported the events of the day to the chamberlain, sending him back to the queen with the message that she was to go before the king to intercede for her people.

But to enter the presence of the king unbidden was to die— unless he held out his golden sceptre in pardon. The queen demurred. She had not been summoned to the king in thirty days. How dare she venture in?

Mordecai somewhat wryly warned Esther not to flatter herself that the royal court would shelter her from the massacre. "Who knows, but thou hast reached the throne only to be ready for such an opportunity as this?" (4:14 Knox) A neater lesson in the way we are manipulated by divine providence is hardly to be found anywhere.

And this decided her. She sent a message bidding Mordecai and all the Jews of the city to fast and pray for three days and three nights and at the end of that time she would risk her life before the king. Mordecai's prayer in 13:8-18 is noble and beautiful, and Esther's prayer in chapter 14 is a magnificent revelation of longing and fidelity crying out with the same anguish as all victims of injustice.

The third day came and Esther, clad most beautifully, approached the throne. The scene is described in rich detail in 15:4-19, and provides us with the lines used on the feast of Our Lady of Lourdes. Far from angry, the king extended his sceptre and offered his beloved queen whatever her heart desired, even to half his kingdom. But all she would have was the king's company and Aman's, at a banquet she had prepared for them. Having dined, again the king asked Esther her wishes and again she asked that he and Aman return the following night to dine.

Aman Undone

Aman, returning home, was puffed with pride until he passed Mordecai at the palace gates and saw that he "would not rise nor stir from his post." (5:9) Infuriated, Aman recounted the insult to his family and friends. Was he not the most honored noble of the kingdom? The wealthiest? All agreed. He was. Was not he alone of all the nobles invited to dine with the king and the queen? He alone. Should this make him happy? All seemed to think it should. He raged. It did not. Not when he saw Mordecai sit by the palace gate and refuse to bow to him. His wife and friends suggested that Aman have a gibbet built in his own yard upon which to hang Mordecai on the morrow, and *then* he could dine with the king and queen "light-hearted enough." And this counsel Aman liked well.

We might remember for just a moment that the same evil spirit that was in Aman tempted another man, a Jew, another time: ". . . if thou wilt worship before me, the whole [world] shall be thine." (Luke 4:7)

Now the king could not sleep that night so he had the annals of his reign brought to be read aloud and he heard again of the loyalty of Mordecai when he betrayed the murderous plot of the two chamberlains. Had this man been rewarded? he asked. No, he had not, was the reply. Then a reward was due. How to reward him?

At that very moment Aman entered to ask permission for the hanging of Mordecai but the king interrupted him. Could Aman advise him on how to honor one of his subjects? Aman reflected that at last the king was going to do him honor. He must suggest truly remarkable honors. He would advise the king, said Aman, to clothe the man in the king's clothes, let him wear the king's crown, give him the king's horse to ride upon and let the next highest noble in the kingdom lead him through the streets of the city crying out that here was a man the king honored.

First rate, said the king. "Lose no time doing all this for Mordecai!" Aman was confounded. And he received no comfort from his wife and friends but on the contrary was reminded that Mordecai was a *Jew*—"thou wilt never get the better of him." (6:13) Even the pagans were convinced that the Jews enjoyed a special divine protection.

The Triumph of Esther and Mordecai

Again the king and Aman dined with the queen, and again the king asked Esther her wish. This time she revealed it. She would have the king spare her life and the lives of her people. There was one in the kingdom, said Esther, who plotted against the very life of the queen. The king was astonished: who was this man? And triumphantly Esther pointed to Aman.

The gallows built for Mordecai were used for the hanging of Aman and to Mordecai went Aman's house together with honor and riches. An edict gave the Jews permission to defend themselves on the day set for the pogrom and in time they resisted and triumphed over their attackers.

The Lord is with us as He has always been with His people: this is one of the messages of the book of Esther. For all those who live His life in the Mystical Body, Esther reminds us anew that but for Our Lady, we should not exist in Him.

The most appropriate time of the year for the family to read Esther is, of course, for the celebration of Purim. We might join our Jewish friends in their rejoicing that this gallant and beautiful queen interceded for His people, and celebrate as well the glorious intercession of Mary, Queen of all queens. Esther is an ideal story to act out, with puppets or charades, and when we see our children revel in the downfall of Aman and the triumph of Queen Esther,

we might remind them that for centuries Jewish children have
shouted and stamped their feet and clapped their hands over her
victory. Jesus probably did, too.

The Book of Jona

Together with Noe and the Ark and David and Goliath, the
story of Jona is one of the few Bible tales that almost every child
knows. Is it a true story? In the past it was considered to be true
and some still hold this opinion. More recent scholarship claims
it is an allegory. Whichever it is does not matter as it makes its
point either way—and its point never was to prove that a man
could live inside a fish.

The prophet Jona is first mentioned in IV Kings 14:25, when
he announces the expansion of the domain of Jeroboam II. It is
not until four hundred years later that he appears in his adventure
with the fish, turning his back on the Lord's command, swallowed
and coughed up, and in the end going to the city of Ninive to do
the Lord's bidding. To hold that the story is not history is not
to say that God could not make a man live inside a fish; not at
all. But the reasons for considering it a morality tale are so con-
clusive that in our family we like this opinion best.[1]

The point of the story of Jona is to instruct the Jews that
God is the God of all men, not just the Israelites, and that His
mercy extends to everyone. And its prophetical application was
made by Our Lord Himself when He cited Jona as a type of
Himself—for as Jona was in the belly of the fish for three days
and three nights, so Christ was in the tomb. (Matt 12:40; 16:4)

The book of Jona is one of the shortest books of the Bible
and in our family we have always saved it for reading Easter Sunday evening, as a kind of retelling of the glory of the Resurrection.
All during Holy Week, the Easter vigil, and the Easter Masses,
the solemn and beautiful language of the liturgy and scripture
have told us the mystery of Christ's death and resurrection. Now on
Sunday night after Easter egg hunts and baskets and even, perhaps,

[1] Stuhlmueller, *op. cit.*

too many chocolate eggs, there is a gaiety and giddiness in the air to which Jona is exactly suited. There comes, with the reading of Jona, a great sense of the divine joke God has played—but only the language of allegory suits this, else we seem to be irreverent and profane.

The little figure of Jona (which one of the boys made of papier-mâché) standing jubilantly with arms extended in *Alleluia!* beside his joyful fish (papier-mâché also) seems to shout. "You men, little and insignificant, rejoice! He has paid a great price for you. He has taken your nothingness and bought it with His own worth and you have become priceless. He has turned all His pain and yours into blessings. He has made tragedy into comedy and joy has come out of sorrow, life has come out of death. Rejoice, little children, for God loves you!"

It is a lovely joke—God loving man so much.

Jona's Adventure

Briefly, the story of Jona goes like this. When the Lord called Jona and bade him go to Ninive and warn the people that he was going to punish their wickedness, Jona was loathe to contaminate himself by contact with the Ninivites, a people whose city was considered by the Jews to be corruption incarnate, and he bought passage on a ship sailing in the opposite direction. No sooner had they set out to sea than the Lord sent a storm to punish Jona and he was forced to admit that the ship and its crew were in peril for his own fault. What to do? Jona himself, perceiving his guilt, bade the sailors to throw him in the sea, which they did, and there he was swallowed by the great fish. From the belly of the fish Jona prayed to the Lord most eloquently in words sublime with hope, and hearing them, the Lord bade the fish cast Jona on the beach.

A second time the Lord sent Jona to Ninive and this time he went, crying out all over the city, "Forty days more and Ninive shall be destroyed." (Jona 3:5) Hearing this the Ninivites, wicked gentiles that they were, believed the word of God and began to fast and pray, from the king down to the very beasts in the stables. And when the Lord saw their repentance, He had mercy on them and spared them. The forty days of fasting and prayer with the salvation of the Ninivites at the end of it is a type of our own Lent followed by Easter.

But Jona, alas, was upset. Not mercy but condemnation was what Jona wanted to see and he turned on the Lord accusingly. This was why he had run away in the first place, he said, because the Lord was too forgiving, because Jona foresaw His mercy to these undeserving sinners. Jona groaned: "Please take my life from me; for it is better for me to die than to live." (4:4) And the Lord asked reprovingly, "Have you reason to be angry?" Well He might; had He not just saved Jona from the belly of the fish?

Then Jona took himself outside the city and sat under a little hut he had made for himself, waiting there to see if doom would fall on Ninive. Now at God's bidding a gourd vine grew up and shaded the side of the hut and Jona was delighted.[2] But on the following day a worm gnawed at the root of the vine and it died, and when the sun and the hot wind came Jona became faint with the heat. Now he truly wanted to die and he cried out to the Lord, "I would be better off dead than alive." (4:8)

But God said to Jona: "Have you reason to be angry over the plant? . . . which cost you no labor and which you did not raise; it came up in one night and in one night it perished. And should I not be concerned over Ninive, the great city, in which there are more than a hundred and twenty thousand persons who cannot distinguish their right hand from their left? . . ." (4:9-11)

It is a brilliant little lesson for us all, accustomed as we are to accepting the Lord's mercy year in and year out as we sin and repent, sin and repent—yet are sometimes so slow to show mercy when others offend us.

The Book of Daniel

The book of Daniel presents us, as do the other story books, with a bit of a problem. Daniel was a real prophet who lived during the Babylonian captivity but the book of Daniel contains, along with its basically historical traditions about the prophet, much original invention contributed by its author. In other words, the

[2] The gourd vine has since become one of the symbols of the Resurrection in Christian art.

story is not a literal history even though about an historical person. In fact the book contains historical inaccuracies which could be disturbing unless one realizes that the author had no desire to present a history of the Babylonian captivity. What he was anxious to do was to encourage the desperate and sorely tried Jews of his own time—the time of the Maccabees, four hundred years later—by pointing to the tyrants of the past and the hopelessness of Israel's situation, and reminding the people that God had been with them then and rescued them, and He would do the same again.

How explain all this without making the warm-up for Daniel so tedious that the children would lose all interest in it even before the reading began?

One is forever underestimating children. I had proceeded about halfway through my involved explanation when Philip, still ten, interrupted.

"I know," he said, "it's like that book I just read about Robert Fulton. Some of it's true and some of it the author had to make up in order to write a whole book about him, but that doesn't mean the man didn't really live or that the book is no good."

Enough said. We started to read.

For all its wonderful tales, Daniel is not entirely an easy book and chapter 4, Nabuchodonosor's vision of the tree, together with chapters 7 through 12, filled with apocalyptic visions and symbols, are much too difficult for children to follow comfortably and are best omitted. This leaves us for family reading the following schedule:

Dan 1 Daniel and his companions, their test
2 Nabuchodonosor's vision of the statue
3 The three youths in the fiery furnace
5 Belsassar's vision of the writing on the wall
6 Daniel in the lions' den
Appendix
13 Daniel and Susanna
14 Daniel and Bel, and the dragon

Daniel is one of the last of the books of the Bible, written less than two hundred years before Christ, and it is a source of much of the scriptural knowledge of angels (both Gabriel and Michael appear in the story) as well as the source of some of the terms and ideas used during the ministry of Our Lord, for example, one of His favorite expressions for Himself, "Son of Man." (Dan 7:13)[3]

Daniel, His Companions and Their Test

Daniel and his three friends, Anania, Misael and Azaria, were taken prisoner at the time of Nabuchodonosor and brought to his palace to be tutored for positions close to the king. Every day their meals were brought from the king's table by a chamberlain, but Daniel was determined not to eat this food which might possibly have been offered first in sacrifice before pagan idols. The chamberlain protested that the king would surely have his head if these important charges began to grow weak from undernourishment, and in reply Daniel begged a ten days' trial. If he and his companions did not look as healthy as the others after ten days on a diet of vegetables, they would eat the royal fare. At the end of ten days, of course, they were sleeker and rosier than before, proving the watchful care of the Lord.

The lesson was strategically designed by the author to encourage his compatriots who, bullied by their foreign administrators to eat impure foods, needed the inspiration of Daniel who faithfully kept the law of the Lord.

Nabuchodonosor's Dream of the Statue

Next, in order to emphasize the superiority of divine wisdom as revealed by God to the Jews over the more sophisticated philosophy of their captors, the author tells how Nabuchodonosor's wise men could not interpret his dream—only Daniel could, with the help of the Lord.

Nabuchodonosor had a dream in which he saw a huge statue with a head of gold, chest and arms of silver, belly and thighs of bronze, legs of iron, and feet of iron and clay. While he gazed on it a huge stone detached itself from a mountain, rolled down the slope and smashed the statue to bits. The wise men of the realm were saved from death only because Daniel, inspired by the God of the Jews, was able to tell the king the meaning of his dream.

The statue represented the nations of the earth, with the

[3] Raymond E. Brown, S.S., *The Book of Daniel with a Commentary* (New York: Paulist Press), price 50¢.

ruler Nabuchodonosor, the golden head, superior to all others. But in time he would be overcome by a ruler inferior to him, represented by the chest and arms of silver, who would be overcome by a lesser ruler, represented by the belly and thighs of bronze, who would be overcome by a yet lesser ruler, represented by the legs of iron. In the lifetime of the last kingdom the God of heaven would set up His kingdom, represented by the rock hewn from the mountain by the hand of God, which would put the others to an end and would last forever.

That the statue personified four successive empires—the Babylonian, the Median, the Persian, the Macedonian—is not as important to us as the prophetical allusion to the reign of Christ in His Church, the rock, over God's kingdom, although naturally the author did not see this in the tale but only the salvation of his people from the cruel tyranny of the Seleucid empire. Here indeed is a tale to help a captive people to keep hope burning high, a tale which might well apply to the successive tyrants who have tried to master the world in our own times.

The Three Youths in the Fiery Furnace

Having just read in chapter 2 of Nabuchodonosor's gracious tribute to the God of Israel, it is strange to find in chapter 3 that he is ordering the Israelites to death by fire because they refuse to worship before one of his own gods—unless we remember that the stories in the book of Daniel do not have any chronological connection but have been chosen to teach important lessons. When we read the books of the Maccabees we will find the Assyrian ruler, Antiochus IV, raising up a statue of his "god of the heavens" in the temple of Jerusalem, to the horror of the devout Jews, and ordering the entire population to worship before it—and lo, the people face the same choice as confronted Azarias, Anania and Misael. This much loved hero tale of the three youths in the fiery furnace was the ideal vehicle to inspire the people to continued resistance.

Nabuchodonosor had set up a great idol and demanded that all the people bow down and worship it, saying, "Whoever does not fall down and worship shall be instantly cast into a white-hot furnace." (Dan 3:6) Now some Chaldeans observed that the Jews who were administrators of Babylon—Sidrach, Misach and Ab-

denago (the pagan names given to Anania, Azarias and Misael)—
had refused to worship the golden god and they reported this to
the king. Sending for the three, the king demanded that they worship or die, to which the young men replied that they would not
worship. Perhaps their God would save them, they said, well and
good; but if He would not, well and good also. He was God and
therefore they would not worship the golden statue.

Into the furnace went Sidrach, Misach and Abdenago, with
their coats, hats and shoes on, and so huge was the fire that it destroyed the very attendants who threw the victims into it, but the
three walked about in the flames, singing to God and blessing the
Lord. And we have the beautiful canticle of the three youths praising all creation as they stand in the furnace, cooled by the "dew-
laden breeze" created by the angel who kept them company. Sun
and moon, stars of heaven, shower and dew, fire and heat, cold and
chill, ice and snow, nights and days, lightnings and clouds, seas and
rivers, mountains and hills—every created thing is called upon to
praise the Lord in one of the most ecstatic prayers of the entire
Old Testament.

This lovely prayer gives the family a pattern for a special kind
of prayer, one that can be extemporized at any time and any place
but especially when walking outdoors and seeing the things God
has made in nature. I remember long ago on a very hot day walking down a lane with a small boy to get the mail when suddenly
a breeze went past, surprising us. We stopped and enjoyed it and
then, laughing a little, he said, "All you breezes, praise the Lord."
Indeed, all the things God has made praise Him and we must help
our children see the praise of God in nature. St. Francis de Sales,
walking in a meadow one time, said to the flowers, "Quiet! Quiet!
—don't tell me that I may love, for I am dying of love!" So loudly
did the flowers praise the Lord to Francis.

Needless to say, the king was edified beyond measure to see
that the God of the Jews protected them and in his speech after
their reprieve, he praises their God in words desperately needed by
the men of the Maccabees' time. "Blessed be the God of Sidrach,
Misach, and Abdenago, who sent his angel to deliver the servants
that trusted in him; they disobeyed the royal command and yielded
their bodies rather than serve or worship any god except their own
God." (Dan 3:95)

Daniel and the Handwriting on the Wall

In this story, Belsassar is king and at a great banquet given for a thousand of his lords, he calls for the sacred vessels taken from the temple of Jerusalem. When these are brought, his guests use them to drink libations praising their own gods of gold and silver, bronze and iron, wood and stone, and such a profanation of the vessels of the Lord draws the Almighty's wrath. Suddenly the fingers of a hand appear writing three mysterious words on the wall of the banquet room. Terrified, the king calls his wise men and seers but none can interpret the handwriting on the wall until the queen remembers Daniel. When he is called to solve the mystery, he first rebukes the king for his affrontery to the Lord.

This is the burden of Daniel's speech. All kings receive their authority from God, are elevated by His suffrance to their thrones and flourish under His watchful eye—as long as they are just. But as Nabuchodonosor had hardened his heart and become proud, and was punished by the Lord, so too had Belsassar offended by bringing out the sacred vessels and profaning them, and he would now be punished. The handwriting on the wall had this meaning:

MENE: God has numbered your kingdom and put an end to it;

TEKEL: You have been weighed on the scales and found wanting;

PERES: Your kingdom has been divided and given to the Medes and the Persians. (Dan 5:25-28)

And the author had a perfect story for the warning of Antiochus, who had also robbed the holy temple of its vessels, an outrage which would inevitably reap doom for him at the hands of the Lord.

Daniel in the Lions' Den

Here is the most famous story of them all, a tale which reminds us no little of the persecution of the Jews in the story of Esther. By this time, according to historical reckoning, Daniel would be about one hundred years old—which again suggests to us that time and historical fact are of no concern to our author. He is a moralist; his intent in this episode is to teach the Jews of the Maccabees' time that in their past the truly great Israelites faced death rather than abandon their obligation to praise the One God.

Daniel served Darius, now king, so brilliantly as satrap (a kind of administrator) that the king thought to elevate him to a position superior to all other satraps. Jealously resenting this, the other officials sought a means to trick Daniel and remove him. As Aman in the story of Esther had beguiled the king, so now these men had Darius pass a law that no one in the realm was to address any petition to god or man for thirty days, save to the king himself—for the king was considered a kind of deity. The king signed the edict without giving a thought to his faithful servant Daniel, the Jew.

As we might expect, Daniel continued to pray to the Lord three times a day, facing Jerusalem, and in due time he was reported to the king. Loathe to condemn him, the king nevertheless could not overstep the law and finally had to order Daniel thrown into the lions' den.

All night the king grieved for his friend and could not sleep, and early in the morning he hurried to the den crying out to Daniel words which spotlight the point of the lesson. "O Daniel, servant of the living God, has the God whom you serve so constantly been able to save you from the lions?" (Dan 6:21) And of course He has. In due time the villains responsible for the plot are thrown to the same lions and before they reach the bottom of the den they are seized and torn to pieces.

Daniel and Susanna

The story of Susanna is too delightful to forego for the sake of the difficulties it proposes if told to small children, so our problem is to discover another way to phrase the evil intention of the elders. We can paraphrase somewhat as we did in the story of David and Bethsabee and keep the elders' sinfulness from scandalizing the children with ideas they have not yet understood.

For example, in 13:9, for "they began to lust for her," we can read, "they gazed at her with immodest eyes and thoughts." In 13:12, "for they were ashamed to reveal their lustful desire to have her," we might say, "for they were ashamed to admit to each other that they wanted to make love to her." A little discussion about the blessedness of love-making for mothers and fathers, and the sinfulness of it for people who aren't married, might be added here. With verse 14, where "they admitted their lust," we could say, "and they admitted that they had all these impure thoughts about her," adding, "Wasn't that shameful of them?" Verses 19-21 might be read to say, ". . . give in to us and let us make love to you, or we will testify that you sent your maids away because there was a young man here with you who wasn't your husband and you were making love to him."

The rest of the story tells how the elders tricked Susanna and had her condemned to death by stoning (the punishment for adultery), and how Daniel, a young boy here, outwitted the two and vindicated the lovely heroine.

But it would be a mistake to think that cleverness alone is responsible for Daniel's triumph. Susanna's worthiness is beautifully spelled out in her choice of death rather than dishonor and disloyalty to the Lord (13:22-23), and in her prayer to God asking for help (13:42-43); and when the boy Daniel cried out that the men had testified falsely against her, we are told he was "stirred by the Holy Spirit." (13:44-45)

This story is an inspiration in a time when virtue is little prized and even laughed at, and honor is often sold cheaply. In addition, its thoroughly delightful denouement is highly satisfying to children who love to point out that "God is very smart and you can't fool Him."

Daniel, Bel and the Dragon

In the story of Bel and the dragon, Cyrus the Persian is king and Daniel is once again the king's favorite. Every day the Babylonians provided six barrels of fine flour, forty sheep, and six measures of wine for an idol called Bel which the king worshiped daily. When asked why he too did not worship Bel, Daniel replied that he worshiped only the living God who made the heavens and the earth and not idols made by human hands. But, the king explained, Bel lived; he devoured great amounts of food daily, and Daniel only laughed that the king should be so easily deceived. Angry, the king called for his priests and said they were to prove that Bel lived and ate or they and their families would die; if they could prove that Daniel was wrong, however, Daniel would die.

When the king and Daniel went to the temple, the priests bade the king himself set the food before the idol and with Daniel seal the doors behind them when they came out—but the priests had no fear, for under the table on which the idol stood was a secret door through which they and their families came nightly to eat the food. But Daniel was not fooled. Before the temple was sealed for the night, he ordered the king's servants to sprinkle ashes all over the floor.

In the morning the food was gone and the king pointed out that Bel had been vindicated, whereupon Daniel laughed and pointed to the floor. "Whose footprints are these?" he asked, and when the king discovered the trickery of his priests, he had them and their families destroyed.

Whatever the lesson the tale was meant to teach at the time, in our own times it seems to be a commentary on the foolishness and naïveté, the vulnerability, of those who do not know God or the order and reason that follow from His divine truth. A world without God is prey to every foolish superstition that pops into the minds of men, and every evil plot that is hatched in the hearts of the wicked. Like Daniel, we are bound to resist and protest bad will and bad thinking.

The Dragon

Robbed of Bel, the king turned to a great dragon worshiped by the Babylonians ("Like a Gila monster?" asked one of our boys) and said to Daniel, "Look, here is a living god, so I adore it." But again Daniel said that he adored only the living God. "Give me permission, O king, and I will kill this dragon without club or sword. (14:26) And Daniel mixed up a potion made of pitch, fat and hair "resembling a cross between a hamburger and a Molotov cocktail" [4] and fed it to the dragon, who literally exploded. There, he showed the king, the god he worshiped was no longer living.

When the Babylonians heard this they were very angry. "The king has become a Jew!" (14:28) they cried, and demanded that he hand over Daniel or they would attack the entire royal family. Once again Daniel was thrown into the lions' den, this time to lions who had not been receiving their daily ration of animals so they now should quickly devour Daniel.

But the Lord watched over Daniel. In Judea, the prophet Habacuc was taking pottage to the reapers in the field when an angel appeared to him and told him to take it instead to Daniel in Babylon. Then the angel seized Habacuc by the hair and transported him to the lions' den where he cried out, "Daniel, Daniel,

[4] *Op. cit.* p. 34.

take the lunch that God has sent you." (14:37) And Daniel's reply is a most beautiful prayer for men in times of distress—perhaps the whole point of the story.

"You have remembered me, O God, you have not forsaken those who love you." (14:38)

On the seventh day the king came to mourn for Daniel and imagine his delight to find him safe and sound. Once again the king was forced to salute the superior power of the Lord God of Israel. "You are great, O Lord, the God of Daniel, and there is no other besides you!" (14:41) And Daniel was removed from the den, while those who had tried to destroy him were thrown to the lions and gobbled to bits.

Although the book of Daniel was written for a specific time in the history of the Jews, and meant to encourage and inspire a particular generation, its message is just as important for our own days. "See, the Lord is our God and He alone rules the earth!"

THE PSALMS
AND
THE WISDOM BOOKS

We had tried to use the Psalms for our family prayers for a long, long time. After all, we said, if they were the favorite prayers of Jesus, Mary and Joseph, they ought really to become the favorite prayers of the Newlands—but after we tried them we had to admit we were much happier saying the Rosary.

These prayers were written by the Holy Spirit, we reminded ourselves, and praised God more perfectly than any other prayer, so we tried them for this reason—and we only felt uncomfortable praising God this way, as though we were doing something strange and affected.

The Psalms were prayers for every situation and season and mood, for every need; they were strong and outspoken and free of sentimentality and posturing, the crown of the spirituality of the Old Testament—surely we would want to pray them for this reason. And we did, yet when we prayed them we often felt *dis*comfited—by the cursing in them and the references to the dark silence of the grave (*sheol*).

The Psalms are beautiful poetry and this we cannot say about all prayers. We tried reading them again—only to conclude that for us to read the Psalms was hardly like prayer at all but more like reading poetry. It was hopelessly stilted and strange.

It was suggested that commentaries on the Psalms would help, but they did not. There was so much to juggle into place, words that meant one thing now and another thing then, statements that were sometimes to be taken literally, sometimes figuratively, names that were interchangeable, ideas that depended upon a vast background of scriptural and historical knowledge. It was no use. We just couldn't get on with the Psalms, and reading them for our family prayer made us feel like phonies. We dropped the Psalms.

But we started to read the Old Testament.

And we found the answer to really loving the Psalms and making them our favorite prayer. One evening a long time afterwards when we asked everyone, "What would you prefer to have for family prayer?" the answer came from the whole family (including four teen-age children): "The Psalms."

Why the Difficulty?

Our experiment in discouragement is not common to everyone, but it is the experience of many families. Why is this?

For those like us it is probably because we come to the Psalms empty-handed.

Consider the way we go about praying the Rosary. For a long time in our young lives before we start reciting the Rosary we have been told stories, seen pictures, heard mention all year around of the mysteries of the Rosary. No little one joining his family at the Rosary for the first time has to be told much more than, "With the first ten prayers we thank God for sending the angel Gabriel to tell Our Lady that she would be the mother of Jesus." A swarm of loved impressions accompanies the recital of this one prayer said ten times, and over a lifetime one who is sincere at prayer explores every inch of these scenes, every spiritual significance, every theological dimension within his reach. We roam through the settings of the Rosary with familiarity and love: the garden at Ain-Karim, the dimly-lit cave at Bethlehem, the vast porticoes of the temple, and more. Our own experiences with joy and pain deepen our understanding of the mysteries in the lives of Jesus and Mary. The Rosary is a success not just because we know the few prayers that are required but because we are at home with its meaning.

For us the Psalms were not a success because we were not really at home with their meaning. It was reading the history of God's people—the story of our salvation—that provided the riches we needed in order to make them our own and pray them sincerely.

Praise of God, the Creator

For example, take the story of Creation in Genesis 1 and 2, followed by Psalm 103. Here in this Psalm is the One Who breathed across the waters, speaking of the works of His hands. But, you might say, this Psalm was never very obscure—why the excitement? Because to read it against the background of Genesis gives ten meanings where we found one meaning before, makes of it a prayer that rises up out of the very act of creation as though we were there.

Noe's Story Helps

The story of Noe tells of God's attitude toward sin and virtue, the just man and the evil. (Gen 6:5-22; 6; 7; 8; 9:1-17) The lines of Psalm 31 are marvelously illumined by the image of the ark resting on the crest of the flood and protecting the just from the storms of the world:

> . . . every faithful man will pray to You
> in times of stress,
> when flood-waters rise high, they will not reach him.
> You are my refuge, You will save me from anguish,
> You will surround me with the joy of freedom. (Ps 31:6-7)

Babel and a Psalm about Corruption

Reading Psalm 13 with Babel in mind pushed back the dimensions of evil from our own times and experiences to the corruption of men in the childhood of the race:

> The Lord looks down from heaven on the children of men
> to find one man who is wise, one who seeks God:
> All have gone astray together, all have become depraved,
> there is not one who does good; no, not one. (Ps 13:2-3)

The lesson of Babel and its divisive pride strikes home in this prayer. We are even in danger of being found among the evil instead of the just; we must trust God to help us.

Abraham, the Promise, the Covenant, the Oath

We could not possibly enjoy Psalm 104 until we made the acquaintance of the patriarchs. The covenant, the promise, the oath that He swore—what meaning had these words without Abraham? But once we knew him they showed us many things: Abraham at Ur listening to the voice of a strange, new, One God; Abraham journeying forth with family and flocks; Abraham at night with the carcasses of the covenant beasts, the divine fire blazing; Abraham gazing at the stars—"Your descendents shall outnumber the stars" (Gen 15:5); Abraham looking up from Isaac bound on the altar, listening. All these pictures run like a thread through such a line as: "Always mindful is He of His covenant . . . the covenant He made with Abraham." (Ps 104:8-9)

Jacob as Israel in the Psalms

And Jacob—whole passages are meaningless without an acquaintance with Jacob. Israel is Jacob, is the house of Jacob, is the twelve tribes out of Jacob: "Then Israel came into Egypt," (Ps 104:23); "For He gave a command to Jacob," (Ps 77:5); "That men may know that God rules in Jacob," (Ps 58:14). And we had learned that the Church is the new Israel.

Exodus and Salvation in the Psalms

We can only limp through the Psalms without a knowledge of Exodus. Psalm 77 is filled with images from this book. "He cleft the sea and led them through, He heaped up the waters like a mount." (Ps 77:13) Here and in so many other Psalms are the water from the rock, the manna, the quail, the plagues, the death of the first-born in Egypt.

God Our Protector

Six times in the Psalms we take shelter under God's wings, recalling the tenderness of the Lord as He spoke to His people at Mount Sinai: "You have seen for yourselves what I did to the Egyptians, how I carried you as if on eagle's wings, and took you into my care." (Ex 19:4 Knox)

The Book of Numbers and Disobedience

There is a mystery in Psalm 94 if we have not read Numbers. "I grew weary of that race through forty years, and I said, 'a people of wandering heart, they do not know My ways.' Then I swore in My wrath: 'Never shall they enter into my rest!'" (Ps 94:10-11) Nor did they, but died on the far side of the land of promise—and the warning is clear.

Josue and the Promised Land

Josue gives life to the lines of Psalm 113:3-4: "The river Jordan turned back its course: the mountains bounded like rams, like little lambs, the hills." Never do we read this but some eager boy explains, "Like an earthquake, you know, with hills bounding and skipping. He could have done it with a word or with an earthquake —He is that powerful."

Judges and Confidence

Confidently we pray extravagant lines like, "I fear not men in their thousands, all around me, all against me." (Ps 3:7) We remember the book of Judges and how the Lord caused Sisera's iron chariots to sink in the mud, his horses to be swept away, while Barac led his tribesmen foot soldiers to victory. None of our family crises have been worse!

Our delight in these songs of God's people grew as we read further into the history of Israel. One night we read in Psalm 59:8, "I will go up to divide Sichem . . ." and Stephen interrupted to say, "We've been there!"

David and His Prayers

We found David and the lessons he teaches again and again. We prayed in his words for confidence in times of danger and we knew he meant terrible danger, because we knew his story. (Ps 53) We spoke of our longing to see God, remembering David's loneliness and heartache in the desert. (Ps 62) We asked for victory and peace in his words, and we knew the extent of his gratitude when he blessed the Lord, "O my soul, forget none of His blessings! He forgives all your faults, heals all your diseases . . ." (Ps 102:2-3) David reminds us of the sin God forgave him and we are confident that He will forgive ours. Because we saw David dance before the Ark we can join in the spirit of Psalm 150, the last of all the Psalms, and sing too of praising God with sounding horns, and zither and harp, with timbrels and dance, strings and pipes, with sounding and crashing cymbals. "Let all that breathes praise the Lord."

The Cursing Psalms

Reading the Old Testament, we became used to the language of the Psalms and difficulties with figures of speech disappeared.

The habit of translating meanings became easy for us. The violent language of the cursing Psalms ceased to shock us for we understood the enemies of the Psalmist, who loves God, to be the enemies of God. To cry anathema on the eternal enemy of God is just: the pit, the lion's mouth, the sword of the righteous is his final end; but should the enemy of God repent and turn his face toward the Lord, as quickly can a blessing come down upon him. Did not God vow to destroy Ninive? Did not Ninive repent and God spare her? Woe to the Israelite who would not forgive the repentant enemy of the Lord. This is the lesson of Jona. The language of the cursing Psalms hurls itself at evil, but does not prevent us from praying for those who yield to it.

The Enemy

Sometimes the enemy cursed is the evil one who roams the earth seeking whom he may devour. "Those who dare to say: 'Let us seize the lands of God!' O my God, treat them like storm-driven leaves, like chaff in the wind! As fire burns up the forest, as a flame sets the mountains ablaze, so pursue them with Your storm . . ." (Ps 82:14-16) Lucifer in all his power is, before God, no more than chaff before the wind. No wonder the saints loved the Psalms.

Death and Sheol

We have learned that for a long time the people of God did not have a clear understanding of life after death but thought of the grave as final—a land of twilight and sleep, of darkness and monotony. Thus the mention of *sheol*, so misty and melancholy, no longer puzzles us. We marvel instead that even so a thread of hope weaves its way through the Psalms.

The King

Then there are the royal Psalms saluting the King. These ought to be understandable, with or without a background, yet this is not all a Psalm must be—understandable. It must be a real experience, and without the riches of the books of Kings with their majestic enthronements and exaltations of the kings, their solemnities and sacrifices, their marchings forth and returnings in victory, their celebrations and thanksgivings with courtly pomp and splendor, the colors, sounds, smells, tastes, sights in the stories of the kings, we only half plumb the riches of the very word *king* as it is used to speak of the Lord Who is King in these Psalms. "With trumpets and sounding horns, sing with joy in the Lord's presence, He the King." (Ps 97:6) Here is a great prayer in praise of Christ, eternal King of the ages.

The Temple

The same is true of the temple. The whole mystery of the temple, from David's dream to its first glory under the reign of Solomon, to the unspeakable desecration and robbery of it by one predator after another, the many restorations, the anguish of the people as they struggled to rebuild it, the love and reverence in which they held it, to its final symbolic meaning in the words of the prophets—"Greater will be the future glory of this house than the former, says the Lord of hosts," (Ag 2:9)—all this enriches our meeting with the Psalms which exalt the temple. "How lovely is your dwelling place, O Lord of hosts! My soul is longing and sighing for the courts of the Lord." (Ps 83:1) The words which refer to the temple speak to us of our own church, of the Church, of the house of the Lord in heaven, and by Our Lord's own application of His sacred person.

Jerusalem

It is the same with Jerusalem, the city that was dearest to the heart of all Israel. To go to Jerusalem was the desire of every Israelite, to walk its streets, relive the glories of its past, to offer sacrifice there, to adore God in the sacred precincts of the temple. *Jerusalem* is full of meanings in the Psalms—the Church, the heavenly Jerusalem, the place of the people of God. Sometimes it is called Sion, sometimes a rock, a strong tower, a fortress, a stronghold, a foundation on the holy mountains. Psalm 67, God's triumphant march, is a glorious hymn resounding with these images and telling of the great victory of Christ over sin and death.

Who Wrote Them?

It was not until we learned to love the Psalms that we really wanted to know who wrote them. We felt we knew the authors very well after reading their words; but now we had a real curiosity to know more about the names ascribed to them together with the rather strange instructions accompanying them. David, the sons of

Core,[1] Asaph, Solomon, Heman, Ethan the Ezrahite, and Moses are listed as authors, and their works are labeled as *maskels, miktams,* songs—of ascents, for the Sabbath, to be sung with stringed instruments, "upon the eighth," "upon the gittith," and more. We learned that traditionally the Psalms are thought to be composed by the men whose names accompany their titles, and that the instructions were for the performance of these songs, showing us that they were used in the Hebrew liturgy as well as privately by the people. In the Fides edition of the Psalms, translated by Mary Perkins Ryan, these notations are explained in accompanying paragraphs which also relate each of the Psalms to the daily needs of the family and the Church, and give the liturgical seasons when each Psalm is prominently featured. This has become our favorite translation and each member of our family owns his own copy.[2]

Literary Form

Further, we at last became interested in the parallelism of Hebrew poetry so often pointed out in the commentaries. Unlike our poetry where vowel rhythm marks the meter of a poem, a thought rhythm is the key in Hebrew poetry. Three forms of parallelism are most frequently found: synonymous, antithetic, and synthetic. An example of synonymous parallelism would be:

> My step has held fast to Your paths,
> my feet have not faltered. (Ps 16:5)

Here the second line restates in another way the first.

An example of antithetic parallelism would be the opposite:

> For the Lord watches over the just,
> but the way of the wicked vanishes. (Ps 1:6)

The second line is a contrast to the first.

An example of synthetic parallelism, which is a broader category, would be:

> Rise up, O Lord, in Your anger,
> rise against the fury of my foes,
> Rise up on my behalf
> for the judgment You have ordained. (Ps 7:7)

[1] Descendents of the Core who was destroyed in Numbers 16:31-33.
[2] The Fides Translation, *The Psalms* (Chicago: Fides Press, 1955).

Here the idea presented in the first line is developed and completed in the following lines, in this case like a staircase rising up step by step (therefore the name "staircase parallelism").

Stopping to examine the Psalms for their external form can seem entirely extraneous to praying them until one knows them rather well; then such an examination is rewarding, for it gives added emphasis to the thought of the Psalmist.

The Psalms as Prayer

Which Psalms do we like best? The answer depends on whom you ask. One of our children answered: "I like best the ones that are about the things we've read. You know, the coming out of Egypt, and the promise, and all that—the ones that mention the stories." A family with children might take its cue from this.

Sometimes the mystery of the season dictates our choice of Psalms. At still other times, the world crises or personal needs within our family or among our friends inspire us in our choice. Recently a much loved friend became desperately ill and we searched out the Psalms which cry to the Lord for help in times of danger and distress.

Prayer should be enjoyable as far as possible. But often it has not been enjoyable—for want of variety, depth, even a sense of freedom. Admittedly the Lord sometimes makes it difficult to pray in order to try us, to lead us in faith into the momentary darkness of an even brighter light, but we are not supposed to court difficulties deliberately. The great spiritual writers have always advised simplicity, naturalness, even a comfortable and relaxed position for the body (although dignified) as an aid to prayer. We ought to choose for prayer that which best lifts our hearts and holds our interest on God, for out of this comes the best meditation.

In the Psalms we have a universe of ideas to fit our prayer needs, from praise of God the Creator to the story of His people where every human situation is set forth. There are words on worship, sacrifice, gratitude, fear, hope, love—words that pay tribute to God's goodness, majesty, justice, mercy; words that hold us in mid-flight as an idea suddenly comes alive for the first time through language that is always noble, dignified, inspired.

Indeed, after reading the history of salvation we understand what has been said for so long and by so many about the beauty and worth of the Psalms. They have become our favorite prayer too.

Reading the Psalms Together

How to read the Psalms together in the family is a matter to be settled by each family. We have tried two arrangements. At first, we divided ourselves into two groups, each group reading a verse alternately, or two verses if necessary to complete the thought. This, however, did not always work out ideally. After a long hard day of work, play and study, a degree of snappishness brought on by differences in the reading abilities among us sometimes disturbed our prayer.

"Read faster!" came from the fast readers.

"You read slower!" was the reply of the slow ones.

"How can we call this prayer if you are going to quarrel?" came from the parents and was largely ineffective. The snapping and barking continued and one Psalm avoided by common consent was that rhapsody on the beauty and harmony of brethren who dwell together. (Ps 132) Some brethren dwelt in harmony, perhaps, but unfortunately not ours.

One evening our then 16-year-old son said, "Say, I have an idea. Why don't we read a different way? We could each take two verses and read around in a circle, clockwise." It was an inspiration and it has worked beautifully. Each member of the group chooses two Psalms (sometimes one if they are long, or if the time is limited) and we usually sit for our reading.

It is important for each member of the family to have his own Psalm book. At first this may seem extravagant, but a copy of the Psalms does not cost as much as most pairs of shoes and lasts much longer (into eternity, really), and unlike food, it is not forever in need of replenishing. The various family birthdays, feast days, and Christmas and Easter are ideal occasions for giving the Psalms for a gift.

In our house, the best time to read the Psalms together is in the evening just before the younger children's bedtime. This is not always possible, however, and we have no hard and fast rule. On nights when homework, meetings, business appointments or other necessities leave only a few free to pray the Psalms together, the absent members simply pray when they can and privately. The two youngest at seven and eight years old could often be heard reading aloud in their rooms alternate verses of their favorite Psalms[3] when guests or other business kept us from reading together. We have found that some guests are delighted to read the Psalms with us, while others would be uncomfortable and we do not even suggest it to them. It should be said that we have not given up saying the Rosary. For all our love for the Psalms, there are still evenings when the Rosary seems the ideal choice of prayer.

It is helpful to kneel for a few minutes of silent prayer after the Psalms, with the lights out if possible to eliminate distractions. The effect of the Psalms is peaceful and calming and we must let the children linger as long as possible in their mood. We might suggest that they fix their minds on one sentiment or idea from the Psalms they have read and let God lead their thoughts along paths He will choose for them.

As with any such family activity, the end of reading the Psalms together is not to perpetuate this group saying these prayers but to acquaint this group with these prayers, so that each one may use them throughout his lifetime. So often we find we are still praying the prayers of our own childhood, prayers which long ago cut their tender beauty into our minds so indelibly that we will never be rid of them. It is urgent that we acquaint our own children with the beauty of the Psalms so that their childhood will be steeped in these prayers. Their minds, as ours were before them, are quick and retentive and hungry; these are perfect prayers for the nurturing of them.

The Book of Job

A long time ago we tried to read the book of Job, thinking it another of the "story books" of the Old Testament. But once past the second chapter we bogged down horribly. Discourse followed endless discourse, all saying pretty much the same thing until finally we mercifully (from the point of view of the children) gave the

[3] A beautiful edition of the Psalms especially suited for children is G. Vauthier's *Here I am, Lord* (Westminster, Md. Newman Press, 1960).

whole thing up. Whoever had told us it was a good idea to read the book of Job? And where, if you please, was Job's fabled patience? He seemed to do nothing but complain.

This, I fear, is a pretty universal experience for any family trying to read this book without some help. Yet it is a shame not to read Job, for once we see what the book is teaching it is quite possible, with a judicious selection of texts, to read it so children will enjoy it.

The book of Job is a magnificent Hebrew poem inserted within the framework of an ancient folk tale, and its point is to show us a man who, in spite of terrible misfortune and suffering, remained faithful to God. Remembering that the Hebrews believed that God rewarded the just with good fortune in this life and punished the evil with disaster, Job's suffering and faith before his final reward is indeed remarkable, and out of this puzzle comes the plot of the story—if it can be called a plot.

Job is an historical person thought to have lived in the times of the patriarchs. The prophet Ezechiel mentions him together with Noe and Daniel as a man of great justice and integrity (Ezech 14:13-20), and he is an ideal choice for the central figure of this story.

Job Is Afflicted

Job is a prosperous, God-fearing man who is suddenly afflicted with enormous sufferings, and he is puzzled. He has not sinned grievously but has been faithful and just; does he deserve this? His wife falls into a fit of despondency: "Curse God and die," is her gloomy advice. (Job 2:9) Job's three friends who come to commiserate with him are stolidly orthodox, and seeing the misfortune of their friend they can only conclude that he has done evil, else why the punishment?

This is the dilemma. Job knows he is just. If God is just, why is Job afflicted? Only God can vindicate Job and evidently God will not. Is God no longer just? Or is Job more righteous than God? Does the justice of the good man no longer prevail with God? Job does not really believe these things—but why does not God answer him?

Now a fourth voice enters the debate. Eliu, a young man who has suddenly appeared in the narrative, scolds Job for his presumption. How dare he speak of God like this? The three friends are also rebuked for failing to perceive why God has afflicted Job. Eliu's premise is that God in His justice afflicts the evil and "saves the unfortunate through their affliction, instructs them through their distress." (Job 36:15) He is not entirely right, but he comes close.

Finally God speaks and in the most glorious passages of all Job perceives that God is the almighty and omniscient creator who watches and weighs the affairs of the entire universe, even to the least particles of His creation. God reveals His transcendency to Job—He the mighty, the Holy One, the One whom man cannot analyze or dissect, Who loves the ice, the rain, the hail, the mountain goat, the lioness and her cubs, the wild ass, the wild ox, the cock, the horse, the hawk. Can He love man less? Hidden in the heart of God is the answer to the mystery of the suffering of the just; can we not trust Him? When a man at last meets God in prayer and faith and love, in the mystery of contemplation, he begins to "see." Thus has God spoken to Job, and Job now "sees."

Job answers with great humility. "I have dealt with great things that I do not understand; things too wonderful for me, which I cannot know. I have heard you by word of mouth, but now my eye has seen you. Therefore I disown what I have said, and repent in dust and ashes." (42:1-6)

A Reading Schedule

The adult reader will enjoy the book of Job in its entirety, but reading it to children poses a problem. After hearing, "The speeches are sort of all the same," and "Yes, and they get awfully long," we ruthlessly cut the rich discourses to the bone rather than lose the children.

Chapters 1 and 2 set the scene and in 1:6, the "sons of god" refers to the angels, while "Satan" is not the devil as we are accustomed to call him, but rather an angel appointed to patrol the earth. This name was not used for the devil until a later period. Satan's challenge to God to try Job is merely a device to get us into the story and not, as we will see when finally God speaks, the reason behind it all.

We have found the following schedule of reading helpful:

1; 2   Job's life, his trials
3:1-6, 24-26   Job curses the day he was born

4:1-9   Eliphaz rebukes Job
6:22-26   Job decries the accusations
8:1-7   Baldad says God will vindicate Job if he is innocent
10:1-3   Job repeats his complaint to God
11:1-6; 13-16   Sophar ridicules Job's innocence
13:13-19   Job will wait until God permits him to defend himself; Job defends himself on the basis of his good works
31:5-8   His honesty
31:1, 9, 10   His chastity
31:13-14   His justice to his servants
31:16-17   His generosity to the poor
31:19-20   His goodness to the wanderer
31:21-22   His justice in court
31:24-25   He was not greedy for gold
31:35-37   His final plea
32:1-7; 11-14; 33:1-2, 8-14; 35:1-12; 36:13-15   Eliu's speech
38:1-7, 12, 16, 19, 22-23, 25, 28-29, 31-35, 39-41; 39:1-9; 38:36; 39:19-22; 26-30; 40:1-5   The Lord speaks
42:1-6   Job answers the Lord
42:7-17   Epilogue

As we read along we wanted many times to step into the story and tell Job about Christ. Since the redemption there are still the Jobs, but now they carry the Cross. In the mystery of a fallen world and Christ's redemptive suffering lies the clue to the suffering of the just—the clue Job sought.

In the end Job is rewarded with double the riches and good fortune he had lost. The writer did not know, as we do, that so shall the just man be rewarded forever in heaven.

Proverbs

The book of Proverbs, rich and wonderful as it is, does not lend itself to family reading. Rather it is a book to be read in solitude, and pondered, and sometimes even quoted (we had forgotten so many familiar sayings came from the Bible!), with of course one

exception. The final verses describing the Valiant Woman (the
Ideal Wife as the new translation calls her) are well-beloved and
familiar from the Mass of a Holy Woman not a Martyr, and make
an ideal reading for feast days of wives, mothers and married
women saints.

Proverbs is a collection of the royal wisdom of Solomon, the
Wise (or the Sages), Agur, and King Lamuel, and in it are advice,
instructions and admonitions for young men preparing for a life at
court which, summed up, also encourage each one of us to live the
good life. Each proverb stands alone. At the time these sayings were
compiled, the Hebrews still had no conception of eternal life in
either heaven or hell, and therefore continually emphasized reward
and retribution in this life as the end of man's deeds. *Sheol*, the
grave, was a place of shadow and mystery and not until the books
of Daniel and Wisdom did a knowledge of eternal blessedness appear in Old Testament literature.

The Canticle of Canticles

This book is called the Canticle of Canticles, or the Song of
Songs, because it is considered to be the greatest and most beautiful
of the canticles of the Old Testament. It consists of a series of
alternating songs, or stanzas, praising the beloved and sung by the
bride and the bridegroom, and it is thought to have been written
by Solomon. There are two ways to view the Canticle—as a poetic
rhapsody on the delights of human love in marriage; and, according to ancient Jewish tradition, as an image of the love of Yahweh
for His people, Israel. With the coming of Christ the allegory was
applied to the love of Christ for His Church, and in time the classic
spiritual writers, among them St. Bernard and St. John of the Cross,
pointed out that its language also speaks of Christ's love for the soul.

Exceedingly beautiful, endlessly contemplative, the Canticle of
Canticles is nevertheless far too obscure for reading to children.
We will let them discover this book themselves when they are
grown up.

The Book of Ecclesiastes

The book of Ecclesiastes—or Coheleth, after its author—is another of the Wisdom books which does not lend itself to reading aloud in the family. Although it contains many familiar reflections —"Vanity of vanities . . . all things are vanity," (Eccl 1:2); "Nothing is new under the sun," (Eccl 1:10)—the author's preoccupation with the instability of wealth, pleasure and even some of the fruits of human endeavor is apt to strike the reader as unsettling if not downright pessimistic. In his seeming pessimism, however, he never betrays his faith that God by His wisdom governs the universe. Had the writer of Ecclesiastes known the teachings of Christ, his puzzle over the injustices and imbalances of life could have been more easily solved. This book shows us clearly that the teaching of the Old Testament was incomplete. In the New Testament Christ answers the questions of the sages by revealing that all the experiences of this life are meant to be used to attain eternal happiness in the next.

The Book of Sirach

It seems almost unnecessary to try to explain the book of Sirach, or Ecclesiasticus, when its translator, in a modest and beautifully written Foreword, has explained precisely what his grandfather (the author) intended his work to be. ". . . Something . . . in the nature of instruction and wisdom, in order that those who love wisdom might . . . make even greater progress in living in conformity with the Divine Law."

This book might be called an anthology of Hebrew teaching, covering such subjects as duties towards God and parents, alms for

the poor, true friendship, conduct in public life, prudence in deal-
ing with other men, advice concerning women, choice of friends,
sincerity, justice, humility, pride, glory, moderation—and much
more. It is written with the careful touch of a man who is wise and
learned, who truly loves God and cares deeply that his fellow men
advance in their knowledge and love of God. It contains nothing
new but rather is like one of our own spiritual treatises written by
a saint or a great spiritual director.

Sirach does not lend itself to reading aloud in the family, although there are many selections which might be chosen to give
unction to a family discussion of virtue or religion. For example,
from Sirach 11:7:

> Before investigating, find no fault;
> examine first, then criticize.

This book could provide the family with short maxims to be
read, perhaps, with morning prayers before everyone leaves for
work or school, before dinner at night, or at evening prayers. We
might choose from Sirach a daily lesson for the great liturgical
seasons of Lent or Advent, letting this holy man instruct us in the
fear of the Lord which is the beginning of wisdom.

Sirach gives Wisdom *being* as it comes from God, and allows
it to speak in the first person—almost as a foreshadowing of the
Word of God Who proceeds from the Father and expresses Him.
The familiar passage, "From the mouth of the Most High I came
forth, and mist-like I covered the earth . . ." (Sir 24:3) is used in
the liturgy to portray Our Lady as the "seat of wisdom," that source
of the humanity of Christ Who cannot be disassociated from Him.

The Book of Wisdom

The book of Wisdom is not especially suitable for family
reading either, but like the other Wisdom (or Sapiential) books it
contains many passages which are already familiar to us. This book
was written about one hundred years before Christ by a pious and
cultivated Jew of an Egyptian community who wished to inspire

his fellow Jews, ever in danger of persecution from both pagans and apostate Jews, to persevere in the pursuit of wisdom as the means to eternal life. In this book there appears at last the promise of eternal life and happiness after death, the answer sought so diligently by the writers who went before it. Written at times under the name of Solomon, the book, it is understood, was not intended to deceive but rather, according to accepted practice, to be identified with the great tradition of Solomon and his teachings on wisdom.

Passages from the book of Wisdom are used frequently in the liturgy, which explains our familiarity with them. For example, Wisdom 3:1-8 is the Lesson in the Mass of Many Martyrs, "The souls of the just are in the hands of God." Verses 4-6 answer the troubled questions of Coheleth and others like him who puzzled over the unequal treatment of the just and the unjust—and they confirm us in the hope made possible by Christ: "For if before men, indeed, they be punished, yet is their hope full of immortality; chastised a little, they shall be greatly blessed, because God tried them and found them worthy of himself. As gold in the furnace, he proved them, and as sacrificial offerings he took them to himself."

Beautiful books, full of riches. We may not read them aloud to our families, yet we can feed our own souls on their thoughts, that we may grow in wisdom ourselves and be an ever abundant source of wisdom for our children.

·XI·

THE BATTLES
OF THE
MACHABEES

"Well now—how do you like the Machabees?" we asked after reading the first chapters of Book I. It had long been promised as a great treat and we were anxious to see if it had measured up to advance notices.

"Great!" was one child's reply. "This is more like it!"

"And what does that mean?" we wanted to know.

He hastened to explain—a little apologetically. "Oh, the rest is good too—except when those long speeches and prayers get kind of dragged out—but these battles! I love hearing about them."

And momentarily we were tempted to regret that with children inspiration always comes out a poor second to action in the history of salvation. But only momentarily, for the sound and fury of the wars of the Machabees show us Israel at her most valiant and perfectly illustrate the spirit that burns so high in those speeches and prayers the young find "kind of dragged out." The day will come when they too will be thrilled by the prophets' exhortation to be faithful to the Lord even unto death, but right now we can show them in the Machabees magnificent examples of men who did die for love of the Law and the Lord. Their stories are classics of heroism.

Historical Background

About two hundred and fifty years had passed since Nehemia had helped rebuild the walls of Jerusalem and together with Ezra had instituted the reforms, and although it is not necessary to supply in detail all the events of those years between Ezra and the Machabees, some background is important if we are to understand why the Jews revolted, and against whom.

The Persian domination of the Jews under which Jerusalem was rebuilt had given way to Greece under Alexander the Great, and when this conqueror died at the age of thirty-two his great empire was fought for and divided among his generals until finally the Jews found themselves subject to the kingdom of Egypt under the rule of a former general, Ptolemy I. After about one hundred years the king of Syria, Antiochus III (descended from the Alexandrian general Seleucis), victoriously fought Egypt for possession of Palestine, and the people of God came under the rule of the Seleucid kings who had adopted in their royal title the name of the capital city of Antioch, founded by their illustrious sire.

After his victory over Egpyt, Antiochus III ventured into Europe, but there he was turned back and roundly defeated by the Romans at Magnesia. And suddenly, to his dismay, he found himself subject to Rome. Among the costly terms settled upon after this defeat was a demand for the king's son, Antiochus IV, and nineteen other hostages to be brought to Rome as surety for the monarch's good behavior.

It was this son Antiochus IV (Epiphanes) who returned after fifteen years in Rome to take over the royal throne and who, anxious to throw off the yoke of the Romans, moved to unify the captive peoples under him by forcing them to adopt Greek customs and worship. He is the first of the long line of villains in the first book of Machabees.[1]

The two books of the Machabees tell of the same struggle but are written by different authors who had different reasons for writing. The first book is a history of the years between 175 and 135 B.C., a straightforward account written by a devoted and loyal Jew who is obviously well-acquainted with army life and tactics. It is rich in detail and action and tells in impassioned words of the cour-

[1] One villain precedes him in the second book of Machabees: Heliodorus, Ch. 3.

age and fidelity of the Machabees as contrasted to the treachery of the Jews who apostatized to the Greeks.

The second book was written in an entirely different style and covers only part of the Machabean period—the years between 174 B.C. and 161 B.C. Its author is intent upon inspiring the Jewish colony in the city of Alexandria in Egypt, and his work is more of a sermon than a history. The name "Machabees" is thought to derive from the Hebrew word for *hammer* and is taken from Judas Machabaeus, the third son of Mathathias, a loyal Jewish priest of the Hasmonean family. Judas was the first and greatest of the leaders this family produced and in time his followers were called by the common name "the Machabees."

The Important Point

The most important point to be made about the Machabees before we begin their story is that their revolt was for freedom to worship the Lord and keep His Law. If we do not make this clear, impatient children will be forever interrupting to ask why Judas and his forces do not push the fight farther afield; why they accept peace terms so readily, why they agree from time to time to resume the role of vassal ruled by a foreign power. Unless we explain, they will fail to see that the story has a relevance to the state of things in the world today.

The issue with the captors of the Jews was always conquest, while the people of God were concerned with their relation to God and His Law, and the working out of His promises. As long as they were free to worship the Lord, the Israelites felt no call to be martyrs for the sake of the changes of fortune brought on the tide of their various conquerors. But let Antiochus, for example, determine that they were to become the votaries of Zeus instead of Yahweh, and they had to resist—or forfeit their reason for being.

Here is the difference between the natural and the supernatural points of view illustrated in a way that helps us to understand better the position of the Church today. Why in one area does she patiently endure the constant harassment of an unfriendly government, while in another, and in an atmosphere of religious and political freedom, she will become exercised over a moral issue considered by some people to be a tremendous trifle? The answer is simple. The concern of the Church for the affairs of the world is determined by God's promise of eternal life for all men. Does a policy, a propaganda attack, a scientific device help men go to heaven, or hinder them? Like the Machabees, she can never tolerate what interferes with this.

The people of God seemed to understand that when the prophets spoke of all nations coming one day to Sion to worship the Lord together, they did not envision military campaigns as the means, and even though they had no profound sense of world mission, it followed that once they had been chosen by Yahweh to know Him and His Law, it was their role to keep His religion alive; to say nothing of course of their conviction that worship was due God once men knew Him.

But we must remember also that men do not die for causes they do not love. Martyrdom for the Machabees was not going to be all give and no get. Their books speak out more plainly than any others in the Bible of life after death and they, like other men who would follow them, found the promise of eternity with the Lord irresistible.

The First Book of Machabees

As we scanned the first book of Machabees before reading it aloud, our impression was of a text so crammed with names and action that one chapter at a time would surely be quite enough, but we reckoned without the audience. By popular request, we ended up reading three and four chapters at a sitting and neither the enormous cast of characters nor the rapid changes of scene posed serious problems. The greatest difficulties came from the translations themselves. The Douay presents no great reading problem but includes a number of archaic words and phrases which often call for the dictionary, while the Knox translation is modern English but set down with such awkward sentence structure that it had to be rearranged to make it smooth for young listeners.

For example, where the Douay has: "And Judas saw all the evils that Alcimus, and they that were with him, did to the children of Israel, much more than the Gentiles." (I Mac 7:23) the Knox has: "Little it liked Judas, to see Alcimus and his crew mishandling

the men of Israel as never the Gentiles did." The moral of this is
that whichever translation is used, a careful preparation of it beforehand is important if reading is to be easy.

The first chapter sets the scene for the story by scanning the
history of Alexander and his successors and bringing us up to the
time when Antiochus IV (here called II) is back from Rome. Already one group of Jews, pro-Hellenists, had acquiesced in the matter of worship and were patronizing a gymnasium built in Jerusalem
where games were conducted in a manner that not only violated all
Jewish standards of modesty but drew many of the people into sin.

Antiochus pillaged Jerusalem, stripping the temple once more
in order to fill his own treasury, and two years later the holy city
was completely wrecked. David's palace became a citadel for Syrian
soldiers, and an order from the king bade the Jews to leave their
ancestral religion and worship the gods of the Greeks, chief of whom
was Zeus (Roman: *Jupiter*). An idol was set up in the temple; all
copies of the Law were destroyed; death by hanging was the sentence for any Jewish mother, child and priest who were caught
being party to a circumcision; and the people were commanded
to eat the flesh of swine offered in sacrifice before pagan idols.
Needless to say, all this was pure horror to the faithful Jews.

As we finished chapter 1 with, "Many a son of Israel refused
the unclean food, preferring death to defilement; and die they
must because they would not break God's holy law," (I Mac 1:65)
Christopher commented.

"That's just like in the story of Daniel and the three young
men in the fiery furnace."

And he touched squarely on the motive of the author for
writing the book of Daniel. He wanted to remind his people that
they had been persecuted like this before, had been as desperate,
and had been rescued by the Lord, as ever.

"Those were their hero tales," said Philip—fixing once and
for all the reason why the book of Daniel should be read before
the Machabees. Had we not read it first, he would not have known
these heroes nor seen how beautifully the story of Daniel and his
friends served as inspiration for the Machabees. More than that,
there was in his remark a small boy's regard for hero tales as
such, and a kind of matter-of-fact expectation that all people must
have them. And so they must. The Machabees themselves ever
after were to serve as hero tales for countless generations.

The Revolt

Mathathias, a Jewish priest of the Hasmonean family and the father of five sons, had left Jerusalem and taken residence in the town of Modin, and now he defied the king and killed not only an apostate Jew attempting to offer sacrifice before the false gods but the king's official also, and sounded the great cry that opened the revolt of God's people.

"Who loves the law? Who keeps the covenant unbroken? Out with you, and follow me!" (I Mac 2:27 Knox) And off he fled with his sons to the hill country.

The very first battle of the rebellion was lost because the Assideans, a group known for their zeal in observing the Law (forerunners to the Pharisees), would not take arms on the Sabbath to defend themselves, so Mathathias and his followers agreed that for the duration of their struggle the law forbidding the use of arms on the Sabbath must be suspended. But the role of Mathathias as instigator of the fight was soon to come to an end and, sending for his sons, he prepared them to take over on the event of his death. Simon would be like a father to them, Judas Machabaeus would be their fighter and leader, and he recommended all to take for their models Abraham, Joseph, Phinees, Josue, Caleb, David, Elias and—here there were knowing murmurs—Ananias, Azaria, Misael and Daniel, and to win a deathless name for themselves in the cause of the Lord.

The Exploits of Judas

Chapter 3 begins the account of the exploits of Judas Machabaeus. "Here was one that brought his race renown, as great a warrior as ever donned a breastplate, or armed himself for the fight, or drew sword to save his camp from peril." (I Mac 3:3) Battles, campaigns, generals, heroes, traitors fairly pack the pages.

First Judas scoured the countryside hunting down both the traitorous Jews and the enemy until his fame reached the ears of Apollonius in the citadel at Jerusalem. This official mustered a great force of men and came out to fight him. He fell in the encounter, his men were routed, and ever after Judas used the sword of Apollonius in battle.

Next Seron, captain of the armies of Syria, came to crush Judas, and he too fell victim to the valor of the Jews. When the king heard of this, he appointed Lysias, administrator at the royal court, to take half his army and dispatch it, as he saw fit to put down this rebel and restore peace to Juda. The outcome of this was the total defeat of Gorgias, leader of one Syrian campaign, and the following year the defeat of Lysias also, who desperately followed Gorgias with another campaign. On the latter occasion, Judas prepared for battle with a prayer which resurrected old and valiant friends for us. "Blessed art thou, Saviour of Israel, who didst make use of thy servant David, a giant's onset to overthrow! Victory thou didst give, over an invading army, to Saul's son Jonathan and the squire that bore him company! So may yonder host . . . unlearn its confidence in strength and in speed . . . sword of thy true lovers be their undoing, triumph-song of thy worshippers their dirge!" (I Mac 4:30) Here Judas reminds us of another valiant Israelite, Judith, whose prayer asking the Lord to help her slay Holofernes sounds very much like the words of Judas. (Jdt 9:12-19)

The Dedication of the Temple

And now, with their enemies repulsed for the time being, Judas and his brethren turned their attention to the work closest to their hearts—the restoration of the holy temple. Jerusalem was in rack and ruin, a wilderness with brush and weeds growing in the very corners of the buildings. Sending a force to harass the citadel while work on the temple got under way, Judas chose priests to remove all that had defiled the temple and its sanctuaries and to cleanse it. A new altar was raised, new furnishings were provided, inside and outside the temple was refurbished, the priests' lodgings were rebuilt, the gates consecrated and great was the rejoicing among Judas and his people on the day it was rededicated. A decree set forth this day to be celebrated from that time forward as the Feast of the Dedication, a feast which is called Hannukah, or the Feast of Lights, and falls in December. Our Lord was in Jerusalem for the celebration of this feast on the occasion of His beautiful parable about the Good Shepherd. (John 10:22)

Once again the walls and towers of Jerusalem were rebuilt and a temple garrison was installed to defend it, and once again the gentiles in the countryside about began to murder and harass the Israelites, determined to be rid of them. Judas had gathered a force to rescue his fellow Jews, especially those under siege in Galaad, when news came that the gentiles of Galilee were also armed and persecuting his people. Dividing his men, Judas put Simon in charge of the contingent to Galilee while he and his brother Jonathan marched off to Galaad. There they crushed all opposition, seized many cities, took spoils, and repatriated the people.

When news of the Syrian defeats and the prowess of Judas reached the king, way off in the country of Persia on a campaign to refill his royal treasury, he took to his bed in a mortal sickness. Why, he mused, should such misfortune fall to him? And then he remembered the havoc he had left in Jerusalem and—like Aman in the book of Esther and Rahab in the book of Josue—he realized that these Jews were no ordinary people and their God no ordinary God; his crimes against them must be the source of all his misery. And sending for his trusted friend Philip, he gave him charge of the kingdom and the young heir, Antiochus Eupator, and then he turned over and died. (The second book of Machabees gives us a very detailed account of his death in chapter 9.)

Meanwhile, the apostate Jews in the citadel at Jerusalem were besieged by Judas and in a desperate effort to save themselves they sent messengers to ask the new king to come to their aid, which he did under the advisement of Lysias, leading a huge army of infantry, cavalry, mercenaries and elephants "blooded to battle with the juice of grape and mulberry." (I Mac 6:35)[1] The description of the maneuvers climaxing in the death of Eleazar, is one of the most exciting passages in the book—"really tops," we have it from our experts. Eleazar, another of the brothers of Judas, gave his life in a bold attempt to kill the enemy king. Thinking he saw him atop an elephant battle tower, he ran beneath the beast, speared it and was crushed to death when the creature fell on him.[2]

But Judas and his followers were forced to retreat to Jerusalem and they survived a siege there only because news from Antioch announced the return of Philip, to whom Antiochus senior had entrusted both the regency and Antiochus the younger until he should come of age—and lo, already the young king had been

---

[1] To provoke the elephants to fight, they were intoxicated with red wine and mulberry juice.

[2] It is thought the claim of thirty-two men atop each elephant tower is an incorrect reading of 2 *or* 3.

enticed into battle abroad by the ambitious Lysias. Now Lysias induced the king to sue for peace, the terms were accepted by the Jews, and the Syrians, treacherous to the last, tore down the battlements of Jerusalem as they departed for Antioch. There Lysias met and conquered Philip and took the city by storm.

The Traitor Alcimus and the Blasphemer Nicanor

Hardly had young Antiochus returned than he and Lysias were slain by his cousin Demetrius, who had come back from Rome to claim the crown. Immediately a pro-Hellenist Jew of Aaron's line, Alcimus, went to the new king and acquired not only the office of high priest but also a task force, under the general Bacchides, to accompany him back to Juda and win control of the land.

Once again the peace-loving Jews walked into a trap and the countryside was the scene of bloodshed and anguish, and once again Judas and his company set about taking vengeance on all who were traitors to their cause. Alcimus complained to the king, who this time sent Nicanor at the head of an army, and he too tried to win the Jews with offers of peace. But Judas, barely escaping his treachery once, was suspicious and forced so costly a battle that the man fled to the citadel in Jerusalem for safety. There some of the temple priests, desiring as always freedom to worship in peace, went to meet him in a gesture of friendship and offered to show him the sacrifice of burnt offerings, but Nicanor angrily blasphemed them and the holy rites and swore to have Judas and his army or burn the temple. In prayer, both Judas and the priests reminded the Lord of that other blasphemer, Sennacherib, in the days of Ezechia, and how He had sent angels to smite his army. (IV Kings 19:35) Cried Judas, "This day a new enemy overwhelm with our onslaught, and let all the world know what comes of threatening thy holy place: for his ill-doing, requite him!" (I Mac 7:42)

And on the evening of the day of their battle, Nicanor's head and right hand were hung up for all Jerusalem to see.

The Death of Judas, the Succession of Jonathan, the Death of John

Chapter 8 tells how Judas sent envoys to Rome to make a treaty of friendship and alliance with the Romans and in chapter 9 we come to the last battle fought by Judas Machabaeus.

Demetrius was angered to learn that Nicanor had been slain and his army dispersed and once again he sent Alcimus and Bacchides to Juda to wipe out the Machabees and restore control of the land to the high priest. This time they came with such numbers that the men of Judas' army were intimidated and began to desert until no more than eight hundred were left. In vain they tried to dissuade him from engaging in the battle, but he would not betray the cause nor be found wanting in valor and so he attacked. Overcoming one flank of Bacchides' army, Judas was overcome by another, and thus fell one of the greatest heroes in all Israel's history.

Once again Alcimus ruled from the temple in Jerusalem and Bacchides established himself and his might to support the pro-Hellenists. "There was no corner in Israel but treason began to show its face there, and lawlessness to abound." (I Mac 9:23) The lives of the faithful few were imperiled not only by informers on every hand but by famine as well, and finally in their anguish they begged Jonathan to be their leader in Judas' place and lead them in battle against their enemies. To this Jonathan agreed and together with Simon he gathered together the remnants of the Machabees in the desert five miles south of Jerusalem. He dispatched his eldest brother, John, with a caravan of camp followers —perhaps families of the fighting men—and their goods to take refuge with the Nabuthaeans to the east, but they were ambushed in mid-journey and John and his party were slain or carried away. Since it was the custom to exact blood vengeance for such deeds, Jonathan and his band went to the district and there waylaid and slew the members of a native wedding party, and the news of these skirmishes drew Bacchides and his troops from Jerusalem to the banks of the Jordan to trap Jonathan on his return. But after a brief encounter, the Machabees swam the Jordan and escaped into the fastness of the desert.

Now Bacchides busied himself fortifying the cities of Juda, and to insure the loyalty of the chieftains he ordered their sons sent to Jerusalem citadel as hostages. Alcimus was busy too with alterations to the temple, and it was during the work of tearing down the dividing wall between the temple's inner and outer courts that he was seized with apoplexy. "Dumbstricken and palsied, he never spoke again, even to dispose of his goods, but died there and then in great torment," (I Mac 9:56) and his death was considered by the devout Jews to be a punishment for having demolished part of the temple.

With Alcimus dead, Bacchides had no call to stay longer in Juda, so for two years he left the Jews in peace; but soon the godless party conspired to be rid of Jonathan and they called on the Syrian general to venture forth a third and final time to put an end to the Machabees. Again his efforts came to naught and finally in disgust Bacchides exchanged peace terms and prisoners with Jonathan and marched away, leaving Jonathan at long last undisputed ruler of Juda.

Jonathan's Friendship Is Sought by both Demetrius and Alexander

Now comes a bit of intrigue which we thought would surely be too complicated for the children to follow—but not in the least. The story of the Machabees is so compelling that we found them not only able to follow, but also making judicious remarks as we read along.

Alexander, son of Antiochus Epiphanes (our very first villain) took possession of Ptolemais, a coastal city often called the "key of Palestine" because it led to the plain of Esdralon and the valley of the Jordan. When Demetrius heard this, he called up a great number of troops and prepared to do battle for the city. At the same time, he reasoned that it would be wise to repair his relations with Jonathan before Alexander got to him first, so he wrote Jonathan—"in such loving terms as should flatter his dignity" (I Mac 10:4)—that he must feel free to return to Jerusalem, call up troops, release the hostages still detained in the citadel (the sons of the chieftains) and make weapons of war. The king's men, hearing this, became so alarmed that they fled their outposts for home leaving only the town of Bethsura still manned—by apostate Jews at that, who had no other place to go.

When Alexander heard of the overtures of Demetrius, and learned the story of Judas, Jonathan and their brethren, he too decided here was a man whose friendship he should court. So he wrote Jonathan also; and with the authority of one who considers himself rightful pretender to the crown, he made Jonathan high priest and sent him a purple robe and golden crown.

Alarmed because Alexander had beat him to the punch, Demetrius now thought to make an alliance with Jonathan that would top Alexander's gifts and favors, and in 10:25-45 we read his prodigious offer—all rights restored, privileges granted, gifts bestowed, even the city of Ptolemais (as though he had control of it)—until Stephen remarked:

"Brother! He's sure giving them a deal."

But Christopher was concerned. "I hope they don't take it."

No fear—10:46 relieved our apprehensions. "In vain were such promises made to Jonathan and the Jewish folk . . . could they forget all the mischief Demetrius had done in Israel, all the tyranny they had endured?" And when the two kings finally met in battle, Demetrius fell.

"Good!" came from all around.

So Alexander became king of Syria, consolidated his position by making friends with the king of Egypt and wooing his daughter Cleopatra (not *the* Cleopatra—there were four in all), and Jonathan rose in high favor while Juda expanded as never before since the return from exile.

Demetrius II and Jonathan

Now Demetrius II, son of the vanquished king, appeared to claim his father's throne. His first move was to send his army under the command of a certain Apollonius to unseat Jonathan in Juda, but this plan came to grief when Jonathan and Simon outmaneuvered him. When Alexander heard that Jonathan had not only triumphed but taken cities, plundered and returned to Jerusalem with spoils, more than ever he honored him.

Real trouble was brewing now, however, for the king of Egypt noted his son-in-law's possessions and began to covet them. He undertook an expedition to visit him, and as he passed through town after town in Alexander's territory, he left guards of soldiers in each one. Even Jonathan was taken in, and went to Joppe to meet the king and escort him part of the way. Formal estrangement came when Alexander was off in Cilicia quelling a revolt and Ptolemy seized the opportunity to take back his daughter and rewed her to Demetrius. Finally the two kings met in battle, Alexander was routed and fled to Arabia and there an enemy cut off his head and sent it back to Ptolemy. But the lord of Egypt, mortally wounded in battle, had only three days left to enjoy his prize and his power, and after his death the realm fell once more into the hands of Demetrius.

Now at long last friendly relations were established between Jonathan and Demetrius and the whole land was at peace.

With peace, Demetrius disbanded his army, keeping only hired soldiers from Crete under arms, and this was his great mistake—"bitterly they hated him for it, the men who had served under his fathers." (11:38) In no time a certain Tryphon, formerly with Alexander, noted the unrest and began to promote Alexander's son Antiochus as the rightful heir to the throne. While this was happening, Jonathan had been urging Demetrius to withdraw the soldiers from the Jerusalem citadel. He now promised to, on one condition: Jonathan must send troops to aid Demetrius in Antioch, for his army had revolted. It was no sooner said than Jewish troops were dispatched and so valiantly did they prove themselves that the rebels called for a truce and the Jews returned home victorious and laden with spoils.

But Demetrius, secure now, conveniently forgot his part of the bargain with Jonathan and "did him much mischief besides," (11:53) until Jonathan in disgust allied himself with the young Antiochus, self-styled king, about whom the disgruntled warriors of Demetrius had rallied. Antiochus confirmed Jonathan in the high priesthood and in possession of the lands he already held, and made Simon lord of the seacoast from Tyre to the frontiers of Egypt.

There follows in 11:60-64 a confusing passage which may be the result of some disturbance in the text. At any rate, it is proposed that it was Antiochus, not Jonathan, who patrolled the cities with the armies of Syria gathered to aid him, and that it was Jonathan who marched out to Ascalon. Learning that Demetrius planned to unseat him, Jonathan marched out to give battle, was ambushed and deserted by many of his men. Then Jonathan, tearing his garments and strewing dirt on his head, threw himself on the mercy of the Lord in prayer, and in the battle that followed he drove off the enemy with great losses among them.

In chapter 12, 1-23, we find the texts of two letters exchanged between the Jews and the Spartans as Jonathan went about the business of hedging Juda round with allies. Verse 11 especially makes Jonathan seem a contemporary of ours as we pray for the peoples of the world today. "Never feast-day passes, nor day apt for remembrance, but you are remembered, as brothers should be, in sacrifice and prayer we offer."

Such a text was often lifted from its place in sacred scriptures and set like a jewel among the prayers of the Mass. Jonathan's words give emphasis to the at-oneness of the sons of God as they worship together and pray for one another, and for those who have yet to know Him. The story of the Machabees has endless applications to our lives today and presents to our children striking new statements of the oldest lessons.

But now the news came to Jonathan that Demetrius was returning to attack, so the Jews marched out to put him off before he could even cross their borders, and the rumor of their preparedness so frightened the enemy that they fled without pressing an encounter. And after skirmishing about and taking spoils, Jonathan returned to Jerusalem to plan for the refortification of Juda.

Jonathan Is Tricked

By now Tryphon, having seated young Antiochus on the throne, had an even better idea: *he* should be king. But he knew Jonathan would never tolerate this, for he and Antiochus were bound together in friendship. So the first step must be the removal of Jonathan. Tryphon marched himself almost midway between the border and Jerusalem before Jonathan came out to meet him with a great band of warriors, and seeing that force would not win for him, Tryphon decided upon trickery. Why had Jonathan come out with such an army, he asked, when there was no threat of war? Let him send home all but a bodyguard and then Jonathan could journey together with him to Ptolemais where Tryphon was bound on an errand. And Jonathan fell for it. No sooner had they entered Ptolemais than the gates of the city were shut, Jonathan's men were killed and the great Machabean leader was captured at last.

With panic everywhere, Simon quickly took command in place of his brother (whom rumor had reported dead), the fortifications at Jerusalem were speedily finished, and when Tryphon marched inland for the taking of Juda, he found Simon and his forces encamped to meet him. Once again resorting to trickery, he sent word that Jonathan was captured only because he was short of tribute owed the royal treasury. Let Simon send money and Jonathan's two sons for surety, and their leader would be returned. Simon, no fool, knew it was madness to believe the man, but he also knew that if he did not meet the ransom demands, forever after his people would say that for want of money and hostages, the great Jonathan was lost. So he sent them both. "But all was treachery; Jonathan never came back." (13:19 Knox)

Vainly Tryphon tried to take Juda, but he failed, and in a rage he put Jonathan and his sons to death, turned about and went home to murder young Antiochus, sit on his throne and wear his crown.

Simon as High Priest

Now that Simon was high priest and the fortresses of Juda were repaired, he sent envoys to Demetrius to ask that the same immunity be granted Juda as she had enjoyed before the usurpations of Tryphon, and this Demetrius confirmed. "Thus . . . Israel was free of the Gentile yoke at last," (13:41 Knox) and the people, in celebration, established a new chronological era, dating coins, "private bonds and public instruments" (13:42 Knox) by the year of their independence. Simon "mopped up," rid Gazara of its idol worshipers, cleansed its houses, finally drove out the gentiles still left in Jerusalem citadel, and put his son John, "grown into a brave warrior," at the head of the whole army.

While Simon looked ahead to a life of honors and peace, Demetrius faced the need to raise money to make war on Tryphon and unseat him, and it was during a campaign to the kingdom of the Medes and the Persians, that he was captured at last by their king and "put safely into prison." (14:3 Knox)

We read on and on, all about Simon's great deeds, his loyalty, his fame, the honor in which he was held by all the world, of the citations from Rome and Sparta, until finally Stephen said, "Holy mackerel. He was the lucky Machabee."

And it began to look as though this Machabee would probably die quietly in his old age.

A week elapsed before we began to read again and as we gathered ourselves together to resume the story, a briefing seemed called for.

"Now a new Antiochus enters the scene, a son of that first Demetrius. Do you remember that Demetrius?" And we wondered —there had been so many names, plots, counter-plots, kings, scions, pretenders, usurpers, rebels, traitors. Who would be surprised if they did not remember that Demetrius?

But someone answered, "How could we forget him?"

And for the hundredth time we marveled at the impact that

these great stories from holy scripture have upon children. Again
and again, all through the historical books, we had questioned their
ability to keep track of the characters, to keep their eye on the
plots, but we did no more. We had reached the last two books of
the Bible and, as they themselves would say, they were still with
it. We had only one regret—that as a family we had not started
reading the Old Testament sooner.

A New Antiochus, Treachery, and Simon's Death

The new Antiochus meant to be rid of Tryphon and regain
the throne of his fathers, and he wrote to Simon confirming all his
privileges and liberties and begging passage through Juda so he
might move up to do battle with the usurper. Simon gave permission and Antiochus chased Tryphon all down the seacoast and
holed him up in the port of Dora, keeping him under siege by
land and blockaded by sea.

Here in 15:15-24 Knox there is an interruption in the narrative with the insertion of a letter from Rome which seems to
reply to a letter from Simon mentioned in 14:24, a passage that is
incomplete. It is thought that 15:15-24 may have been placed ac-
cidentally in chapter 15 instead of 14 through a copyist's error.

The account of Antiochus continues with 15:25 and we find,
to our surprise, that suddenly Antiochus' sentiment toward Simon
and the Jews changed. With Tryphon bottled up, he had become
demanding and full of threats. He sent an envoy to Jerusalem with
this message: Let Simon pay back tribute, return cities and com-
pensation for damages done, or Antiochus would make war on
Juda. And furious after Simon's refusal, he sent an army under a
certain Cendebaeus to harass the Jews and prepare to battle for
Juda. Now Simon called his elder sons, Judas and John (named
for their valiant uncles) to take up the cause in true Machabean
tradition.

"Still young we were, I and my brothers and my father's kin,
when we began that war on Israel's enemies which is being fought
yet; under our banners once and again came victory, and the day
was saved for Israel. I am an old man now, and it is yours to do
what I and brothers of mine did; march out, fight in our people's
cause, and heaven's aid be with you!" (16:2-3 Knox)

And their performance must have filled the old man's heart
with fire, for they were true Machabees—both leaders, dedicated

and without fear. The enemy fled at great cost to himself and the Machabees returned victoriously once again to Jerusalem.

In the end it was another Jew who killed Simon—Ptolemy, son-in-law of a former high priest. Determined to be high priest in his place, he plotted to murder Simon and his sons, and on a Sabbath day when Simon, his sons Mathathias (named for his grandfather) and Judas, were on an official visit to Jericho, Ptolemy treacherously welcomed them to a banquet arranged in their honor. After they had dined, had toasted and been toasted, armed men broke into the banquet hall and slew the three—and the inspired writer laments: "Never saw Israel so good a service so ill rewarded." (16:17 Knox)

Hastily Ptolemy reported these events to the king and asked that the rule of Juda be turned over to him, meanwhile sending a band of men to Gazara to murder John, and another to Jerusalem to take the city and the temple hill. But news of his father's death had reached John and, once on the alert, he seized his executioners when they arrived and made an end of them. Thus John ruled in place of Simon and followed in the tradition of the Machabees —Judas, Eleazar, John, Jonathan and the gallant old Mathathias.

This brings us to the end of the first book of Machabees. Chronologically, it brings us almost to the threshold of Our Lord's times, for the strength of Syria was waning and the Jews would remain relatively independent from that time until the coming of the Romans—less than one hundred years away.

The Second Book of Machabees

The second book of Machabees certainly merits reading at any time and for many reasons *except* if you are young and have just finished hearing about the same things in the first book, told in a style that is far more attractive. This we discovered when we started to read the second book. After proceeding just a short while, there was a discreet cough from someone who shall remain nameless.

"Maybe I shouldn't say this, but this book isn't as interesting as the other."

It was getting "kind of draggy," and Heaven preserve us from draggy scripture readings!

Rather than risk spoiling their enthusiasm for the Machabees, we swiftly scanned the book and chose the three most exciting passages: new episodes which were not included in the first book, plus a short but important postscript to the story, leaving the rest for another time. The stories we chose were:

II Mac 6:18-31: The story of Eleazar who preferred death to defilement

7 The mother of the Machabees and her seven sons

9 The death of Antiochus

As a postscript to the defeat of Gorgias, about which we read in I Machabees 4:1-25, we read II Machabees 12:38-46, which tells how Judas sent offerings to Jerusalem for sacrifices to be made for the souls of the dead, showing us that the Jews believed in Purgatory.

The Martyrdom of Eleazar

The time and place for the story of Eleazar are already familiar to us. Antiochus IV (the first one in our story) was king and had ordered the Jews to forsake the religion of their fathers. Vicious punishments were meted out to those who had their children circumcised, who continued to observe the Sabbath, who would not eat the unclean meats forbidden by the law, and more. Eleazar, a man of great age and nobility, one of the chief scribes, was bade to eat swine's flesh but he refused to do so, even though they held his mouth open and attempted to force him to swallow. He would rather die. Friends prevailed upon him: let him eat other meat, merely giving the appearance that it was swine's flesh, this would satisfy the king's men. But the old man refused, and in a most noble speech pointed out his obligation before those younger than he to give heroic example of fidelity to the Lord. He preferred to die with a clear conscience. As he lay dying, he uttered a last prayer.

"Lord, in thy holy wisdom this thou well knowest; I might have had life if I would, yet never a cruel pang my body endures, but my soul suffers it gladly for thy reverence." (6:30 Knox)

What a sobering story for parents and teachers, stressing so dramatically the obligation to give right example to those who look to us for their training, and those who watch from the sidelines. And for children the lesson of martyrdom, whether in the Old Testament or today, is always the same: when men must choose between God and man, martyrdom is the choice of men who love God terribly because they have discovered how much God loves them.

The Mother of the Machabees

The story of the mother of the Machabees and her seven sons is one of the most magnificent in all the annals of the martyrs. No matter how familiar, it never ceases to be profoundly moving and the counsels of this great mother to her sons should be read from time to time by all parents so they may rededicate themselves to forming their children first of all in the knowledge of things that are eternal.

This family had also refused to eat swine's flesh, were arrested, tortured, and still they refused. The king in a rage ordered frightful torments for the eldset son and he died while his mother and brothers looked on. Undaunted, the second died, and the third, until one after another the Machabees died rather than submit to the will of a tyrant and break the law of the Lord.

"And here was the greatest marvel of all . . . that the mother of the seven children should be content to lose them all in one day, for the hope she had of God's mercy . . . One by one she put heart into them: Into this womb you came, she told them, who knows how? Not I quickened, not I the breath of life gave you, nor fashioned the bodies of you one by one! Man's birth, and the origin of all things, he devised who is the whole world's Maker; and shall he not give the breath of life back to you, that for his law's sake hold your lives so cheap?" (7:20-24 Knox)

This is what matters, that God has made us for Himself, that from Him we received the breath of this life, and when it is gone He can give us eternal life—would we but love Him with all our strength. The great women of the Old Testament always show forth in type one or another of Our Lady's virtues and the mother of the Machabees helps us better to comprehend the silent courage and generosity of Our Lady who stood at the foot of the Cross

and with no word demurred the sacrifice of her own Son in order
that eternal life be put within our reach.

When at last the littlest son was about to die, the king, moved
by the child's tender years, assured the woman that she had but
to plead with him to yield and he would. And so the mother
agreed to dissuade her son, and tricking the king she lapsed into
her own dialect and said: "Look around at heaven and earth and
all they contain; bethink thee that of all this, and of mankind too,
God is maker. Of this butcher have no fear; claim rightful share
among thy brethren in yonder inheritance of death; so shall the
divine mercy give me back all my sons at once." (7:28 Knox)

What an indictment her speech is to parents who will not
let their children give their lives to God in the religious vocation
or in apostolic service elsewhere. What an inspiration she is to
parents who want with all their hearts to encourage in their children the spirit of self-discipline, service, sacrifice. And for children,
the lesson goes straight to the heart—and their hearts are so generous while they are still little. This is a story for all families to
know and to cherish.

The Death of Antiochus

Chapter 9 tells in great detail of the death of Antiochus, already reported in I Machabees 6:8-17. Pity Antiochus; in his dying
frenzy wildly he promised the Lord everything but His own moon,
would He but cure him. All privileges he would give back to the
Jews, could he but live; choice gifts and rich furnishings he would
send to the temple, could he but live; he would even become a Jew
himself, could he but live! But he did not live. And the lesson he
teaches is old, old, old. One must take heed of the Lord and
keep His word while one lives. There will be no time for it when
one dies.

Judas Has Sacrifices Offered for the Dead

The last selection we chose from the second book of Machabees
brings our portrait of Judas—and his brothers and his people—to
a perfect completion. This passage tells that, following the defeat
of Gorgias and after they had been cleansed and kept the Sabbath,
Judas and his troops returned to recover the bodies of his slain
warriors and found to his dismay that under their shirts each had

worn some token of one of the false gods of Jamnia. No one doubted but this was the cause of their undoing, and yet in their love for these men they begged God to forget their sins. Here is the passage that speaks so clearly of the Jewish belief in Purgatory. Judas took up a collection among his troops and sent it to Jerusalem to have sacrifices offered for these dead companions.

"Here was a man kept the resurrection ever in mind; he had done fondly and foolishly indeed, to pray for the dead, if these might rise no more, that once were fallen! And these had made a godly end; could he doubt, a rich recompense awaited them? A holy and wholesome thought it is to pray for the dead, for their guilt's undoing." (II Mac 12:43-46 Knox)

It is exactly where our story should end, for it brings us to that promise of eternal life that had been the destiny of the race before ever Adam disobeyed.

The story of Judas and the Machabees restates the role of Israel in the plan of salvation and shows us her faithful ones fulfilling it. In the new dispensation the new Israel is militant in the same way. She too can exist under different forms of rule and government, and her members too fight and even die for the same cause—that God may win on the frontier of men's souls, capture them with His truth, fill them with His life, that they may prosper everlastingly in His kingdom.

The history of the Machabees is ideal for closing the Old Testament—for leading us up to the final moments in His plan for our salvation.

·XII·

THE NEW TESTAMENT
AGAINST
THE BACKGROUND
OF THE OLD

It would be a rash thing to say that the New Testament alone is not enough for anyone seeking to love the Lord and discover the meaning of the Christian life, but it is quite true to say that there are things in the New Testament which we cannot discover without a knowledge of the Old and that one is always more aware of Who Christ is after reading the Old Testament. Therefore it is wonderfully satisfying, after reading the story of salvation, to turn again to the Gospels. Now we see not only the familiar truths but things which we have been totally unable to see before, and might never have seen if we had not taken ourselves through the story of God's people.

With the Jews, of course, it was the other way round. They could never have understood Who He was if He had not based His teaching on their tradition of promise, covenant and expectation. Since He was the fulfillment of all this, His teaching depended upon their consciousness of it, and this in itself hints that there must be much in what Christ said that we missed all these years for want of familiarity with the background of His people.

Why Didn't He Tell Them?

With everything spelled out so clearly in prophecy and tradition, why didn't Our Lord simply sit down with His people and explain Who He was right at the beginning, as it has been explained to us? It would have been so simple. "I am the promised one, the messiah, the very Son of God, don't you see?"

That is what we used to think before knowing the Israelites and their attitude toward God. Now we can see that it was never that simple. If they *had* believed Him, they'd have been terrified; they might have fallen flat or even run away. Besides their own quite understandable awe in the presence of the All-Holy One, they thought no man could see God and live. What was it God said to Moses on the mountain? "But my face you cannot see, for no man sees me and still lives." (Ex 33:20) After his struggle with the "angel of the Lord," Jacob named the place where he wrestled *Phanuel*, "face of God," and he said, "I have seen a heavenly being face to face yet my life has been spared." (Gen 32:31) When the parents of Samson were visited by the angel, they said: "We will certainly die, for we have seen God." (Judg 13:23) And He couldn't have them running away when He had so much to teach them.

So Our Lord revealed Himself to His people slowly, and our knowing why makes us a hundred times more sensitive to the clues He gave them.

The Storm on the Lake

For example, not long ago we were reading the Gospel about the storm on the lake of Genesareth. (Mark 4:35-40) The apostles, frightened, awakened Christ crying, "Master, does it not concern thee that we are perishing?" And rising up, Jesus rebuked the wind and said to the sea, "Peace, be still." The apostles marveled, saying, "Who then is this, that even the wind and the sea obey Him?"

Someone asked, "But for men who knew the Psalms, why didn't they see Who He was?" Who is it in the Psalms Who alone commands the elements? The Lord God.

Perhaps the apostles guessed the answer to their question the moment they asked it, and for the same reason that now seems apparent to us, but the point is that *this* reason was never apparent to us before. We had always loved the story and the display of Christ's power in the miracle but we had never seen that it revealed Him as the God of the Old Testament, the same voice that commanded order out of chaos on the day of creation. Of course Christ was God, but still we thought of Him as somehow separate from the God of the Old Testament—as though the one were old and the other young—which is not true. It is the same God and the same voice. The only difference is that in the New Testament God has become Man.

Christ in the Fire and the Cloud and the Jordan

St. Paul and his "Christ was the rock," (I Cor 10:4) startled us another time, turning our minds back to the crossing of the Red Sea. Then it was also Christ in the pillar of fire, we thought, and Christ in the pillar of cloud. We had seen God there—but not as *Christ*. Going before them through the waters, He had brought them out of a land of death and into a new life, fore-shadowing Baptism in the New Testament when Christ went down into the waters of the Jordan and came out, in the pillar of His own flesh, and for all time water became the handmaid of a new and divine life for men. Now not only when we read the Baptism of Christ (Matt 3:13-17), but when we see a Baptism, we see also Christ and John as they stand in the torrent, and behind them we see the mighty exodus through the sea with the fire and the cloud, and we understand that the voice that speaks out over this binds together all three events. "This is my beloved Son . . ." Both Old and New Testaments exist to teach us this, that we are once again the sons of God.

The Canticle of Zachary

Everywhere familiar things took on deeper meanings. Here are verses from Zachary's canticle which had been known to us for a long time:

> Blessed be the Lord, the God of Israel,
>> because he has visited and wrought redemption
>> for his people,
> And has raised up a horn of salvation for us,
>> in the house of David his servant,
> As he promised through the mouth of his holy ones,
>> the prophets of old . . . (Luke 1:68-70)

We had heard these words for years. They have the noble ring of scripture, speaking of prophets, David, redemption, as one expects scripture to speak of such things. But not until we knew Abraham and Isaac and Jacob and Moses, and David and the tortuous existence of his line through good times and bad, good kings and bad, could we marvel that God had kept the threads of promise, covenant, nation and house disentangled (though it was very easy for us to become entangled as we read along) and had been weaving, weaving down the generations until this moment when the plan was beginning to be revealed. We will never read this canticle again without scanning the whole history of Israel, which is precisely what Zachary was doing—looking down thousands of years from promise to fulfillment and praising God for it all.

The Withered Fig Tree

To have made the acquaintance of the prophets sets alight many texts we have skimmed by before. For example, the little incident where Our Lord looked in a fig tree to see if it showed any signs of bearing fruit. Being God, He was not unaware that it was too early in the season for figs, so we can only conclude that He was teaching something, not with words but in a way we often teach in our families, by "acting it out." It was a kind of charade, and if we ask ourselves where we have read something like this before, we may recall a passage from the prophet Jeremia. First, let us remember the anguish and anger of Our Lord as, for many months prior to this incident, He had tried in every way to cut through the complacency and pride and jealousy of the Scribes and the Pharisees. Now turn back to the 8th chapter of Jeremia. Here is the prophet speaking to the people of God in his own time:

> How can you say, "We are wise,
>   we have the law of the Lord"?
> Why, that has been changed into falsehood
>   by the lying pen of the scribes!
> The wise are confounded,
>   dismayed and ensnared;
> Since they have rejected the word of the Lord,
>   of what avail is their wisdom? (Jer 8:8-9)

Three verses later we read this:

> I will gather them all in, says the Lord:
>> no grapes on the vine,
> No figs on the fig trees,
>> foliage withered! (Jer 8:13)

Did the disciples get the point? The text does not say. But the next morning as they were returning to the city from Bethany, they passed by the tree and were astonished to see that it had indeed withered right down to its roots. When Peter commented on this to Jesus, He said that if they (unlike the Scribes and Pharisees) would have faith and not waver, not only would they be able to wither fig trees but more—they would be able to move mountains. Thus the issue was clearly drawn. The teachers and wise men of Israel had proven themselves men too proud to hear the truth and believe in it, and the faithful remnant was once more revealed. Always, always, the people had suffered for the sins of their leaders, but always a remnant was steadfast, and out of these would come the fulfillment of the promise. It was not the Jews as a people Who rejected Our Lord but the everlastingly proud ones among them (as among all men), and if we wonder at this we have only to see that it was to other Jews that He entrusted the task of moving mountains—of founding His Church and extending it to the ends of the earth.

If we read on to Jeremia 8:18, we find the prophet weeping over his people.

> My grief is incurable,
>> my heart within me is faint.
> Listen! the cry of the daughter of my people,
>> far and wide in the land!
> Is the Lord no longer in Sion,
>> is her King no longer in her midst? (8:18-19)

Strangely enough, the episode of the fig tree took place the day after Our Lord had ridden triumphantly into Jerusalem. As He approached the city that day He too wept. "If thou hadst known, in this thy day, even thou, the things that are for thy peace! But now they are hidden from thy eyes. For days will come upon thee when thine enemies will throw up a rampart about thee, and surround thee and shut thee in on every side, and will dash thee to the ground and thy children within thee, and will not leave in thee one stone upon another, because thou hast not known the time of thy visitation." (Luke 19:42-44)

They would call Him King that very afternoon—but before another week was out, well might Jeremia cry: "Is the King no longer in her midst?"

The Panoramic View

It is but one step back from Jeremia to the whole panorama of God's people and all the way back to Adam, and from there we can see that the specific men, soldiers, crowds, followers who held specific roles in the most titanic event in history before the Resurrection, are like all the men who have ever lived, and ever will, and have ever faced God to choose for Him or against Him in their own hearts. The Old Testament is like a mirror held to our souls, with God's people the image of ourselves, and seeing this makes reading the Gospels something more than just a devotion. In the figures that walk beside Him, comfort Him, question, pause, turn away, come back, we find ourselves. Here we face Christ. The Old Testament shows us how men have behaved with God in the past, and the New Testament shows us how God is with men in the present.

The Bridegroom

How many times in our reading of the Old Testament have we come upon the mention of Israel as Yahweh's bride, of Yahweh as Israel's spouse? We remember the evening when we read in Isaia, "See, upon the palms of my hands I have written your name . . ." (Is 49:16) and one of the children concluded that it meant the marks of the nails.

But this is exactly right, for Christ refers to Himself as the bridegroom in the first three Gospels, while St. John the Baptist speaks of Him as the bridegroom in the fourth. It is odd how one can grasp only part of a meaning. I must confess that years of hearing St. Paul speak of Christ loving the Church as the bridegroom loves the bride had interfered with my seeing that Our Lord was really identifying Himself as the Yahweh of the Old Testament. Certainly He is the Second Person of the Blessed Trinity, but He is also One God, and to understand Christ as the bridegroom of the Church is enormously enriched when we see that long before St. Paul came along to explain it this way, the prophets spoke of Yahweh as the bridegroom of Israel.

Here is Isaia speaking of the Lord and Jerusalem:

> As a young man marries a virgin,
> your Builder shall marry you;
> And as a bridegroom rejoices in his bride
> so shall your God rejoice in you. (Is 62:5)

And here is Jeremia instructed by the Lord:

> Go, cry out this message for Jerusalem to hear!
> I remember the devotion of your youth,
> how you loved me as a bride,
> Following me in the desert,
> in a land unsown. (Jer 22:1-2)

Now let us reread the words of John the Baptist:

> I am not the Christ but have been sent before him. He who has the bride is the bridegroom; but the friend of the bridegroom, who stands and hears him, rejoices exceedingly at the voice of the bridegroom. This, my joy, therefore is made full. He must increase, but I must decrease. (John 3:28-30)

This last of the prophets was repeating the thoughts of his predecessors when he spoke of Christ this way. No wonder that in time the Pharisees began to suspect Christ of blasphemy.

Plucking the Grain on the Sabbath

We found many allusions to stories told in the Old Testament without which one can only half guess the meanings of lessons taught in the Gospels. Some of these we have mentioned in earlier chapters, such as Our Lord's reference to the widow of Sarepta and Naaman the Syrian in the synagogue in Nazareth (Luke 4:16-30), the question of John's identification with Elias (Matt 17:12-13), Jona as a type of Our Lord's resurrection, and the condemnation of the Pharisees by the Ninivites and the queen of the South on the day of the last judgment (Matt 12:38-42), and many others. One such passage, the account of the disciples plucking grain on the Sabbath, combines a number of texts from the Old Testament. (Matt 12:1-8)

On this occasion the criticism of the Pharisees was not aimed

at the disciples' eating, for the law provided that men could pluck
grain and eat it if they were hungry, but at their plucking—a work,
they claimed, forbidden on the Sabbath. In His reply, Our Lord
reminded them of the time David ran away from Saul and, being
without food, was allowed to take the bread offering from the
sanctuary at Nobe. (I Sam 21:1-6) Next, He reminded them that
on the Sabbath the priests have the work of offering the Sabbath
holocaust in addition to the established holocaust and its libation
even in the temple. (Num 28:9) Then He continued: "But I tell
you that one greater than the temple is here," and this reminded us
of what the prophet Aggai had said to his discouraged people when
they rebuilt the temple after the exile and saw how poor it looked
in comparison to the temple of Solomon.

Our Lord continued with a reference to words spoken by the
prophet Osee: "It is love that I desire, not sacrifice, and knowledge
of God rather than holocausts." (Osee 6:6) If they had remembered this, He said, they would not have condemned these men,
contriving to catch them by one of the minute additions to the Law,
and He concluded by referring to Himself in a favorite way, using
a title out of the book of Daniel: "For the Son of Man is Lord
even of the Sabbath." (Dan 7:13)

One of the most satisfying discoveries of all is to find that
having read the Old Testament in a family fashion, which is not
the same as a scholarly fashion, we have already become well
enough acquainted with it to identify many of these references and
to reach much deeper into Our Lord's teaching. It is like a
rediscovery of the Gospels.

And It's All True

We talked a lot about these things, and thought a lot, and
we asked the different members of the family to tell us how they
thought reading the Old Testament had helped their understanding of the Gospels.

One boy said, "I think it helps a lot to know who He came
from and to know their stories. You know—Joseph was the son
of someone, and he was the son of someone, and he was the son
of someone, and all the way down through the people we've read
about."

He was thinking of the genealogy of Christ in the third
chapter of St. Luke, 23-38. It starts with Jesus "being—as was

supposed—the son of Joseph," (3:23) and goes back through a long list of names, many of which are familiar now but never were before—Zorobabel, Salathiel, Nathan, David, Jesse, Obed, Booz, Aminidab, Judas, Jacob, Isaac, Abraham, Thare, Nachor, Sem, Noe, Lamech, Mathusale, Enoch, Jared, Cainan, Enos, to Seth who was "the son of Adam, who was the son of God" (3:38). We could see how this would be especially satisfying, for it describes the full circle—from Adam, son of God; to Jesus, Son of God; to all men, once more the sons of God. And we thought this a good place to end a book. But one of the little ones said something else which seems an even better way to end a book; in fact, one man before us ended his book in somewhat the same way.

The smallest boy of all said, "I think it helps you to know all about the Old Testament because then you know it's all true."

I could understand perfectly what he meant because when I was little there was a great emptiness before the story of Jesus and it made me uneasy. I believed in Him, but a child likes to be anchored and secure and not to know the Old Testament is to lack an anchor and to be the least bit insecure. It is as though Our Lord appears out of the air, hovering on the edge of an abyss; in spite of great faith, one wants to see what went before Him.

The Old Testament went before Him and it shows us that He did come from both God and a family of men, that He had a people and a history and a tradition and He was part of our world, one of our race. It tells us why He had to come—because He loved us so He could not bear to be without us—and how He made it happen. And it leads us in a nice orderly, satisfying way to the New Testament, where He finally appears and wins us back and invites us to help Him win back all the others that He loves.

It would be easy to go on and on but one must stop somewhere. We will stop with what the little boy said: "And it's all true."

It's very much like the ending to another book about Him, written by someone who calls himself a disciple "who bears witness concerning these things, and who has written these things, and we know that his witness is true. There are many other things that Jesus did; but if every one of these should be written, not even the world itself, I think, could hold the books that would have to be written." (John 21:24-25.)

APPENDIX

SCRIPTURE REFERENCES FOR STORIES AND LESSONS

The following list of scripture references will help families find texts for story-telling and lessons. Many more texts will be discovered as they read together and apply the scriptures to daily living.

The Sacraments

Baptism:
>God's life (the state of grace): Creation of man in God's image and likeness (Gen 1:26)
>
>Loss of God's life (sin): the Fall (Gen 3:1-9)
>
>Man's rebirth to God's life (Baptism): Noe—a type of Christ regenerating the life of the race; Noe and the just saved by the waters (Gen 6, 7, 8)
>
>>Moses in his basket of reeds (one saved by the waters) (Ex 2:1-10); type of Christ
>>
>>Flight through Red Sea—type of Baptism (Ex 14)
>>
>>Naaman the Leper (healed of sickness as he bathes in the waters)—type of Baptism (IV Kings 5:1-15)
>>
>>Baptism of Christ in the Jordan (Matt 3:1-17)
>>
>>Christ explains Baptism to Nicodemus (John 3:1-8)
>>
>>Ethiopian receives Baptism into the Church (Acts 8:35-39)
>>
>>The baptized are the salt of the earth, the light of the world, a leaven (Matt 5:13, 14-15; Luke 13:20-21)

Confirmation:

> Babel—example of disharmony and confusion among men when they substitute their own powers for God's (Gen 11:1-9)
>
> God promises to make available to men His own wisdom, understanding, counsel, strength, knowledge, etc., in the coming of His Spirit (Is 11:1-5)
>
> Solemn importance of anointing (in Baptism as well as Confirmation) making us sharers of Christ's Kingship and Priesthood
>
>> Saul's anointing (I Sam 10:1)
>>
>> David spares Saul, the anointed king (I Sam 24:1-12)
>>
>> David's anger with man who killed Saul (II Sam 1:1-16)
>
> God's promise to pour out His Spirit on His people (Joel 3:1-2)
>
> Pentecost, "the undoing of Babel" and the first Confirmation (Acts 2:1-18)
>
> The apostles confirm by laying on of hands (Acts 8:14-17; 19:1-7)

Holy Eucharist:

> The Food of Life: like tree of life available to Adam (Gen 2:9; 16-17)
>
> Adam deprived of the food of the tree of life by sin (Gen 3:22)
>
> St. Paul warns against eating the Holy Eucharist unworthily (I Cor 11:23-24)
>
> Joseph feeding his brothers—type of Christ and Eucharist (Gen 45:1-8)
>
> Passover meal celebrating the Israelites' freedom after slavery —type of Mass celebrating our freedom and new life in Christ (Ex 12:1-28)
>
> Christ eats the Passover meal—it becomes the Mass (Mark 14:22-25)
>
> Manna, the miraculous food of the desert—type of Holy Eucharist; miraculous food on the altar (Ex 16:1-15)
>
> Christ teaches of manna and Eucharist (John 6:22-59)
>
> Manna disappears in the promised land—we will not need Eucharist in heaven (Jos 5:10-12)
>
> David and Miphiboseth. We too eat at the King's table (II Sam 9)

Penance:

    Moses, intercessor for the sinful people, a type of Christ (Ex 32:30-35)

    Miriam's punishment and re-entry into the divine community —a foreshadowing of Penance as sacrament of restoration to the Church (Num 12:1-15)

    David's sin and sorrow for sin (II Sam 12:1-6, 13-14)

    Mary Magdalene's sorrow for sin and forgiveness (Luke 7:36-50)

    The Prodigal Son (Luke 15:11-32)

    Christ forgives sin (Luke 5:18-26)

    Christ empowers apostles to bind and loose sin (John 20:19-23)

Matrimony:

    Adam and Eve (Gen 2:21-25)

    Prayer of maiden Sara (Tob 3:12-22)

    Counsel of angel Raphael to Tobias (Tob 6:14-18a, 22b)

    Marriage of Isaac and Rebecca (Gen 24)

    David and Michol—David wins her hand (I Sam 18:12-28); Michol despises David's love for God (II Sam 6:11-23)

    Daughter of Jephte mourns because she will not marry and bear children (Judg 11:29-40)

    Miracle at Cana (John 2:1-11)

    Christ's teaching on marriage (Matt 19:3-12)

    St. Paul's teaching on marriage (I Cor 7:1-10; Eph 5:22-23)

Holy Orders:

    The people of God a priestly people (Ex 19:6; I Peter 2:9)

    Melchisedech—type of the priesthood in the Church (Gen 14:17-24)

    Aaron and his sons consecrated priests (Ex 29:1-9)

    Aaron's staff sprouts, a sign that the priesthood belonged to his family alone (Num 18:16-26)

    God ordains that the priests shall offer sacrifice for the people (Lev 1:1-9)

    Once a year the high priest atones for the sins of the people with the blood of animals (Lev 16:1-19)

    The Son of God sheds His blood on the cross for the sins of men (Mark 15:20-38)

    St. Paul teaches that Christ is Eternal High Priest (Heb 9:1-14)

Sacrament of the Sick and
Extreme Unction:
>   Elias cures the widow's son (III Kings 17:17-24)
>   Eliseus cures the widow's son (IV Kings 4:18-37)
>   Tobias' death (Tob 14:16)
>   Our Lord and the man with the withered hand (Mark 3:1-5)
>>   the daughter of Jairus (Mark 5:21-24; 35-43)
>>   Peter's mother-in-law (Matt 8:14-15)
>>   the centurion's servant (Matt 8:5-13)
>>   the woman with a hemorrhage (Mark 5:25-34)
>   The sacrament of anointing the sick (James 5:14-15)

The Mass:
>   Cain and Abel offer sacrifice (Gen 4:2b-7)
>   Noe offers sacrifice (Gen 8:20-22)
>   Abraham offers sacrifice (Gen 12:5b-7)
>   Abraham and Isaac (Gen 22)
>   Moses asks Pharaoh's permission to take the people to offer
>   sacrifice (Ex 3:18; 5:1-3; 7:14-16, 26-27; 8:17; 8:21; 8:25-28;
>   9:13; 10:3; 10:7-11; 10:24-27)
>   Passover meal (Ex 12:1-20)
>   God makes a covenant with the people (Ex 24:3-8)
>   Josue and people celebrate Passover (Jos 5:10-12)
>   Christ eats the Passover meal, celebrating the first Mass (Mark
>   14:22-24)

Faith:
>   Abraham, man of faith (Gen 12:1-5a; 15:1-6)
>   St. Paul cites the faith of the men of old: Abel, Henoch, Noe,
>   Abraham, Sara, Isaac, Jacob, Joseph, Moses, Rahab,
>   Gideon, Barac, Samson, Jephte, David, Samuel, the
>   prophets (Hebrews 11)
>   Jesus praises centurion's faith (Matt 8:5-13)

Hope:
>   St. Paul tells of Abraham's hope (Rom 4:18-25)
>   The hope of the Syrophoenician woman (Mark 7:24-30)
>   Judith's hope in deliverance (Jdt 8:21-27)

Charity:
>   God has loved the people, and they must love in the same way
>   (Deut 10:15, 17-19; 14:29; 15:7-11)
>   The Good Samaritan (Luke 10:25-37)
>   The New Commandment of Love (John 13:31-35)

Good example: Eleazar's martyrdom (II Mach 6:18-31)

Prudence: The story of Judith

Courage (Fortitude): David and Goliath (I Sam 17:22-58)

Chastity: Joseph and Phutiphar's wife (Gen 39:1-12)

Sixth Commandment, and Ninth: David and Bethsabee (II Sam 11; 12:1-13)

Types of Our Lady: Rebecca (Gen 24:16, 67), Judith (15:9-10), Esther (7:1-4), Mother of the Machabees (7:27b-29), Dew on the Fleece of Gideon (Judg 6:36-40)

BOOKS AND STUDY AIDS

Many fine texts on scripture are currently available to help families with their reading of the Bible, and to include everything of value would be impossible here. The following is a list of the books and study aids we have found helpful in our family, arranged as they might be referred to throughout this book.

Atlases

Atlas of the Bible, by Luke H. Grollenberg, O.P., Nelson, New York, 1956

Lands of the Bible, A Golden Historical Atlas, by Samuel Terrien, Simon & Schuster, New York, 1957

Books

A Path through Genesis, by Bruce Vawter, C.M., Sheed & Ward, New York, 1956 (includes text of Genesis as well as commentary, very easy to read)

The Conscience of Israel, by Bruce Vawter, C.M., Sheed & Ward, New York, 1961 (on the prophets)

Beginnings, Genesis and Modern Science, by Charles Hauret, Priory Press, Dubuque, 1955 (on creation, Adam, Eve, the fall, Paradise)

The Story of the Bible World, in Map, Word and Pictures, by Nelson Beecher Keyes, C. S. Hammond & Co., Inc., 1959 (very easy to read)

Everyday Life in Old Testament Times, by E. W. Heaton, Charles Scribner's Sons, New York, 1956 (lore and details of O.T. life)

Unless Some Man Show Me (reprint), by Alexander Jones, Sheed & Ward, New York, 1960 (on Old Testament interpretation)

God's Living Word, by Alexander Jones, Sheed & Ward, New York, 1961

The History of Israel, Vols. I and II, by Guiseppe Ricciotti, trans.

Clement Della Penta, O.P., and Richard T. A. Murphy, O.P., Bruce Publishing Co., Milwaukee, 1955

Israel and the Ancient World (reprint), by Daniel-Rops, Eyre & Spottiswoode, London, 1960

Ancient Israel, Its Life and Institutions, by Roland de Vaux, O.P., McGraw-Hill, New York, 1961

A History of Israel, by John Bright, Westminster Press, Philadelphia, 1952

God's Word and Work, by Kathryn Sullivan, R.S.J.C., The Liturgical Press, Collegeville, 1958 (easy to read)

The Lord of History, by Jean Daniélou, S.J., Henry Regnery Co., Chicago, 1958

The Outspoken Ones, by Dom Hubert von Zeller, O.S.B., Sheed & Ward, New York, 1955 (on the minor prophets)

The Christian Approach to the Bible, Dom Celestin Charlier, Newman Press, Westminster, Md., 1958

The Two-Edged Sword, An Interpretation of the Old Testament, John L. McKenzie, S.J., Bruce Publishing Co., Milwaukee, 1956

Seven Books of Wisdom, by Roland E. Murphy, O.Carm., Bruce Publishing Co., Milwaukee, 1960

Introducing the Old Testament, by Frederick L. Moriarty, S.J., Bruce Publishing Co., Milwaukee, 1960

The God of Israel, the God of Christians, The Great Themes of Scripture, edited by J. Giblet, trans. by Kathryn Sullivan, R.S.C.J., Desclee Co., New York, 1961

The Jews and the Gospel, A Re-examination of the New Testament, by Gregory Baum, O.S.A., The Newman Press, Westminster, Md., 1961

Symbols of Christ, Old Testament and New Testament, by Damasus Winzen, O.S.B., P. J. Kenedy & Sons, New York, 1955

Understanding the Bible, by Ignatius Hunt, O.S.B., Sheed & Ward, New York, 1961 (easy to read)

Meet the Bible, John J. Castelot, S.S., Helicon Press, Baltimore, 1961 (easy to read)

What Is the Bible? by Daniel-Rops (a volume of the Twentieth Century Encyclopedia of Catholicism), Hawthorn Books, Inc., New York, 1958

The Liturgy and the Word of God (papers by Martimort, Jounel, Daniélou, von Balthasar, Bouyer, Roguet, Gelineau, Coudreau,

Moeller, Lécuyer, Spuelbeck) Liturgical Press, Collegeville, 1959

The Bridge, Vols. I, II, III, IV, edited by John M. Oesterreicher, Pantheon Books, 1955, 1956, 1958, 1961

Key to the Psalms, by Mary Perkins Ryan, Fides Publishers, Chicago, 1957

To Know Christ Jesus, by Frank Sheed, Sheed & Ward, New York, 1962

Reading the Word of God, by Lawrence Dannemiller, S.S., Helicon Press, Baltimore, 1960

Commentaries

A Catholic Commentary on Holy Scripture, Thomas Nelson & Sons, New York, 1953

The Word of Salvation, by Alfred Durand, S.J., and Joseph Huby, S.J., trans. John J. Heenan, S.J., Bruce Publishing Co., Milwaukee, 1957

(*See also* Pamphlets, Magazines)

Concordance

Complete Concordance to the Bible, by Newton Thompson and Raymond Stock, B. Herder Book Co., St. Louis, 1957

Encyclopedias

Catholic Biblical Encyclopedia (2 Vols., Old Testament and New Testament), by John E. Steinmueller and Kathryn Sullivan, R.S.C.J., Joseph Wagner Inc., New York, 1950 (N.T.), 1959 (O.T.)

Encyclopedia of Bible Life, by Madeline S. and J. Lane Miller, Harper & Bros., New York, 1944

Translations of the Bible

Confraternity of Christian Doctrine Translation of The Holy Bible, St. Anthony Guild Press, Paterson, N.J. (the books of Samuel, Kings, Paralipomena, Esdras, Nehemias, Tobias, Judith and Esther not yet completed)

A Gospel Harmony (CCD translation), by John E. Steinmueller, W. H. Sadlier, Inc., New York, 1942

Monsignor Knox Translation of the Old Testament, Sheed & Ward, New York, 1952

The Psalms, The Fides Translation, Introduction by Mary Perkins Ryan, Fides Pub., Chicago, 1955

Magazines

The Bible Today, The Liturgical Press, Collegeville, Minn.

Worship, The Liturgical Press, Collegeville, Minn.

Current Scripture Notes (4-page folder), Marist College, 3875 Harewood Rd., N.E., Washington 17, D.C.

The A. P. I. Bulletin (Archconfraternity of Prayer for Israel), (8-page publication), Archconfraternity of Prayer, Kansas City 9, Mo.

The Catholic Biblical Quarterly, The Catholic Biblical Assoc. of America, Washington 17, D.C.

Maps

Plastic contour map of Palestine, The Liturgical Press, Collegeville, Minn. ($15)

The Life of Christ in the Holy Land Map, The Liturgical Press, Collegeville, Minn. ($5)

Pamphlets

New Testament Reading Guide, The Liturgical Press, Collegeville, Minn.

Introduction to the New Testament—Roderick A. F. MacKenzie, S.J.

The Gospel of Saint Mark—Gerard S. Sloyan

The Gospel of Saint Luke—Carroll Stuhlmueller, C.P.

The Gospel of Saint Matthew—David M. Stanley, S.J.

The Acts of the Apostles—Neal M. Flanagan, O.S.M.

Introduction to the Pauline Epistles—Bruce Vawter, C.M.

I Thessalonians

II Thessalonians

The Epistles to the Galatians and to the Romans—Barnabas M. Ahern, C.P.

First Corinthians, Second Corinthians—Claude J. Peifer, O.S.B.

St. Paul's Epistles to the Philippians, Philemon, Colossians, Ephesians—Kathryn Sullivan, R.S.C.J.

The Pastoral Epistles, I Timothy, Titus, II Timothy—Robert T. Siebeneck, C.PP.S.

The Epistle to the Hebrews—John F. McConnell, M.M.

The Epistles of Saints James, Jude, Peter—Eugene H. Maly

The Gospel of St. John, the Johannine Epistles—Raymond E. Brown, S.S.

The Book of the Apocalypse—William G. Heidt, O.S.B.

Pamphlet Bible Series, Paulist Press, New York

The Law Given through Moses, Introduction to the Pentateuch —Neil J. McEleney, C.S.P.

The Book of Genesis, Part 1 and Part 2, with a Commentary —Ignatius Hunt, O.S.B.

The Book of Exodus, Part 1 and Part 2, with a Commentary —Roland E. Murphy, O.Carm.

The Book of Leviticus with a Commentary—Carroll Stuhlmueller, C.P.

The Book of Numbers, Part 1 and Part 2, with a Commentary —Frederick L. Moriarty, S.J.

The Book of Deuteronomy, Part 1 and Part 2, with a Commentary—George S. Glanzman, S.J.

The Book of Josue with a Commentary—Joseph J. De Vault, S.J.

The Book of Judges with a Commentary—Rev. Philip J. King

The Book of Proverbs with a Commentary—J. Terence Forestell, C.S.B.

The Book of Ecclesiastes and The Canticle of Canticles, with a Commentary—Roland E. Murphy, O.Carm.

The Book of Isaia, Part 1 and Part 2, with a Commentary— John E. Huesman, S.J.

The Books of Amos, Osee and Michea, with a Commentary —Marcian Strange, O.S.B.

The Book of Jeremia, Part 1 and Part 2, with a Commentary —Neal M. Flanagan, O.S.M.

The Books of Lamentations, Baruch, Sophonia, Nahum and Habacuc, with a Commentary—Edward J. Crowley, C.S.S.R.

The Book of Ezechial, Part 1 and Part 2, with a Commentary —Edward F. Siegman, C.PP.S.

The Books of Aggai, Zacharia, Malachai, Jona, Joel, Abdia, with a Commentary—Carroll Stuhlmueller, C.P.

The Book of Daniel with a Commentary—Raymond E. Brown, S.S.

The Book of Job, Part 1 and Part 2, with a Commentary—Myles M. Bourke

The Book of Wisdom with a Commentary—Eugene H. Maly

The Book of Sirach, Part 1 and Part 2, with a Commentary—Bruce Vawter, C.M.

The Book of Psalms, Part 1 and Part 2, with a Commentary—Rev. Philip King

The Book of Psalms, Part 3 and Part 4, with a Commentary—Robert North, S.J.

God's Love Songs (*The Psalms*), by Dom Rembert Sorg, O.S.B., Pio Decimo Press, St. Louis, Mo.

Hesed and Hasid in the Psalms, by Dom Rembert Sorg, O.S.B., Pio Decimo Press, St. Louis, Mo.

Meditating Like a Dove (*on the Psalms*), by Dom Rembert Sorg, O.S.B., Pio Decimo Press, St. Louis, Mo.

PRONUNCIATION OF NAMES

Note: It would be impossible to include a complete list of pronunciations. The following were helpful to our family, after we discovered that we rarely guessed right about the pronunciation of names in the Old Testament. A complete list of names with explanatory notes can be found in *The Catholic Biblical Encyclopedia, Old Testament.*[1]

A

Abdemelech: ab-deh-meh-lek
Abdenago: ab-den'-uh-goe
Abdia: ab-dye'-uh
Abdon: ab'-don
Abesan: ab'-e-san
Abia: uh-bye'-uh
Abiam: uh-bye'-um
Abiathar: uh-bye'-uh-thar
Abiel: ay'-bi-el
Abiezer: ab-i-eh-zer
Abihaiel: uh-bi-ha-yel
Abimelech: uh-bim'e-lek
Abinadab: uh-bin'-uh-dab
Abiram: uh-bi-rum
Abisag: uh-biss-sag
Abisai: uh-bis'-a-eye
Abiu: uh-bye'-yew
Absalom: ahb-sal'-om
Accad: ak'-ad
Accaron: ak'-uh-ron
Achab: ahk-ahb
Achan: ay'-kun
Achaz: ay'-kazz
Achias: uh-kye'-us
Achimaas: uh-kim'-a-as
Achimelech: uh-kim'-e-lek

Achior: ay'-ki-or
Achis: ah-kiss
Achitophel: uh-kit'-o-fel
Achor: ay'-kor
Adonai: uh-doe'-nay
Adonia(s): uh-don-i-yuh(s)
Adonibezec: uh-doe'-nye-bee'-zek
Adoniram: ad-o-nye'-ram
Agag: ay'-gag
Aggai: ag-gay
Ahimelech: uh-him'-e-lek
Alcimus: al'-si-mus
Amalec: am'-uh-lek
Amalecites: ah-mal'-e-sites
Aman: amy'-an
Amasai: ah-mah-say
Amasias: am'uh-sye'-us
Amathi: am-ah-tee
Amelech: am-eh-lek
Aminadab: uh-min'-uh-dab
Amraphel: am'-ruh-fel
Amri: am'-rye
Anania(s): an'-uh-nye-us
Anathoth: an'-a-thoth
Andronicus: an'-dron-nye'-kus
Antiochus: an'tye'-o-kus
Antipater: an-tip'-uh-tur

[1] Steinmueller and Sullivan, (New York: Joseph F. Wagner, Inc., 1959).

Asaa: a-sa'-ah
Asael: as'-a-el (or ay'-sa-el)
Asaph: ay'-saf
Aser: ay'-sir
Asiongaber: ay'-si-on-gab'-bur
Asmodeus: as'-mo-dee'-us
Asor: as'-or
Assideans: as'-i-dee'-uns
Assuerus: as-yu-ee'-rus
Astaroth: as'-tuh-roth
Astarthe: as-tahr'-tee
Azael (or Hazael): az'-a-el
Azareel: uh-zay'-re-el

B

Baal: bay'-uhl
Baal-Phogor: bay'-uhl-fuh-gor
Baasa: bay'-uh-suh
Babel: bay'-bel
Bacchides: ba-kye'-dees
Balaam: bay'-lam
Balac: bay'-lak
Balthasar: bal-thayz'-er (or tayz'-er)
Banaias: buh-nay'-yus
Barac: buh-rahk'
Baruch: bayr'-uk
Basan: bas-an
Bathuel: buh-thew'-el
Beelzebub: bee-el'zuh-bub
Behemoth: bee-hee'-moth
Bela: bee'-luh
Belial: bee'-lee-ul
Belsassar: bel-sa'zar
Benadad: ben-ay'-dad
Beroth: bee'-roth
Bersabee: ber-say'-bee
Berzellai: bur-zel'-a-eye
Besor: bee'-sor
Bethel: beth'-el
Bethsabee: beth-say'-bee
Bethulia: beth'-yu-lye'-uh
Booz: boh'-ahz

C

Cades: kay'-dez
Canaan: kay'-nun
Carioth: kay'-ri-oth
Carmel: kahr'-mel
Cedar: see'-dar
Cedes: cee'-des
Cedron: see'-druhn
Cendebeus: sen'-de-bee'-us
Cetura: se-tew'-ruh
Chaldeans: kal-dee'-uns
Cham: kam
Chanaan: kay'-nun
Chodorlahomor: kod'-ur-lay'-ho-mur
Chus: kus
Chusai: kew'-sye
Chusi: Chew'-sye
Cin: kin
Cinites: kinites
Cis: sis
Cison: ki-son
Cleopatra: kle'-o-pay'-truh
Coheleth: koe'-hel-eth
Core: kohr
Cozbi: kos'-bye
Cyrene: sye-ree'-nee
Cyrus: sye'-rus

D

Dagon: day'-gun
Darius: duh-rye'-us
Dathan: day'-thun
Debbora: deb'-o-ra
Demetrius: dee-mee'-tre-us
Deuteronomy: dew-ter-on'-o-mee
Diaspora: dye-ass'-poe-ruh
Dina: dye'-nuh
Dodau: dod'-a-ewe
Doeg: doh'-eg
Dorymenus: duh-rim'-i-nus
Dothain: doh'-tha-in

E

Ecbatana: ek-bat′-a-nuh
Ecclesiastes: e-klee′-zee-ass′-teez
Ecclesiasticus: e-klee′-zee-ass′-ti-kuss
Egeus: e-gee′-us
Ela: ee′-luh
Elam, Elamites: ee′-lum, ee′-lum-eytes
Elcana: el′-kuh-nuh
Elchanan: el-kay′-nun
Eleazar: el′ee-ay′-zer
Elia: ay-li′-ah
Eliab: e-lye′-ab
Eliachim: e-lye′-uh-kim
Eliacim: e-lye′-a-sim
Eliada: e-lye′uh-duh
Eliam: e-lye′-am
Elidad: e-lye′-dad
Eliel: ee-lye′-el
Eliezar: el′uh-ee′-zer
Elim: ee′-lim
Elimelech: e-lum′-e-lek
Elioda: e-lye′-o-duh
Eliphalet(h): e-lif′-uh-let(h)
Eliphaz: el′-i-faz
Eliseus: el′-e-see′-us
Eliu: ee-lye′-yew
Elohim: el′-o-him
Elon: ee′-lon
Emmanuel: eh-man′-yew-el
Emmaus: eh-may′-us
Endor: en′-dor
Engaddi: en-gad′-eye
Enoch: ee′-nok
Enos: ee′-nos
Epha: eh′-fuh
Ephod: ef′-od
Ephraim: ee′-fray-im
Ephrata: ef′-ruh-tuh
Epiphanes: eh-pif-on′-eez
Esdrelon: es-dree′-lon
Eupator: yew′-pa-tohr
Eupolemus: yew-pol′-e-mus
Ezechias: ee-zeek′-e-as
Ezechiel: ee-zeek′-yell
Ezion-Geber: ee′-zi-on-gay′-ber

G

Gaal: ga-al
Gabaa: ga-ba-ah
Gabaon: ga-ba-on
Gabelus: ga-bee′-lus
Galaad: gal′-uh-ad
Gamaliel: guh-may′-lee-el
Garizim: gar′-uh-zim
Gaza: gay′-zuh
Gedeon: ged′-ee-on
Gehenna: gee-hen′-uh
Gelboe: gel-boh′-uh
Godolias: god′-o-lye′-us
Goel: goh′-el
Gorgias: gohr′-jee-as

H

Habacuc: hab′-uh-kuk
Hadriel: hay′-dri-el
Hai: hay′-eye
Haman (Aman): hay′-mun
Hananias: han-an-i-as
Hasmonean: has-moe′-nee-an
Hazael: has′-uh-el
Heber: hee′-ber
Helchias: hel-kee-us
Helcias: hel-sye′-us
Heli: hee′-lye
Heliodorus: hee′-lih-o-doh′-rus
Heman: heh-man
Henoch: hee′nok
Hesebon: he-se-bon
Holofernes: ho-lo-fer′-neez
Horeb: hoe′-reb

I

Isai (Jesse): eye′-sye
Isaia: eye-say′-uh

Isboseth: is-boh'-seth
Ismael: is'-muh-el
Israel: is'-rah-el
Issachar: is'-uh-kahr

J

Jahel: jah'-el
Jahweh: yah'-weh
Jair: jay'-er
Jamne: jam'-nuh
Jaziel: jah'-zi-el
Jebusite: jeb'-yew-zyte
Jecemia: jeh-kem-yah
Jechelia: jeh-kel'-yah
Jechonias: jek'oh-nye'-us
Jehiel: jeh'-i-el
Jehovah: jee-hoe'-vuh
Jehu: jee'-hew
Jehus: jeh'-hus
Jemini: jem'-i-nye
Jephte: jef'-tee
Jeremia: jer'-eh-mye'-yah
Jerobaal: jer'-o-bay-al
Jeroboam: jer'-o-boh'-am
Jethraam: jeth'-ra-am
Jezabel: jez'-eh-bel
Jezonias: jeh-zo-ni-as
Joab: joe'-ab
Joachaz: joh-a-kaz
Joada: joe-ah-dah
Joakim(n): joe'-uh-kim(n)
Joas: joe'-as
Joatham: joe'-uh-tham
Joiada: joy'-ah-da
Josaia: joe-sah-ee-ah
Josaphat: jose'-uh-fat
Josias: joe-see'-as
Juda: joo'-dah
Judea: joo-dee'-uh

L

Laban: lay'-ban
Lachis: lay'-kis
Laisa: lay'-uh-sa
Lamech: lay'-mek
Lamuel: la-mew'-el
Levi: lee'-vye
Leviticus: li-vit'-i-kus
Lia: lee'-a
Libanus: lib'-uh-nus
Lysias: lis'-e-us
Lysimachus: lye-sim'-uh-kus

M

Maacha: may'-uh-kuh
Maala: may'-uh-luh
Maasias: may'-uh-sye'-as
Machabees: mak'-uh-bees'
Machabeus: mak'-uh-bee'-us
Machpela: mak-pee'-la
Madian: may'-di-un
Mageddo: muh-gid'-oe
Magi: may'-jye
Magog: may'-gog
Mahalath: mah-hah-lath
Mahanaim: may'-huh-nay'-um
Maharai (Marai): may'-huh-rye
Maheleth: may'-huh-leth
Malachia(s): mal'-uh-kye'uh(s)
Malaleel: muh-lay'-luh-el
Mambre: man-reh
Manasse: muh-nas'-i
Manasses: muh-nas'-eez
Manue: muh-new'-i
Maon: may'-un
Mara: may'-ruh
Mari: mah'-ree
Mathania(s): math'-uh-nye'-uh(s)
Mathathias: math'-uh-thye'-us
Matthias: muh-thye'-us
Melchia(s): mel-kye'-uh(s)
Melchisidech: mel-kiz'-uh-dek
Meribaal: mur'-ib-bay'-al
Meribah: mer'-uh-buh
Merodach: muh-roe'-dak

Michaia: mye-kay'-yuh
Michea(s): mye'-kee'-yuh(s)
Michol: mik-hol
Miphiboseth: mi-fib'-oe-seth
Mesach: mi-sak
Misael: mis'-uh-el
Moab: moe'-ab
Mordecai: mor'-deh-kye'
Moreseth: mo-reh-seth

N

Naaman: nay'-uh-man
Nabal: nay'-bul
Nabat: nay'-bat
Naboth: nah'-both
Nabuchodonosor: nab'-yew-ko-
    don'o-sor
Nachon: nay'-kon
Nachor: nahk'-or
Nadab: nay'-dab
Nahaliel: nuh-hay'-liel
Nahath: nay'-hath
Nahum: nah-hum
Nehemia(s): nee'-huh-mye'-
    uh(s)
Nepheg: nee'-feg
Nephthali: nef-ta-li
Nicanor: nik'-an-ohr
Ninive: nin'-uh-vuh
Nisan: nye'-san
Noe: no-ah
Nobe: nobh
Noemi: noh'-ee-my

O

Obadia: oh'-buh-dye'-uh
Obdia(s): ohb'-dye-uh(s)
Obededom: oh'-bed-ee'-dum
Ochozia(s): ok'-o-zye'-uh(s)
Odollam: o-dol'-um
Omrai: om'-rye
Onam: oh'-nam
Onan: oh'-nun

Onias: uh-nye'-us
Ophel: oh'-fel
Ophni: of'-nye
Osaias: oh-zay'-yus
Othoniel: oh-thoh'-ni-el
Ozias: oh-zye'-as

P

Paralipomena: par'-uh-li-pom'i-
    nah
Pasch: pask
Pentateuch: pent'-tuh-tewk
Phacee: fay'-se-ee
Phadaia: fuh-day'-yuh
Phaleg: fay'-leg
Phanuel: fan-u-el
Phicol: fye'-kul
Philistia: fi-lis'-ti-uh
Phinees: fin'-i-hus
Phison: fye'-son
Ptolemais: tahl'-uh-may'-is
Ptolemy: tohl'-uh-mee
Purim: poo'-rim
Putiphar: pewe'-ti-fur

R

Rages: ray'-jiz
Raguel: rah-gewe'-el
Rahab: ray'-hab
Rama: rah'-muh
Ramesses: ram'-uh-sees
Ramoth: ray'-muth
Raphael: ray'-fi-el
Raphaia: raf'-a-eye-uh
Rasin: ra-sin
Rechab: ree'-kab
Rehoboth: ree'-hoe-'buth
Roboam: roe-boe'-um
Romelia: roe'-muh-lye'-uh

S

Sadoc: say'-doc
Saducees: sad'-jew-seez

Salamiel: suh-lay'-miel
Salathi: sa-la-thy
Salathiel: suh-lay'-thee-el
Salem: say'-lim
Salmanasar: sal'-muh-nay'-sur
Salphaad: sal-fah-ad
Salumith: sa-lew'-mith
Samaaias: suh-may'-yas
Sanhedrin: san'-he-drin
Saphat: say'-fat
Saphathia: saf'-uh-thye'-uh
Sarep(h)ta: suh-rep'-tuh
Sargon: sahr'-gon
Sarvia: sar-vye'-uh
Sassabasar: sa-sab'-uh-sar
Satrap: say-trap
Sechenia(s): sek'-e-nye'-uh(s)
Sedecias: sed'-e-sye'-us
Segor: se-gor
Sehon: si-hon
Seir: see'-ir
Selemia(s): sel'-uh-mye'-uh(s)
Seleucia: see-lew'-she-uh
Seleucus: se-lew'-kus
Semaia: se-may'-uh
Semei: see'-mee-eye
Sennacherib: se-nak'-e-rib
Sephora: se-foe'-ruh
Seraphim: ser'-uh-fim
Shalleketh: shal'-e-keth
Shekinah: she-kye'-nuh
Sheol: shee'ohl
Siceleg: sis'-e-leg
Sichem: sye'-kem
Sidon: sye'-dun
Sidrach: sid-rak
Silo: si-lo
Siloe: si-loh'-ee
Sin: (desert, wilderness) tsin
Sinai: sye'-nye
Sion: sye'-on
Sirach: sye'-rak
Sisara: sis'-ur-uh

Sobochai: so-bo-kay
Soccoth: soe'-koth
Sochoth: suh-coth'
Sodi: soe'-dye
Sodom: sod'-um
Sophonia: sof'-o-nye'-uh
Sunam: suh-nem

T

Tabeel: tab-eh-el
Tanis: tay'-nis
Thabor: tay'-bor
Thamar: thay'-mar
Thare: thair
Thares: tair-es
Thecua: the-kew'-uh
Theglath-Phalasar: theg'-lath
  fuh-lay'-sur
Thola: toe-la
Timotheus: ti-moh'-the-us
Tobia(s): to-bye'uh(s)
Tryphon: trye'-fon

U

Ur: oower
Urias: yew-rye'-us
Uriel: yew'-ri-el
Urim and Thummim: yew'-rim
  and thum'-im
Uthai: yew'-thye

V

Vagao: vuh-gay'-o
Vashti: vash-tee

X

Xerxes: zerks'-ees

Z

Zabad: zay'-bad
Zabadia: zab'-uh-dye'-uh
Zabdias: zab'-dye'-us

Zabud: zay'-bud
Zabulon: zab'-yew-lun
Zacharia(s): zak'-uh-rye'-uh(s)

Zambri: zam'-brye
Zoheleth: zoe'-he-leth
Zorobabel: zoe-rob'-a-bel

ABOUT THE AUTHOR

Seven children of her own give MARY REED NEW-LAND an ideal private audience on which to test her books on family life and the children's books that she both writes and illustrates. The Newlands and a small menagerie of animals—wild and domestic—occupy a fourteen-room house and 103-acre farm in southern Massachusetts. Mrs. Newland studied art at the National Institute of Design, Pratt Institute and the New School for Social Research, training she later utilized in many ways, such as illustrating the stories she told on her own television program. Her books for parents include one on the cycle of the liturgical year and another on the lives of the saints. Other activities include making lecture tours and participating in many Catholic programs and conferences in her own diocese and elsewhere in the country. She has been awarded two honorary degrees of humane letters. Her writing, says Mrs. Newland, evolves from her desire to give to her own children "the riches of the faith together with the fullness of life in Christ."